IN PUTIN'S FOOTSTEPS

ALSO BY NINA KHRUSHCHEVA

The Lost Khrushchev:
A Journey into the Gulag of the Russian Mind

Imagining Nabokov:
Russia Between Art and Politics

ALSO BY JEFFREY TAYLER

Siberian Dawn:
A Journey Across the New Russia

Facing the Congo

Glory in a Camel's Eye

Angry Wind:
Through Muslim Black Africa by Truck, Bus, Boat, and Camel

Murderers in Mausoleums:
Riding the Back Roads of Empire Between Moscow and Beijing

Topless Jihadis:
Inside Femen, the World's Most Provocative Protest Movement

· IN ·
PUTIN'S
FOOTSTEPS

Searching for the Soul of an Empire
Across Russia's Eleven Time Zones

·

NINA KHRUSHCHEVA
AND JEFFREY TAYLER

St. Martin's Press
New York

www.stmartins.com

Design by Kathryn Parise

Map by Paul Pugliese

Song lyrics from "Land of Bones and Ice" in chapter 11 © Vladimir Vysotsky, reprinted by permission of the Estate of V. Vysotsky (translated 2019 by Nina Khrushcheva).

LIBRARY OF CONGRESS CATALOGING-IN-PUBLICATION DATA

Names: Khrushcheva, Nina L., 1962– author. | Tayler, Jeffrey, author.
Title: In Putin's footsteps : searching for the soul of an empire across Russia's eleven time zones / Nina L. Khrushcheva and Jeffrey Tayler.
Description: First edition. | New York : St. Martin's Press, 2019. | Includes bibliographical references and index.
Identifiers: LCCN 2018039821| ISBN 9781250163233 (hardcover) | ISBN 9781250163240 (ebook)
Subjects: LCSH: Russia (Federation)—Description and travel. | Khrushcheva, Nina L., 1962– —Travel—Russia (Federation) | Tayler, Jeffrey—Travel—Russia (Federation) | Russia (Federation)—History, Local. | Putin, Vladimir Vladimirovich, 1952– —Political and social views. | Regionalism—Political aspects—Russia (Federation) | Russia (Federation)—Politics and government—1991– | Russia (Federation)—Relations.
Classification: LCC DK510.76 .K53 2019 | DDC 947.086/2—dc23
LC record available at https://lccn.loc.gov/2018039821

Our books may be purchased in bulk for promotional, educational, or business use. Please contact your local bookseller or the Macmillan Corporate and Premium Sales Department at 1-800-221-7945, extension 5442, or by email at MacmillanSpecialMarkets@macmillan.com.

First Edition: February 2019

10 9 8 7 6 5 4 3 2 1

To Nina's mother, Julia Khrushcheva,

who vehemently opposed our plan to travel across Russia

and then became a passionate supporter of the project,

but didn't live to see the publication of this book

CONTENTS

IN PUTIN'S FOOTSTEPS

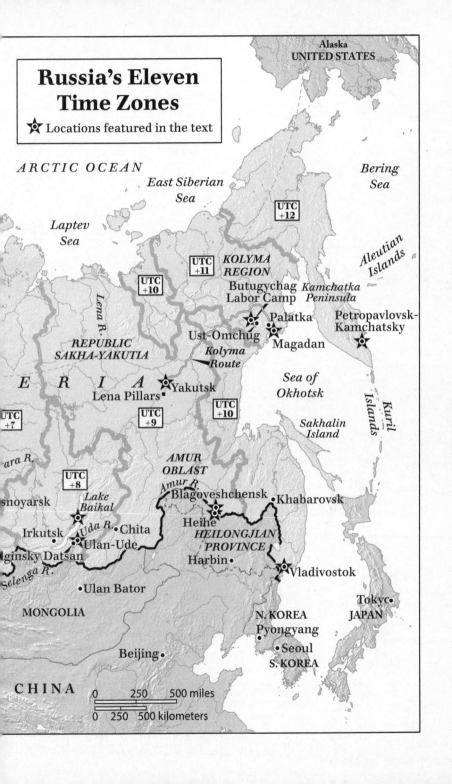

Russia's Eleven Time Zones

⭐ Locations featured in the text

ARCTIC OCEAN

East Siberian Sea

Laptev Sea

Bering Sea

UTC +12

UTC +11

UTC +10

KOLYMA REGION

Butugychag Labor Camp

Kamchatka Peninsula

Palatka

Aleutian Islands

REPUBLIC SAKHA-YAKUTIA

Ust-Omchug

Kolyma Route

Magadan

Petropavlovsk-Kamchatsky

E R I A

⭐ Yakutsk

Lena Pillars ▪

Sea of Okhotsk

UTC +7

UTC +9

UTC +10

Sakhalin Island

Kuril Islands

ara R.

UTC +8

Lake Baikal

AMUR OBLAST

Amur R.

Blagoveshchensk

Khabarovsk

snoyarsk

Irkutsk ▪

Uda R. ▪ Chita

Ulan-Ude

Heihe

HEILONGJIAN PROVINCE

ginsky Datsan

Selenga R.

Harbin ▪

⭐ Vladivostok

▪ Ulan Bator

Tokyo ▪

JAPAN

MONGOLIA

N. KOREA

Pyongyang ▪

▪ Seoul

S. KOREA

Beijing ▪

| 0 | 250 | 500 miles |

| 0 | 250 | 500 kilometers |

CHINA

SOLOVKI,
THE SOUL OF RUSSIA

We will drive humanity to happiness with an iron hand!
—Soviet slogan from the Stalin era

A t dusk, a forty-seat propeller plane from the 1970s circles around the islands, pale masses in an indigo sea. One circle, two, and then three. A flight that should take forty minutes has now dragged on for an hour and a half. We can't land.

The pilot announces over the speakerphone: "It's the wind. The Solovetsky Islands' landing strip is too short. With such a wind, we'd be blown right into the White Sea." He pauses, and then requests, in all seriousness, "Pray to the Solovetsky Islands that they accept you."

It is a few nights before Christmas—the Russian Orthodox Christmas, that is, which falls in early January. The plane is filled with religious tourists and nuns in black habits, with their hair hidden beneath black kerchiefs, and shod in, surprisingly, posh black hiking boots. Nowadays it is cool to be Orthodox Christian in Russia.

Everyone lowers their eyes and prays.

Ten minutes later the plane, wobbling in the fierce erratic winds, manages to touch down.

Welcome to Solovki (as the Solovetsky Islands are called, in Russian, for short)—an archipelago in the White Sea about a hundred miles south of the Arctic Circle. The remote abode of a monastery and a colony of exiles under the czars, a forced labor camp and military barracks under the Soviets, the Solovetsky Islands these days are a Kremlin-patronized religious sanctuary where the past and the present collide.

The landing field terminates by a single-story, gable-roofed blue brick airport waiting hall that abuts a white, onion-domed chapel (converted into an outhouse during the early part of the Soviet era) topped with a gilt Russian Orthodox cross. Waiting is a crowd of bearded, black-clad monks who greet the arriving passengers.

It is three in the afternoon, and the pale orange sun is setting, the violet sky darkening, the cross losing its glint and luster. Mid-winter days last just five hours at this subarctic latitude. (Summer days, in contrast, linger endlessly, with several weeks of sublime "white nights" ending with the sun rising obliquely, infusing the pale firmament with golden light that eventually gives way to the softest of azures.) Ahead of us the monastery's domes, towers, and crosses—lots of crosses—rise, almost black against the sky, composing an image fit for a postcard. A postcard, as it happens, from both heaven and hell. For much of the past century, communist red stars topped these Christian domes—a violent juxtaposition, a clash between God and Bolshevism. The Bolsheviks murdered, among other political outcasts, scores of monks, nuns, and priests and smashed the bronze bells. The bells chiming here so regularly are in fact of more recent provenance.

Solovki once held the prototypical labor camp—the first of, eventually, many that formed a sweeping crescent of outposts of toil and misery across the most inclement parts of the Soviet lands. The Soviet dissident writer Alexander Solzhenitsyn would dub them, collectively, the Gulag Archipelago, in his eponymous magnum opus on prison life during the Stalin decades. Solzhenitsyn served his time in Ekibastuz, now in Kazakhstan, and wrote his semiautobiographical documentary masterpiece in the 1970s. But the metaphor for *The Gulag Archipelago* title came from the arch of labor camp sites established in these northerly latitudes in the 1920s. The new Soviet government opened the first forced labor camp of its Gulag—the grim acronym standing for the USSR's Chief Administration of Labor Camps—on these islands where, since the 1500s, the czars had already held their first religious and political prisoners.

"Zheleznoi rukoi zagonim chelovechestvo k schastyu" (We will drive humanity to happiness with an iron hand) was the Soviet slogan emblazoned on banners once festooning the dirt lanes of the main settlement, Solovetsky. The brutal saying accorded with the violent legend of how humans came to settle the islands in the 1430s. Two angels are said to have beaten to death a fisherman's wife because she landed on the islands' holy terrain, which God, supposedly, had reserved only for the devout. A legend most likely created by monks, who first came here to establish their refuge for prayer and meditation. What is this legend if not a precursor to communism, with its mix of millennial, quasireligious belief in a dogma and the violence used to enforce it?

Surrounding us is the barren landscape of winter—frozen lakes become vast snowfields, exuding a glowing whiteness in the crepuscular evening light; dark, brooding pine forests; and, above all this, gold crosses, glinting with the faint rays of the dying sun. Yet in summer the sun awakens the sleeping land, invigorating life in the forests and bogs and raising clouds of giant mosquitos that torment all warm-blooded creatures. These creatures used to threaten the sanity and the lives of humans wandering the wilds here unprotected, turning their days into merciless crucibles. They still do.

The locals say, nevertheless, that "Cold is the primordial state of Solovki, the islands of utopia and dystopia, both blessed and cursed."

They might as well be talking about all of Russia.

In Putin's Footsteps

The Kremlin warned that if the West further expands the sanctions, the Kremlin will further increase Putin's ratings.

—A contemporary Russian joke

O n New Year's Eve, 1999, journalists in the Russian president's press pool had a feeling that things were going to change. They were right: the feeble and aging Boris Yeltsin, who could barely board a plane or stand for a fifteen-minute press conference, was about to deliver his End of the Year Address, in which he resigned and ceded power to his prime minister and handpicked successor, Vladimir Putin. Once head of the Federal Security Service (FSB), the post-communist "democratic" version of the dreaded KGB, Putin was indeed an unusual choice, having served as the head of the government for only a few months. But the forty-eight-year-old ex-spy, who would become the youngest Kremlin leader since the Soviet Union's founders, Vladimir Lenin and Joseph Stalin, had a quiet energy that seemed boundless. As boundless as the geographic expanses contained within Russia's eleven—yes, eleven—time zones.

After taking over from Yeltsin as acting president on the first day of the new millennium, and after winning, by a landslide, presidential elections three months later, Putin, in the year to come, held over a dozen press conferences and traveled to almost two dozen countries and at least a quarter of Russia's eighty-nine regions, which are spread out over eleven time zones. Altogether, he was seen in public and on television more often than Yeltsin during most of his eight-year presidency.

Suddenly the press had something to report. The new stories were no longer those of Yeltsin's Russia, which was perceived, both at home and abroad, as a weak, insignificant, and corrupt bogeyman reeling from its Cold War defeat. These were stories of an enigmatic young technocrat tirelessly crisscrossing the country and meeting with workers, farmers, and cultural figures, attending theater galas and factory openings.

All that uplifting travel—Russia was starving for the Kremlin's attention—connected Putin to ordinary people and gave him the idea of delivering a rousing New Year's Eve televised address to the nation. Standing before the Kremlin's Spassky Tower, just before the giant bells rang in the year 2001, under starry winter skies in front of a large, snow-dusted Christmas tree, he pledged to counter the negativity of the post-Soviet decade and set the country on a new, positive course.

This he did. In his address, the ardent young leader looked both charming and in charge when he spoke of Russia's great future, heroic past, and enduring spirit.

Putin had often appeared a reserved technocrat, but soon he would demonstrate a talent for finding opportunities to impress the heartland. He knew the best way to get to people's hearts: showing them that his priority was returning Russia to the world stage as a major power of formidable dimensions.

Originally, he had an even bolder plan for his New Year's address, and he had run it by journalists in his press pool during one of his trips around Russia. Without a hint of doubt in his voice, Putin told them that "Russia is an enormous country, a great country. We need to remember that our strength is our size. What if I were to travel through Russia's limitless land in one night, through all its eleven time zones, stopping in each one at midnight local time to record the New Year's message to show our nation's greatness, our riches, the diversity of our Mother Russia, our unity, our worth?"[1]

Even though Russia's time zones are exaggerated in number (there should only be seven, according to generally accepted geographic markers of Greenwich Mean Time's [GMT] twenty-four-hour cycle, also called Coordinated Universal Time and abbreviated as UTC), maintaining them is not only a political matter; it is reflective of the national identity, state power, and international influence. Russia has eleven time zones, more than any other country, and that, as Russians would have it, bespeaks its status in a way no one can deny.

Often the time that appears on a nation's iconic clock—Big Ben in the United Kingdom, for instance, or those daunting dials on the Spassky Tower, in Russia's case—is a subtle way of representing where power lies. In Russia, every time zone is first referenced in relation to MSK, Moscow Standard Time, with UTC only following. Moreover, many countries don't even adhere to the twenty-four-hour GMT-UTC's neat meridians. China's huge landmass should straddle five different time zones, yet operates according to just one. Inhabitants of western China, if they follow their clocks, have dark mornings and light evenings, but nobody doubts that only the Beijing time matters. When Hugo Chávez became president of Venezuela in 1999, he decided to create a new time zone that would set Venezuela thirty minutes apart from neighboring countries. That was his way to let the world know that Venezuela was striking out on its own.

But Putin's idea of showcasing his country's temporal and geographic diversity in just one night was certainly unique, and it accorded with his plans to return Russia to its lost great-power status. It also sprung from what Putin knew Russians expect of their leader: something close to godlike status. Keen on creating a leader's image steeped in tradition, history, and mythology often associated with the uniqueness of the "Russian soul"—spiritual endurance, persevering patience, belief in miracles, and material sacrifice—he wanted to be seen as the *Ded Moroz* ("Granddad Frost," the Russian Santa Claus) bearing gifts of renewed national importance and self-confidence.

Capitalizing on Russia's size—six thousand miles from east to west—Putin hoped to begin restoring his country's grandeur, once czarist, then Soviet, and now Russian. The idea was bold and beautiful but, unfortunately, unrealizable. The young leader soon had to abandon his "across Russia in one night" plan, because covering eleven times zones in eleven hours, indeed, could only be done in a magic sleigh, not in an actual airplane.

Now, eighteen years later—it is worth recalling that he first became president when Bill Clinton sat in the White House—after last year comfortably securing his fourth presidential term with a formidable 77 percent public support,[2] Putin is even more determined to present Russia as a formidable nation. In his 2017 New Year's Address, he promised to bring all of Russia to the world stage, asserting that his country has finally "risen off its knees" and has truly become "vast, unique, and wonderful."[3] He remains firm in his conviction that his country's geographic dimensions play a vital role in projecting power, which he has done, lately, in close-by Ukraine and as far afield as Syria.

For the past few years the world's eyes have set on Russia, with the same intensity as they did during the 1962 Cuban Missile Crisis with Soviet premier Nikita Khrushchev, or the 1991 collapse of the Soviet Union following Mikhail Gorbachev's Perestroika. The reasons have been manifold: Russia's 2014 annexation of Crimea and the consequent Kremlin-supported secession from Ukraine of the Donetsk and Luhansk People's Republics; the alleged Russian meddling in the 2016 U.S. presidential elections; the European and American diplomatic crisis in 2018, after former GRU spy Sergei Skripal and his daughter were said to be poisoned in the United Kingdom with the nerve agent Novichok.

Putin has taken a tough stance in responding to these occurrences and allegations. He has been driving both the events and the rhetoric around them in Russia and across the globe. The very picture of a statesman, he has offered the West partnership around the world's hot spots, be they Syria or North Korea. The more the West chastises Russia for its rogue behavior, though, the more combative Putin's rhetoric has become.

As have so many in many countries, we, too, wanted to know how Putin's idea of restoring pride to his once powerful nation has been playing out across its vast expanses. The great-granddaughter of Premier Khrushchev, Nina Khrushcheva, now a New Yorker, was brought up in elite circles in Moscow and is eager to see and understand her native Russia beyond the capital's bounds. Jeffrey Tayler, living in Moscow and married to a Russian woman, Tatyana, felt the same way, his last trans-Russia journey having taken place in 1993.

Both of us wondered if the Kremlin had really managed to impose its writ on a hinterland traditionally impervious to change, but nevertheless having undergone three dramatic political and social upheavals in the past century alone. Determined to find out, in the spring and summer of 2017 we did something close to the sequential trans-Russia journey from which Putin found he had to desist. We followed, though in the warmer, more comfortable months, in what would have been his footsteps, visiting all of Russia's eleven time zones in search of the factors—among them, natural resources, educational institutions, ethnic and religious diversity, and strategic assets—that define Russia and its place in the world. Do they, in fact, make the country an "indispensable nation," to borrow a phrase former Secretary of State Madeleine Albright used to describe the United States? And it was not just in Putin's footsteps we traveled; we followed the historical footprints of other Kremlin leaders, who, too, left lasting imprints on this giant land and on the people.

We announced our plans to our families in Moscow and upset them greatly. To those safely ensconced within the capital's confines, traveling out into the hinterland—almost anywhere besides Moscow—seemed like a risky, grueling undertaking. The press in Russia and abroad had been reporting on cases of arrests or prosecution of those critical of Putin, and on animosity toward foreigners. In fact, even in Moscow we heard an occasional drunken outburst. On a bus one of us witnessed a young man in a T-shirt emblazoned with RUSSIA (in English) slur his words and shout at a group of unruffled Italian tourists, "Yankee, go home!"

"At least don't speak English to each other!" pleaded Nina's mother, Julia, a Muscovite. She worried that widespread Russian support for Putin's annexation of Crimea would bring us unwanted attention. After all, it was Khrushchev who, in 1954, had transferred Crimea (Russian from 1783 until then) to Ukraine. This was at Khrushchev's time an administrative move, which shifted control of the area from one Soviet socialist republic to another, with the aim of improving its governance—the Crimean Peninsula lies to the Ukrainian mainland's south, without a land connection to Russia. That, of course, changed in May 2018, when the Crimea Bridge opened with pomp and circumstance over the Kerch Strait that divided the peninsula from the Russian territory.

In his Granddad Frost–type travels, Putin had planned on moving east to west, but we would do the opposite, because despite its grandstanding as a unique power, Russia's definition of itself begins in

Europe, with the arrival, in the ninth century, of the Ruriks. The Ruriks were Nordic princes who came to rule over the eastern Slavs, the proto-Slavic people speaking Old Russian, the language from which Russian, Ukrainian, and Belorussian would emerge. A century later, Russia further anchored its identity in Europe by adopting Christianity from the Byzantine Greeks. Moreover, once Byzantium had fallen to the Ottoman Turks in 1453 and the devastating era of Tatar-Mongolian rule over Russia ended in the 1470s, the country declared itself the Byzantine Empire's successor, the Third Rome, as the last bastion of Orthodox (that is, true, spiritual) Christianity. Russia appropriated the Byzantine Empire's emblem—its imperial coat of arms, with the double-headed eagle. From then on, the country began expanding (both east and west) thanks to the successful efforts of the early czars. Its growth was further assisted by Europeanizing reforms of Russia's first emperor, Peter the Great. The young sovereign undertook these reforms after visiting Europe in the late seventeenth century and encountering countries vastly more developed than his own.

The keys to understanding Russia's geopolitics, its people and its leaders, have been the nation's faith—the stress on the communal rather than the individual in either Christian Orthodoxy or communist brotherhood—and its giant territory and what it holds. With the collapse of the Soviet Union, Russia shed satellite nations in Eastern Europe and republics in the Baltics and Central Asia. Abroad, it then began to be seen not as the center of a Eurasian civilization, but as an extension of the West.

The Putin decades, however, have changed that perception as Russia, once again, began to reimagine itself in civilizational, not just national or geographical, terms. The country that Barack Obama dismissed as a "regional power" after the Crimea annexation looks set to rival the United States. Not least because Russia, like the

United States, occupies a "region"—a continent, actually—verging on two oceans.

Also like the United States, Russia, contrary to its convictions, does not constitute a separate civilization—civilizations, as those of Persia or China, possess independent frames of reference. Russia derives much of its identity from the West, either in imitation of it or in opposition to it. It has both striven to define itself as Western and what the West is not. The pro-Russian patriots who became known as the Slavophiles in the nineteenth century believed in Russia's religious and spiritual uniqueness, which set it apart from the West and assured it future glory. Another group, the Westernizers, argued for the rational, European approach to Russian matters. Even though at least half of Russia's landmass is in Asia, it does not see itself as Asian.

Russia, then, is a mutant, an oxymoron of geography, a self-enclosed empire defined by its central government and its rule over an extensive territory on which dwell dozens of peoples speaking many languages. However, Russian is the mother tongue of eight out of ten Russian citizens, and the lingua franca of virtually everyone.

Russia's gross domestic product stands at $1,283 billion, which makes its economy the world's twelfth, behind those of India, Brazil, and South Korea.[4] It spends $70 billion annually on its military, less than China does, and only one-seventh of the defense budget of the United States.[5] In economic terms, Russia hardly seems like much of an empire.

But either way, relatively few outsiders have seen much of it. How many foreigners, or even Russians, have made a concerted effort to traverse its vastness, as the American song has it, "from sea to shining sea"?

Demonized as a dictator, at least in the United States, Putin has nevertheless overseen a turn in Russia's fortunes that was impossible to imagine during the chaotic Yeltsin years of the 1990s, often deemed democratic in the West. Stepping in to reverse the excesses produced by the collapse of socialism and the sudden introduction of the free market, Putin nationalized, or rather took under the Kremlin's control, Russia's hydrocarbon industry, assuring his almost bankrupt government of much-needed revenues. Aided by high world energy prices, he was able to pay pensions and salaries owed to miners, railroad workers, and teachers, and so many others whom the Yeltsin administration had largely abandoned. Under Putin, roads and bridges were built, factories began functioning, and the jobless index fell to below 5 percent by 2017,[6] and this is despite the many rounds of sanctions imposed by the West after the Crimea annexation.

The Russia Putin built has largely survived notwithstanding the government's self-punishing response when it decided to levy its own countersanctions. These retaliatory measures—blocking import of European food and agricultural products and barring certain American politicians and businesspeople from visiting Russia—hurt the Russian economy and its partners much more than those at whom the countersanctions were aimed. But such was Russia's state of mind—when dealing with the West it often addresses matters emotionally, not pragmatically.

Such harmful actions add to the many already existing problems—an undiversified economy, graft, nepotism, aging infrastructure, in addition to shrinking space for free speech, free assembly, and the press. Despite these infringements on democracy, however, many Russians appear to share Putin's belief that only a centralized Russia can achieve the desired greatness, or at least the mythology of it. That mythology is mostly based on the idea of Russia's superior soul and its imperial stature as a unique nation straddling the East and West. The president recently confirmed this: "We are less pragmatic

than other people, less calculating. But then we have a more generous heart. Perhaps this reflects the greatness of our country, its vast
size."[7]

Russia's other enduring myth is that of a caring and benevolent
czar—be it Ivan the Terrible; Peter the Great; or Nicholas I, who announced that the three pillars of Russia's empire were *pravoslavie,
samoderzhavie, narodnost* (the Russian Orthodox faith, absolute state
power, and the people). After the March 2018 presidential elections,
with Putin winning an impressive 77 percent of the votes,[8] and a subsequent inauguration fit for a czar, many Russians have begun to see
Putin as Putin the First.

Do the three imperial pillars of Russia's past still uphold an empire of Putin's present? We were determined to find out.

1

THE AMBER-TINTED GAZE
OF AN EMPIRE

TIME ZONE: MSK-1; UTC+2

When Kant assumes that something outside of us, a thing-in-itself,
corresponds to our ideas, he is a materialist. When he declares this
thing-in-itself to be unknowable, transcendental, other-sided, he is
an idealist.

—Vladimir Lenin, *Materialism and Empirio-Criticism*

Kaliningrad, formerly the German city of Königsberg, has often
been called Russia's western door, yet this door is not always a
welcoming one. From here, the country's exclave (officially, the Kaliningrad Oblast, or region) that borders Poland, Lithuania, and the
Baltic Sea, the empire gazes with suspicion at anyone who may doubt
its superiority and strength.

We arrived late one cool, clear-skied April afternoon at Kaliningrad's shambolic, undersized airport—an architectural remnant from
Soviet times when it was a "closed" city (off-limits, that is, to non-
residents, owing to its strategic significance as the Soviet's westernmost military outpost) and had just a handful of visitors. We found

ourselves greeted with distrust. As we walked off the runway and entered the terminal building, stern blue-uniformed border guards brusquely took all the passengers' passports. The guards divided us into two lines, one for foreigners, the other for Russians. One guard detained Jeff, an American citizen, and led him up to a "detention" office—a room on the second floor that was empty, save for a fluorescent light and a desk. The guard handed his detainee over to his two colleagues, who questioned him about why he had come to Kaliningrad and the people on his contact list for the city.

"What do you think of Putin?" one of the officers demanded, his doughy face, slack paunch, and diminutive stature belying the seriousness of his expression. His comrade noted down Jeff's answers. The short man's questions were coming at a rapid pace.

"What are you doing here?"

"How is it that you speak Russian?"

"You say you're writing a book about Russia. About *what*, exactly?"

"Where are you staying in Kaliningrad?"

"Who's accompanying you?"

"What flight are you taking out of here, and on what date?"

The Western press was reporting that Russia, in apparent violation of a decades-old arms control treaty signed with the United States, had been busy stationing nuclear-capable intermediate-range Iskander missiles in the oblast, so such scrutiny was to be expected. Yet the guards relented when they learned that Jeff was a frequent foreign-policy commentator on the Russian airwaves and was married to a Russian.

Then the officers asked him to call Nina, a Russian citizen, and have her come up for her own cross-examination.

Easier said than done. The airport officials, when she had asked for directions, did not know where the apparently "secret" facility was located. Impatient, the border guards finally sent the American subject of their interrogation down to find her himself.

Nina found it hard to take her interrogator seriously, given his resemblance to the Pillsbury Doughboy. But then it dawned on her—this clever, persistent young man had overcome his looks to turn himself into a duty-bound Guardian of the Motherland, though, as it turned out, a polite and apologetic one. Nonetheless, his questions were still intrusive, a point-by-point verification of all the answers Jeff had given; the guard treated Nina as if she were Jeff's minder, as they would have done to most women seen with foreign men during the Cold War. They paid particular attention to his feelings about Putin.

"Does he approve of him? Do you?"

"Sometimes," she answered.

The point came, though, when she had had enough.

"Why all these questions?" she asked. "Kaliningrad isn't a closed city anymore, right?"

"Of course not," he replied. "We're very sorry. You see, this American *is* a *foreigner.* You do understand, don't you?"

Nina nodded, recalling similar interviews by American border officials when she first arrived in New York almost three decades earlier. And now, with relations between the two countries worsening by the day, a guarded approach to Western visitors was back in vogue again.

Jeff, for all intents and purposes a Muscovite now, didn't bat an eye at such a suspicious reception. Nina, living in New York, was choking with disgust.

"I feel violated," she said, shaking her head.

Finally we made our way out of the terminal. From the various souvenir stalls and a medley of amber amulets and portraits of varying dimensions made in his image, Vladimir Putin's stern gaze was fixed upon us with icy distrust. In addition to the amulets, the stalls held an array of amber bracelets, statuettes, and portraits of the double-headed eagle—Russia's coat of arms.

Amber, colloquially known as *Baltiyskoye zoloto* ("Baltic gold," except that it is fossilized tree resin), was everywhere on display, crowding shelves in the terminal's cluttered arrival hall. Artisans had turned the oblast's signature treasure into a local strategic resource on a par with oil and gas but utilized it to glorify the nation's president and insignia of state. It is, of course, a valuable resource. Nine-tenths of the world's supply of this unique substance originates in the oblast; Kremlin insiders hold a monopoly on its trade, worth more than a billion dollars a year.

Annexed by the Soviets after World War II—in Russia most commonly known as the Great Patriotic War—the Kaliningrad Oblast had previously belonged to the seven-hundred-year-old East Prussian region of Germany. Königsberg was the region's serene redbrick capital. Renamed Kaliningrad in 1946 to honor the just-deceased Soviet prime minister Mikhail Kalinin, the ceremonial head of state under Lenin and Stalin, the city became the capital of the Soviet Union's westernmost territory. Yet, apparently, some young people nowadays do not even know the origins of its name. We asked a twenty-five-year-old resident if he knew who Kalinin was, but, flustered, he admitted he did not. In any case, Kaliningrad's history is fraught with contradictions: the city has retained a Soviet functionary's name but has removed its hulking Lenin statue from its main square. In its place, municipal authorities have erected an obelisk to the Great Patriotic War. Nobody here would argue with that.

We took a taxi into town, approaching its skyline of mostly ten-story concrete apartment blocks and then trundling down often mud-splattered, potholed, and at times unmarked roads busy with slick, foreign-made cars. Some cars—especially BMWs, Audis, or Volkswagens, bore bumper stickers that read as an exhortation to attack: ON TO BERLIN, AGAIN! That militancy—Russians had defeated Nazi Germany and now use their automobiles to relive the victory—also displayed deep insecurity and evoked a sad, telling irony: they prize German automobiles above their own. The war had dealt cruelly with the city: the old cobbled German streets and quaint, gingerbread German houses remain intact almost exclusively in the Amalienau and Maraunenhof districts. Elsewhere, Kaliningrad, two and a half decades after the demise of the communist state, is Soviet and gray.

A Soviet war trophy of sorts, the Kaliningrad Oblast was, oddly, never formally transferred to the communist government; although Germany has never officially demanded its return, it has never renounced it, either. Perhaps, because of this, the fear of "re-Germanization" looms. Today, the Kremlin uses the exclave's very ambiguity to ratchet up anti-Western rhetoric.

But what does the fear of "re-Germanization" mean, exactly? Germanization in Kaliningrad—as understood by Russians—is the belief that Germany is eager to relocate ethnic Germans back to Kaliningrad, actively and aggressively infusing the territory with German culture. If such were to occur, it would surely be as bad as the Nazi occupation, the state insists. This fear of "re-Germanization" isn't novel; it was a constant undercurrent in Kaliningrad's Soviet history. And even though people here frequently travel to the Baltics, Poland, and Germany on long-term Schengen visas and witness little evidence of this "threat" while there, in a country where the state is so imposing, how does one disregard the propaganda? The Western menace is often discussed on television and the harrowing memory of Nazism is never allowed to quite fade into historical oblivion. And, the argument goes, just about the only thing protecting the country from this threat is Putin.

The next day was rainy and cool—typical Baltic weather. Maxim, the enterprising, thirtysomething son of a Moscow acquaintance of ours, kindly offered to give us a tour of the city and the surrounding towns. We drove out in his slick black Audi through morning traffic into the rain-sodden fields and forests of the countryside, briefly stopping at the military hamlet of Pionersky, our first encounter with Putin's specter on this trip. Rumor has it that the Russian president, who visits frequently, stays in a villa behind a tall green wall. We also dropped in on Svetlogorsk, an up-and-coming resort hardly renowned during the Soviet era. Then, the Soviets boasted of Latvia as their major Baltic vacation spot.

Maxim had previously worked as an engineer in the ports of Kaliningrad and Baltiysk (formerly the German town of Pillau) but now finds himself employed by the Chinese, preparing their soybean oil containers for shipping. These two ports shelter Russia's Baltic fleet and have, since the Soviet era, formed the epicenter of the region's military-oriented economy. Maxim told us that he was disappointed to have lost his state-related job recently owing to the Kremlin's shift of resources toward the Crimean Peninsula.

Crimea—in 988 it became the cradle of Orthodox Christianity for Kievan Rus, the original protostate for both Russia and Ukraine—had been officially Russian since 1783, when Empress Catherine the Great seized it from the Crimean Khanate, then a vassal state of the Ottoman Empire. In the Soviet Union Crimea remained under the Kremlin's jurisdiction, but in 1954 Nikita Khrushchev, who succeeded Joseph Stalin after his death, transferred it to Ukraine, which was, just like Russia, one of fifteen Soviet Republics within one country, the Union of Soviet Socialist Republics (USSR). There were many reasons for that transfer, administrative and economic, but uppermost was the desire to overcome Stalin's legacy of central control. Khrushchev thought of Ukraine and Russia as equal nations; he assigned historical primacy to ninth-century Kiev, not to Moscow, which until the 1100s was just an obscure village in the woods.

But following the Euromaidan protest movement in Kiev that led to the 2014 overthrow of Ukrainian president Viktor Yanukovych, a Putin ally, Russia annexed Crimea with a stealth invasion. Announcing the annexation in March 2014, Putin insisted that "in people's hearts and minds, Crimea has always been an inseparable part of Russia."[1] He thereby vilified Khrushchev—by whose action Russia was not "simply robbed, it was plundered." The speech set up a dichotomy that now stands at the core of Russian identity: strong-hand rulers like Putin or Stalin—those who collect Russian lands—standing against reformers like Khrushchev or Mikhail Gorbachev, who give them away. Kievan Rus, too, was eventually torn apart—Great Russia versus Small Russia ("Malorossiya," an old Russian name for Ukraine).

Arguing that for sixty years the Crimean dream has been to return under the wings of Mother Russia, the Kremlin had to deliver on its promise to improve life on the peninsula. The minimum monthly cost of living on the peninsula has been around 14,000 rubles ($240), which is more than half the average salary and 10 percent higher than that of Russia's southern regions bordering Crimea.[2] Moreover, the price for upgrading or rebuilding the peninsula's economic and social infrastructure has been calculated—so far—as anything from $10 billion (300 billion rubles) to $85 billion (3 trillion rubles).[3] And since Crimea lacked an overland connection to Russia (one of the reasons for Khrushchev's transfer), Russia constructed a bridge across the Kerch Strait, which consumed funds (almost $4 billion) that would have gone to other regions of the country. The bridge opened last year, shortly after Putin's triumphant win in presidential elections and his inauguration; its opening was, as one would expect, a grand affair, with Putin the first to cross it—in a giant Kamaz truck, an event broadcast throughout the country. The almost twelve-mile-long steel structure—the longest bridge in Europe— physically reunited Russia and Crimea. Or "Russia's birthplace,"[4] as Putin called it in his remarks.

To build that bridge and accomplish everything else it planned to do, the Russian government had been awarding contracts to Crimean businesses to keep them afloat as they went through the transition from Ukrainian to Russian sovereignty. And even though the military has been aggressively returning to the Kaliningrad exclave—as a strategic territory inside the West it has recently become one of Europe's most militarized places—the city's ports, which had once been thriving shipping centers, have slowly been abandoned as commercial entrepôts and taken on an important status as military installations. Replacing the Baltics, Crimea has become the new Russian showcase.

Maxim, displaying all the staple attributes of Russian (actually foreign) "cool"—Ray-Ban sunglasses, Polo jeans, and a blue quilted Barbour jacket—told us that his father, a Kaliningrad-born naval officer, had made a fortune on deals with the armed forces during the Putin years. Although unable to advance his own career, Maxim was certainly benefiting from his father's success: he owned a nice car and traveled abroad frequently. The young man both criticized and supported the Kremlin, thereby evincing an attitude we would encounter elsewhere in Russia—people neither demonized nor deified Putin but viewed him and his administration in light of their achievements and failings.

"Putin is a smart man," Maxim said admiringly, as his Audi carried us through the austere Baltic landscape—here, mostly coniferous forest. The air was redolent of the calming scents of pine cones and the nearby sea.

He spoke at length about the Kaliningrad Oblast's status as Russia's paramount "strategic zone."

"Do you believe that the Germans are really planning on invading?" we asked.

He did not, but he understood why the Russian government needed to send such a message—to instill in the oblast's population a mind-set for potential confrontation, so that no one would be taken by surprise if the West did attack. This might seem like a far-fetched notion, but the dramatic deterioration of relations between the West and Russia following the outbreak of the Ukraine crisis, and the buildup of North Atlantic Treaty Organization (NATO) forces in the Baltic region, made it a justifiable concern for the Russian government.

Yet Maxim was disillusioned. Since the 2014 annexation, life had become so much more expensive in Kaliningrad that shopping for food in Poland was cheaper. The ports, once bustling with trade, were now less busy. If at times they were employed, it was for the purpose of impressing on German cruise ship passengers the purportedly formidable might of the Russian navy.

"Once the cruise ships dock," Maxim told us, "a submarine, already retired from the fleet, surfaces within their view. The tourists don't know it's been retired. It's just used to show off, to tell them, 'See what Russia can do against your NATO!' And the Germans are frightened," he added with a chuckle, "and start taking pictures."

Although Maxim only half believed in the threat supposedly emanating from NATO, an older taxi driver we later struck up a conversation with unquestionably did. "In Russia, with all the history we have had, why should we be afraid of NATO? Of the Germans?" he asked sarcastically. Such is the sentiment prevailing throughout

Russia, as we would discover during our travels across the country's eleven time zones. Fears dormant for two decades have been reemerging with the renewed volatility in relations with NATO countries. In a country thrice invaded from the West in recent centuries—the last time in 1941, within living memory of so many Russians—the scars of war are real, the fear of it is hard to appreciate for those living with a more peaceful past.

The Kaliningrad Oblast, home to almost a million people, is now about 80 percent ethnically Russian, yet its Russian identity seems more fragile than elsewhere in the country. Perhaps this derives from a profound sense of cultural dislocation: through a program of coercion and promises, after the war the Soviet Union encouraged its peasants from central Russia to relocate as urban dwellers to the newly obtained exclave by way of tax credits and internal passports. Peasants didn't have such passports at the time, but urban dwellers did. They were also lured with a promise of comfortable homes and better supplies of food. Roughly 400,000 peasants moved to Kaliningrad between 1947 and 1950, to restart their lives and rebuild the city in the Soviet image.

Kaliningrad residents have since been taught to celebrate and, moreover, take credit for the legacy of a history that is not their own—for example, the fourteenth-century Königsberg Cathedral; the eighteenth-century philosopher Immanuel Kant; the famed Romantic writer E. T. A. Hoffmann, author of a fairy tale that the world-famous story "The Nutcracker" is based on, made even more famous by the ballet set to Pyotr Tchaikovsky's music. Marvelous, these—but not all Russian.

The currently Russian Kaliningrad region, with so little of its own Russian history, strikingly manifests the split personality disorder afflicting the country as a whole. Nothing symbolizes this division more than the bicephalous eagle. The eagle is a vestige of the Russian Empire, which claimed to be the successor to the Byzantine Empire from which Russia adopted its Christian beliefs. The Soviet Union abandoned the bird after 1917, but it was revived again when the new Russia was searching its past for a new identity.

Following the fall of Byzantium in the fifteenth century, Russia, fortified with its new double-headed eagle emblem, began seeing itself as the Guardian of the True Faith, in opposition to "heretical" Rome-based Catholicism. The eastern and western churches had excommunicated each other in the Schism of 1054, an event that would have momentous consequences for Russia and its relations with the West. Russians dubbed their own capital, Moscow, the "Third Rome" (the first Rome having been Rome, the second Constantinople). After the collapse of the Soviet Union in 1991, the Russian Orthodox Church reemerged from the shadows. During the Soviet era, after initial persecution, the church was tolerated; in post-1991 Russia, it has been celebrated and recognized in the country's otherwise secular constitution for the special role it had played in Russian history. As it had in bygone Byzantium, the double-headed eagle signifies Russian domination over a territory encompassing parts of both Europe and Asia. Russia's borders, after all, extend from Kaliningrad in Europe to the Kamchatka Peninsula in Asia (on the Pacific Ocean) and Chukotka, just across the Bering Strait from Alaska.

In the Putin years, the eagle's significance has come to rival that of the communist-era red star. The not-so-subtle idea behind the Byzantine connection is that Russia can (and should) exist only as a counterweight to the West; the West had troubled, often competitive relations with Byzantium just as it does now with Byzantium's spiritual heir, Russia. Nowadays, more than ever before, the double eagle embodies the country's split personality, the deep-rooted anxiety of a former superpower torn between the old and the new, between the past and present. We are Western, *European*, people told us in

Kaliningrad, yet their behavior, both haughty and insecure, could not have been more Russian. They argue that Russia, a continent of its own, doesn't need approval from abroad to prosper. Yet, simultaneously, they crave that approval.

In Kaliningrad a Western lifestyle has emerged, at least as residents understand it. They pass long hours in cafés and go on frequent shopping sprees to Poland. The "Westernness" of Russian towns and cities may be evaluated, to an extent, by the ease with which they have accepted the café culture of Europe—the sharing of leisurely moments over a cup of coffee, something less substantial than a meal or a drink. This, we would see, varies greatly from place to place. When, for example, people have disposable income in Tyumen (the capital of Siberian oil), they mostly spend it on furs, jewelry, and appliances; there, cafés are hard to come by. But in Kaliningrad—so close to the West and bearing a history that makes it Western—café culture exists, yet only in a superficial, inchoate form. Naturally, it has not cured the paranoid attitude of the authorities.

When asked how they feel about being Russian in this once so Prussian a city, the locals responded, "Well, *Krym nash* [Crimea is ours]!" In other words, "What we've taken we keep and make ours, by virtue of our strength, our military power; we took back Crimea, and we will not give it up!"

Many Russians indeed believe in their inherent ownership—97 percent of Crimeans voted for the annexation in March 2014; 88 percent of all Russians supported the move at the time, and in March 2018 the number is almost unchanged—86 percent.[5] The takeover has not only pitted Ukraine and the West against Russia, it has also divided many families. Even Khrushchev's son Sergei, Nina's uncle, once said that for the Russians, the public referendum that supported Crimea's takeover was as legitimate as throwing out Yanukovych was for the Ukrainians.

"*Krym nash*," the typical Russian response to any militant or oppressive move by the Kremlin, we saw as a display of feelings of insecurity and superiority all at once. Again, think of the double-headed eagle, the split-personality syndrome.

This newly revived fear of foreign associations—somewhat odd in an exclave so proud of its Western heritage—may well have been shared by one of our potential contacts, Andrei Klemeshev, the rector of the Immanuel Kant Baltic Federal University. Despite our repeated attempts to arrange an interview for this book, he avoided meeting us. We did not expect this: after all, his university was once the open-minded Albertina (as the University of Königsberg was formerly known), where Kant himself served as rector and taught logic and metaphysics; it was also the alma mater of Hoffmann and the birthplace of German Romanticism. Cordial on the phone at first, Klemeshev soon stopped answering our calls and ignored our texts. In a militarized city on the border, he might have decided that meeting with us would create problems for him with the authorities. This was a reasonable, if a slightly paranoid, supposition: after all, we—one of us an American, the other a Russian critic of Putin living in New York—might have served to incriminate him by mere association. His response reflected the increasing animosity between Russia and the West and was reminiscent of suspicions that made Russians wary of entertaining Westerners during the Cold War era. Others in Kaliningrad, too—including the head of the German Relations Center—refused to see us, citing busy schedules or forthcoming trips.

Our difficulties in arranging meetings put us in mind of a scene from Russian literature. In Mikhail Bulgakov's novel *The Master and Margarita*—which for so many Russians was, during the atheist decades of communism, a Soviet gospel of sorts—a theater administrator, Varenukha, dodged phone calls from those hoping to secure tickets to a scandalous show featuring Satan (the character Woland, in Bulgakov's telling). Spoofing Goethe's *Faust* and Kant's *The Critique of Pure Reason*, Bulgakov, writing in the Stalin era, depicted Woland as surveilling Muscovites en masse. Perhaps Klemeshev, too, thought he was being watched, and that we had come to town to ask him probing, even judgmental, questions.

One person, though, did agree to meet with us—Igor Rudnikov, a deputy of the Kaliningrad City Council and the editor of the popular opposition newspaper *Novye Kolesa* (New Wheels). (He would pay dearly for his political views; in November 2017 he was arrested on trumped-up charges of extortion.)

On an afternoon of rain and whipping wind we found him in his office in a nondescript suburb, which, like so much of Kaliningrad, resembled a construction site. A balding, trim bespectacled man in his early fifties, Rudnikov seemed excited. He had just returned from a court case that pitted him and his clients against a "criminal businessman" who wanted to build a fourteen-story hotel without the requisite permits. There had been two murders in Kaliningrad recently, he explained, but "The police are on the side of killers, of course."

Rudnikov was eager to talk to an American. In him, as in others we would encounter on our travels, Westerners—especially Americans—still inspire reverence and often receive preferential treatment, despite the xenophobic attitude of the authorities. The Soviet Union was largely closed to foreigners, and curiosity is still evident in now rather common encounters. Moreover, Russia has felt inferior and envious toward the West throughout its history, hence its often-militant display of grandstanding and superiority in human relations translates as fascination and desire for contact.

Receiving the American's attention, for an hour and a half, Rudnikov lectured us on Russian politics: "For a century, our country has been in the grip of total lies." As had the border guards at the airport, he treated Nina as Jeff's helper—a reflection of sexist bias still so common in Russia. Sure, women write books in Russia all the time, but a male foreigner is in any case worthier of serious attention than a Russian female. (We did not advertise Nina's Khrushchev connection.)

Rudnikov was particularly concerned about the vulnerability of an American writer traveling around Russia, believing that such an American would inevitably provoke suspicion. "Yesterday you Americans were our friends. Today, you aren't, and no one will want to talk to you. The way it is nowadays," he added, channeling the state's message, "if you explain you're writing a book, you'll be immediately considered a spy, a provocateur. You have to come up with a better cover."

Cover? The odd, very Cold War choice of words made us doubt what he was saying. The expressions on our faces surely reflected this, possibly prompting him to clarify: "But here in Kaliningrad it's different, of course. Europe is a stone's throw away. Here we see Russian patriots only at soccer matches."

This was not quite our impression. Rudnikov was a member of the opposition, after all, but as it turned out, he had it wrong. In places we were to visit farther east, which we expected to be more nationalist and patriotic, people were, in fact, much less suspicious than in Kaliningrad.

We told him of our travails in attempting to interview people in town. He offered an explanation that contradicted what he had just said. In his view, what made some in Kaliningrad so closed-minded, was the oblast's proximity to the West and, therefore, at least as the authorities saw it, the distinct possibility that Kaliningrad might succumb to Western influence.

Rudnikov told us that in the early 2000s Kaliningrad was proud that Putin's then-wife Lyudmila hailed from here.

"Putin was no stranger to this town," he said. "What's more, for the first two terms of his presidency, Kaliningrad was supposed to become Russia's European enclave, a qualitative test for Russo-European relationships that would then be replicated in the rest of the country." In fact, he explained, in 2005 Königsberg/Kaliningrad celebrated its 750th anniversary as a joint German-Russian city. This reflected a dramatic change in the authorities' attitude toward Kaliningrad's history, which they had previously depicted as beginning, basically, only in 1945. Germany welcomed the inclusive continuity of the "new" view of the city's past; German tourists whose families were originally from the area could now visit without feeling burdened by the Nazis' crimes in the Soviet Union. The government then proclaimed Kaliningrad a Free Economic Zone (appropriately nicknamed *Yantar*, or Amber) and dubbed it Russia's Hong Kong, with tax tariffs lower than elsewhere in the country. Rudnikov detailed for us the inevitable distortions to which such status led: clever entrepreneurs imported goods—from foodstuffs to automobiles—from Germany and other European countries only to repackage and relabel them "Made in Kaliningrad," so that they might sell them as authentically Russian.

Kaliningrad's pro-Western orientation, however, began to change in 2002, when President George W. Bush announced that the United States was unilaterally withdrawing from the Anti-Ballistic Missile Treaty (a cornerstone arms control agreement of the Cold War) it had signed with the Soviet Union. He further decided to deploy missile defense systems (supposedly against threats emanating from Iran) in Poland and other Eastern European countries. Relations soured further after the Russian annexation of Crimea and the subsequent imposition of Western economic sanctions on the Russian economy. Kaliningrad set about converting itself into a fortress of sorts, in preparation for conflict with the NATO alliance. Russia accomplished this easily; after all, it had never fully dismantled the oblast's military infrastructure and continued sheltering its Baltic fleet there. In addition to basing Iskander missiles in the oblast, which became official in 2018, it has recently set about building long-range anti-missile radar installations.

During the Prussian centuries, the city was a fortress, too, then facing the Russian frontier. In the Soviet decades, the old German forts—seven in total, grim, all built of grimy red brick—were converted into Great Patriotic War museums and operate as such today. The tanks and submarines strategically placed by these forts serve as a reminder to visitors of the threat from the West.

Rudnikov insisted that actual warfare was not looming; instead, a virtual combat involving a "hybrid" war of perceptions and information was on, because neither side—for obvious reasons—actually wants to fight. Nevertheless, "This threat," he said, "helps bolster the state's propaganda. After the Soviet collapse there was talk that Kaliningrad might split from Russia, just as parts of Yugoslavia broke away, and became independent." He termed the "threat of Germanization" a convenient political tool, nothing more.

During the war the Soviets decimated large parts of the city in retaliation for the Nazi destruction of so much of western Russia. The city had been laid to waste: infrastructure was in ruins, there was no running water or electricity, and a shortage of food and medical supplies persisted. Stalin, however, saw an opportunity amid the destruction. He would have Königsberg completely rebuilt to represent the New Soviet City. This transformation—from a "fascist" city embedded in almost a millennium of German culture into a Socialist dream town devoid of German influence—necessitated a complete erasure of its past.

Nevertheless, the Soviet government followed political considerations in determining what it destroyed and what it left standing.

Miraculously surviving both the Nazi and the Soviet assaults, Königsberg Cathedral is still the focal point of the city. It stands on the stone embankment of the lightly wooded Kant Island (once Kneiphof Island) in the Pregel River, amid Kaliningrad's Soviet-style concrete apartment blocks. Kant is interred beside its north wall, in a triple-plinthed grave supporting an elongated pyramidal slab. The Bolsheviks considered Kant a precursor to Karl Marx, and Kant's *The Critique of Pure Reason* was seen as an argument against the existence of God. Hence, the Soviet government decided to leave the cathedral intact.

During the Soviet decades the house of worship fell into disrepair, but under Putin, the maintenance of Kaliningrad's cultural heritage became a priority. The Gothic cathedral was renovated and restored to much of its glory.

Much, but not all. One drizzly morning, we took a taxi to the cathedral, passing by older women selling flowers, fruits, and vegetables from little stands on the sidewalks, and noting scruffy men of all ages bundled up against the weather, fishing for pike in the canal's pewter-colored waters. We walked around the massive redbrick structure, where, despite ten years of restoration, many of its windows still sported shoddy slabs of cardboard instead of the original stained glass. Approaching Kant's tomb, we heard a Russian guide addressing a group of fifteen Russian tourists. After informing her guests that Kant lay buried in front of them, she added, with a schoolmarm's imperiousness, "And now I invite you to honor the memory of the great philosopher Immanuel Kant with a moment of silence."

The group fell silent, and so did we—out of shock. After all, who honors a philosopher, a thinker whose legacy consists of words, with silence? Such a practice was eerily familiar from Soviet days, when it was common to observe "moments of silence" for the memory of

Lenin, Stalin, or Leonid Brezhnev, who succeeded Khrushchev after his ouster in 1964. We half-expected her to refer to Kant as "our Soviet comrade."

After some seventy years of communism, during which the state told its citizens not only how to think about politics, but what to make of history, philosophy, and pretty much everything else, Soviet bureaucratic jargon still has a grip on the Russian psyche. When czarist-era peasants became post-1917 proletarian revolutionaries, they adopted this officialese to convince themselves and others of their new status, affirming their transformation from peasant to urbanite. One of Bulgakov's satirical masterpieces, *The Heart of a Dog*, recounts just such a phenomenon. The writer had a Russian scientist transmogrify a lovable mutt into a despicable communist functionary spouting militantly officious lingo to humorous effect. After the Soviet Union's collapse such language still permeates the interactions between citizens and state employees—and even those in the private sector.

We found evidence of this at the cathedral's elaborate lavatory, where a sign outside indicated its *rezhim raboty*, or "work regime." "Regime" is a holdover from the Soviet past, when all sorts of institutions, from airports to factories to local bakeries to corner cobblers, were governmental entities serving the nation in accordance with criteria laid out in five-year plans. The economy was planned, and everything was ready for potential militarization. (Twenty-five years since the end of communism, a good number of cafés and restaurants—and not only in Kaliningrad—still present themselves to the public as if they were national security installations.) Inside the lavatory, the middle-age female attendant, when we complimented her on the lush, even exotic, potted flowers gracing the atrium between the men's and women's rooms, replied gruffly that they exist *"po rasporyazheniyu administratsii."* She meant that the flowers were arranged according to the instructions of the church's administration. State planning has not only failed to fade away, it has extended to public toilets.

The cathedral opens every day starting at ten in the morning. Much more than a church, it now hosts, on its upper stories, a museum devoted to Kant. On the ground floor it houses a spectacular music hall staging concerts in the evenings and featuring a Baroque organ dating back to the 1800s; two chapels are in operation just inside the entrance portals. Yet here, even religious faith bears traces of history and politics: one chapel is Lutheran, a tribute to the Protestantism of its builders; the other, Russian Orthodox.

We were among the first to walk in that morning. By the ticket office we immediately found ourselves witness to a conversation reflecting Russia's internal tensions—between its history and its ideology, its geography, and its identity.

An elderly cleaning woman saluted the uniformed guard on duty and wished him a pleasant Border Guard Day. In fact she was a month early; Border Guard Day falls on May 28. No matter: in Russia, holidays honoring members of various professions—journalists, teachers, postmen, the armed forces, and so on—sprinkle the calendar.

The man replied, "I'm guarding the cathedral, not the border."

"No," the woman said, "we're surrounded by borders. We must be vigilant! We're all border guards here!"

A passing Lutheran priest, stern and silver-haired, jumped into the conversation. "Why do they even bother to worship God when the only person they truly worship is Stalin?"

The cleaner answered, "Well, we have to pray to someone, and Stalin is the worthiest. He instilled the fear of God in everyone." The incongruity of describing an atheist tyrant—in the 1930s alone almost 200,000 priests were arrested,[6] and half were shot to death—as capable of arousing piety eluded her, as it eludes many increasingly patriotic Russians. She then turned to an icon of Christ above the entrance to the Orthodox chapel and crossed herself.

Once inside the Lutheran chapel, we looked to the priest—also a tour guide, as it happened—for an explanation. Why would Stalin be so openly worshipped in such a "Western" city? Moreover, in a cathedral the Bolsheviks might have leveled, had they governed the oblast in their first decades in power? Even in Moscow, adoration for the tyrant—many Russians do hold him in high regard and his rating as the "most outstanding" Russian tops everyone's list, including Putin's—finds expression in subtler ways.[7]

The priest shrugged. "She's a drill sergeant," he said sarcastically. "So is everyone here."

He had a point. A base, Soviet mind-set survives in much of Russia, even in a place as un-Soviet as a cathedral. We soon encountered further evidence of this. We sat down on a bench in front of the music hall to check the concert schedule, only to be ordered by an elegantly dressed attendant to get up and move—now!

"You can't sit here!" she barked.

"Why not?"

"You just *can't!*"

We could hear music—musicians rehearsing for their evening concert?—coming from behind the door to the concert hall. Perhaps, we thought, she didn't want us to listen for free. Still, there were polite ways of asking us to leave. The underlying assumption of Soviet life, and much of Russian life, too, is that things are forbidden—unless you are advised otherwise.

The Lutheran priest, who turned out to be ethnically German, informed us that he's "here because of my German roots." His mien displayed the arrogance of a Westerner certain that his right to reside in Kaliningrad trumped that of the presumably "inferior" Russian usurpers surrounding him. He went on to tell us that he descended from Germans who, some 250 years ago, heeded the call of the Prussian-born empress Catherine the Great to her former countrymen to come to Russia and establish orderly, German-style farming amid disorderly Russian peasants, mostly along the Volga River. (His family ended up in Kaliningrad after the war, possibly uprooted by Stalin's forced transfer of potentially "treasonous" populations.) Catherine the Great's invitation marked the beginning of the country's Russo-German history, and thereby set up a dichotomy within Russia itself—enlightened *European* Russia versus ignorant *Russian* Russia—the very Russia embodied, at least for this priest, by the "drill sergeant" janitor.

We ascended the stairs to the cathedral's Kant museum, walking in past a table where a vendor sold Kant chocolate, Kant kitchen magnets, and Kant mugs, alongside Putin portraits, Putin mugs, and a variety of badges and paraphernalia bearing the eagle. Inside the museum proper, we examined Kant busts, Kant sculptures, and books by and about Kant in many languages. Soon we came upon a diorama of old Königsberg, with its miniature brick buildings and cobbled streets laid out in perfect order beneath churches with soaring spires—all in all, a placid, quaint depiction of a past era.

The blind arrogance of such a display here was cynical indeed; after all, it was the Russians who reduced the city to rubble in 1945 to stamp out traces of its German past.

And Stalin's vision of rebuilding the city was a far more complicated affair than the display let on; it involved cultural nuances, propaganda, and ethnic cleansing.

It is important to remember that as the Russian peasantry rebuilt their new city, Stalin was effectively convincing Soviet citizens that the biggest enemy facing the Soviet Union often came from within the country—and particularly from ethnic minorities such as Germans, Chechens and Dagestanis in the Caucasus, and others elsewhere. Ultimately, both the Soviet Union and the newly relocated Russian peasants of Kaliningrad blamed ethnic Germans for the war. By that time, many people, and not just the Soviets in fact, had come to believe that Germans were inherently fascist. So the Germans had to be blamed for difficulties suffered in Kaliningrad's struggle to become the New Soviet City.

Through locally taken decisions the Russian peasants occupying the city began removing traces of Germanness: the boulevards were widened, the German-like facades of buildings were removed, the ruins of castles were destroyed, and monuments were taken down. The final step was the expulsion of 100,000 Germans from Kaliningrad. Some were either expelled to East Germany; others became forced laborers or starved.

Effectively, within five years, the city had wiped out the greater part of its historical legacy.

The diorama in the cathedral's museum appeared designed to tout Russia's ability to bridge the old and the new, as if Russia had nothing to do with the death of the past. That death was evident as soon as one stepped outside the cathedral. As the contrast between the idyllic diorama of the museum and the roughshod cement cityscape demonstrated, Russia was neither at ease with its history nor capable of entirely rejecting it. Despite all the efforts made—by both the state and its people—the idea of a new Soviet Kaliningrad was never fully realized, nor did the city fully erase its German roots.

And yet nowhere was this visible in the idyllic diorama. Nor, of course, was Kaliningrad's most prominent present-day feature: the gigantic twenty-one-story House of Soviets. The building calls to mind a shoddily designed modernist office chair built in the 1970s. Built during Brezhnev's time, it is the embodiment of an era once known as "developed socialism." So developed, in fact, that it ended with the collapse of the Soviet Union, the building never completed as a result.

Kaliningradians joke that the House of Soviets is their most prominent landmark. At least, we learned, it is a useful one. For a reasonable price, they told us, you can bribe a guard to enter it at night for wall climbing or to throw a drinking party with a view of the city and the sea.

After sifting through two floors of the museum's Kant memorabilia, we mounted a steep staircase leading up to a half-empty chamber where the philosopher's openmouthed plaster death mask, so fragile and delicate, lay under glass. The mask left us with the impression that we had come across a more refined version of Lenin embalmed in his mausoleum on Moscow's Red Square. Indeed, Kant's iconic presence here and throughout the museum and town, is almost Lenin-like, appearing when least expected, yet almost omnipresent. To paraphrase an old Russian saying—first it was the nineteenth-century poet Alexander Pushkin who was *nashe vse* (our everything); then it was Lenin; and here in Kaliningrad it is Kant.

Our stay in Kaliningrad drew to a close. Early on the first sunny afternoon we had experienced since landing, we arrived at the city's airport to find its departure hall in chaos. Unruly lines of passengers shifted between registration counters—inexplicably, check-ins for flights were first announced at one counter but then switched to others without warning. No one could say why. Loud gaggles of Chinese students showed up and barged in, pressing around us, leaving us little hope of making our flight. We managed to reach a counter only by cutting into lines, as did everyone else. So much about traveling in Russia has become easier, but the Russians' behavior made sense here, and was a reversion to historical norms: in the past, the Russian version of standing in line was akin to storming a cattle wagon. Putin's stern gaze set in amber fixed us from the souvenir stands as, just barely, we managed to check in and head for the gate to board our flight. Even in the city Putin once hoped to transform into a tiny "Europe within Russia," chaos Russian style was still, at least in places, a fact of life.

We flew out over the sea, circled around, and turned east. From high above we saw the land beyond Kaliningrad's concrete bounds sweep away into rain-drenched countryside—the Baltic Plain, a band of sandy-soiled terrain and pine forests stretching from Germany in the west across Poland all the way to Saint Petersburg in the east. Seen from the sky, the plain offered somnolent vistas promising a tranquility that surely helped men of letters, including Kant and Hoffmann, in their meditation and creative labors. We even spotted the resort town of Svetlogorsk that we had visited earlier with Maxim in his Audi. There, we had found the facades of new shops and markets copying the old, resembling Disney-like re-creations of the pre-war Prussian buildings surrounded by drab Soviet suburbs; for us, the scene stood for the spirit of Putin's country, a country often in contradiction with itself.

2

THE MOTHER OF ALL RUSSIAN CITIES OR THE THREAT TO MOTHER RUSSIA?

TIME ZONE: MSK-1 FROM NOVEMBER TO MARCH AND MSK FROM MARCH TO OCTOBER; UCT+2

The brightest light of all [in Kiev] was the white cross held by the gigantic statue of St. Vladimir atop Vladimir Hill. It could be seen from far, far away and often in summer, in thick black mist, amid the osier-beds and tortuous meanders of the age-old river, the boatmen would see it and by its light would steer their way to the City and its wharves.

—Mikhail Bulgakov, *The White Guard*

A hundred years after the Bolshevik Revolution and the subsequent Civil War between the Reds and the Whites, so well described by the Ukrainian-born Russian writer Mikhail Bulgakov in his classic 1924 novel (quoted in the epigraph), Kiev's prince Vladimir the Great has only grown in stature and symbolism. Ruling from 980 to 1015, the prince brought Christianity to his land, Kievan Rus, importing it from the Byzantine Greeks. He has now come to personify the current rift between Russia and Ukraine, two countries locked in a conflict over territory and asserting primacy in their shared Slavic heritage.

Who is senior, the Ukrainians or the Russians? Prince Vladimir ruled over the regional proto-Slavic state, Kievan Rus—a name bespeaking this historical dilemma. It's worth noting that at the time Rus was a voluntary conglomeration of independent city-states with elements of nascent democracy—a democracy laid waste by Mongol invaders in the thirteenth century and eventually stamped out entirely by Russian rulers in Moscow.

A city of some three million, Kiev shares a time zone with Moscow from March to October (during daylight savings time, which, since 2014, Russia has not observed). This one-hour time difference lasting just half a year connotes both the connection between these once brotherly nations and Ukraine's revolt against control by the dominant imperial Russia. Spring is the best time to visit Kiev, so we chose to arrive in April—and pay our respects. And respects were due: Kiev is, after all, *mat gorodov russkikh*—the mother of all Russian cities. Given the critical role Ukraine has played in Russia's history—and especially the dilemmas with which it presents Russia in the present—it cannot be ignored.

One needs to be fit to make even an unhurried ascent to the summit of Vladimir's Hill from Khreshchatyk, Kiev's broad, chestnut-tree-lined central avenue, which the Soviet authorities—under the direction of Nikita Khrushchev—transformed into the capital's main thoroughfare after the Great Patriotic War. From Khreshchatyk's Independence Square, or *Maidan Nezalezhnosti*—the famed Maidan from which Ukrainians launched their Euromaidan protest movement in late 2013—it takes thirty minutes to mount the hill to the station from which an oft-crowded funicular car spirits passengers up to Kiev's highest terrain. Once having disembarked atop Vladimir's Hill, though, visitors may survey the Dnieper River bisecting the city below and enjoy a magnificent view of the age-old waterway so vital to Ukraine's history.

Fresh off the funicular, we walked out onto Mikhailov Square, noting the tony restaurants and posh hotels that have sprung up around it in recent years. The square, dating from the twelfth century—even if known by several other names since then—was once the site of demonstrations and uprisings. It is a host of contradictions: it has both the gray, imposing, oddly concave Soviet-style Ministry of Foreign Affairs; an incongruous, ornately decorated, yet entirely empty children's carousel; an angel-shaped monument to the Holodomor, the Great Famine of 1932–1933 (Kiev has a number of these sculptures); and Saint Michael's Monastery, with its white-trimmed lapis lazuli facades and soaring, cross-topped golden domes.

Just outside the monastery's portals, along its western wall, a long, glass-encased pictorial memorial stands honoring the Ukrainians who have died fighting for their country in its east against the rebel troops of the self-proclaimed republics of Donetsk and Luhansk—officially, the single Confederate Republic of Novorossiya ("New Russia"). The Confederate Republic's founders resurrected the czarist-era name Novorossiya for these territories, which have ethnic Russian majorities and a strong sense of Russian, as opposed to Ukrainian, identity.

In Moscow, one hears a good deal about the war for Novorossiya, which has allied itself with the Kremlin. However, so far away in the Russian capital, the conflict seems almost imagined—little more than conjured-up fodder for patriotic propaganda. Ukraine's break with Russia in 2014 has been, nevertheless, very real and wrenching both for those in the Kremlin nostalgic for control over the large Slavic state on Russia's southern flank, and also for a good number of ordinary Russians, who view Ukraine as Malorossiya ("Little Russia," a subordinate Slavic "little brother"). All Russians, though, understand that the land Ukraine occupies was the wellspring of Russian civilization, the hallowed locus of the *Kreshcheniye Rusi* (the Baptism of Rus) that Prince Vladimir brought about more than a thousand years ago.

The Orange Revolution of 2004, which after rigged presidential elections overturned the victory of the Kremlin-compliant Viktor Yanukovych (who hailed from the Donetsk Oblast, now part of Novorossiya), ended with installing in power two pro-Western politicians: President Viktor Yushchenko and Prime Minister Yulia Tymoshenko. Although eventually doubts grew about the two leaders' commitment to democracy, the pro-European Union Euromaidan uprising still proved that the independent Ukraine is no longer Malorossiya.

We walked along the memorial wall surveying the faces and names of men and women who went to eastern Ukraine to defend their homeland, and the reality sank in: Ukraine is at war, and with Russia—a once-inconceivable notion.

Our stroll eventually led us away from Mikhailov Square, down a path to a headland overlooking the Dnieper, where a daunting, sixty-seven-foot-high statue of Prince Vladimir (Volodymyr, in Ukrainian) surveys the island-studded river and the parks and apartment blocks on the right bank. The statue dates from 1853, the era of the Russian Empire under Nicholas I. Constructed of iron and bronze in neo-Byzantine style for the four hundredth anniversary of Byzantium's fall to the Turks, Prince Vladimir holds aloft a fifteen-foot cross, as though baptizing the land anew. The monument was meant to both highlight Russia's spiritual ties to the Eastern Roman Empire and to establish continuity between Emperor Nicholas I and Vladimir the Great. Though what is less advertised is that following his conversion to Christianity, Vladimir led a less than pious lifestyle that induced one medieval chronicler to dub him *fornicator maximus.* One version of history has it that the still-pagan Vladimir seized the Crimean town of Chersonesus from the Greeks and agreed to return it only if the Byzantine emperor Basil II would grant him the hand in marriage of the emperor's sister, Anna Porphyrogenita. The Greeks acceded to this demand, on the condition that Vladimir convert to Christianity, which he did, with some historians placing his baptism in Chersonesus, others in Kiev, and with the instatement thereafter of Christianity as Kievan Rus's religion. For having inducted Rus into Christendom, the church canonized him.

Some medieval Russian sources put it differently: the Russians sent envoys to neighboring lands to assess their faiths for possible adoption. Vladimir rejected both Judaism and Islam—the latter because of its prohibition against alcohol. (*"Veseliye Rusi piti est* [drinking is the joy of Rus]," purportedly declared Vladimir.) Yet, it was the ethereal, spiritual beauty of the Greek Orthodox liturgy that won over the Russians. Conversion ensued.

In fact, Byzantine Christianity was already making inroads into Kievan Rus and its adoption would have made eminent sense, given Kiev's trade contacts with Byzantium. However it came about, the acceptance of Christianity by Kievan Rus from the Byzantine Greeks and not the Roman Catholics would have momentous consequences for world history. Ultimately, it placed Russia, spiritually, if not civilizationally, outside Western Europe and fostered a faith-based isolationism, which included the rise of the messianic notion of Moscow as the Third Rome and of Russia as the country destined by God to determine the fate of mankind.

Admiring the pugnacious Vladimir the Great, the atheist Soviets left the statue that Nicholas I erected to him in Kiev, sparing it the fate they reserved for most other monuments glorifying the monarchy or religion. Gazing up at Vladimir's weathered bronze grandeur, we could not help thinking that the statue looked remarkably Stalinesque. Its baroque laurel wreaths and the bas-reliefs on its pedestal recall Stalinist classicism, which itself derived from Byzantine models. Some have speculated that the bas-relief—just beneath Vladimir's feet—of a meat cleaver crossed with a torch signifies power and truth, a tribute to Masonic fashions of the nineteenth century.[1] In fact, the meat cleaver and torch bear an eerie resemblance to the Soviet hammer and sickle, which also stood, in their own way, for power and truth. Even Vladimir's hand, raised to grip the majestic cross blessing the city, conjures up the thousands of statues of another Vladimir—Vladimir Lenin—whose giant marble, iron, or bronze right hands all reached out toward the bright communist future across the Soviet Union. In many places in Russia, they still do. Ever inclined to humor, Russians often joke that what Lenin was really trying to do was hail a cab.

Even at the dawn of his rule over the Soviet Union, Stalin, too, admired the ancient Vladimir. He considered Bulgakov's *The White Guard* his favorite novel, presumably because it conveyed the grandiosity of the monarchical attributes of statues, state rituals, and military ceremonies. He read the book numerous times. When Bulgakov refashioned it into a play, the dictator frequented its performances at the Moscow Art Theater. In his later years, and especially after the war, Stalin paid a great deal of attention to the symbolism of the imperial Russian state and desired to root his own Soviet empire in Russia's historical legacy. Vladimir the Great—Saint Vladimir, the Baptizer of Russia—served as his intermediary with Russia's distant past. To cement the connection, the statue was renovated in 1953 for its one hundredth anniversary—ironically the year of Stalin's death.

The Ukrainians now view Prince Vladimir differently, having begun, after the 1991 Soviet collapse, to claim him for themselves. For them, he is the Kiev-born prince Volodymyr, the medieval Ukrainian leader who established Kievan Rus a century before Moscow even existed. In *The White Guard*, Bulgakov wrote,

> In winter the cross would glow through the dense black clouds, a frozen unmoving landmark towering above the gently sloping expanse of the eastern bank, whence two vast bridges were flung across the river. One, the ponderous Chain Bridge that led to the right-bank suburbs, the other high, slim and urgent as an arrow that carried the trains from where, far away, crouched another city, threatening and mysterious: Moscow.[2]

The author, in this and other passages, confirms the timeless dichotomy between the Russian center and its rebellious Ukrainian periphery. In the novel, the action unfolds in 1918 in Kiev, before the Bolsheviks took control, and where Saint Vladimir's Christian legacy was still intact, as opposed to the soon-to-be-Stalinist Moscow, where another Vladimir, Lenin, would become the god of communism.

The themes with which Bulgakov dealt in his work resonated with us throughout our journeys around Russia. Bulgakov, once a journalist who covered politics and human interest news for the Moscow daily *Gudok* (The Whistle), famous for its satirical pages, in his later fiction addressed the relations between people and state power. How do they react to the sudden replacement of the monarchy with a dictatorship of the proletariat, which transforms them from being subjects of the czar into members of the proletarian masses?

A similar question concerned us: Russians, as a rule, adore leaders who flaunt their power—and even deploy it, as did Putin in annexing Crimea. Are Russian subjects subordinating their lives to the greatness of the state? Or are they citizens holding individual rights? Now more than ever, almost a hundred years after Bulgakov's novel, the conflict between open-minded, liberal-spirited Kiev and imperial, autocratic Moscow rages on, both literally—as in the current conflict between Russia and Ukraine—and figuratively, in the Russian mind-set.

Fittingly, the double-headed eagle inherited from Byzantium has been playing into the rivalry. One could say that the Ukrainian head wants to turn toward Western democracy, with Ukraine becoming an enlightened European state. The Russian head, however, remains as it has been for centuries, facing the empire in the east. After all, following the fall of Byzantium, Moscow, not Kiev, assumed the historic mantle of the Third Rome and bore the torch of Christian Orthodoxy. Moreover, since the monument was built for the Russian emperor Nicholas I, St. Vladimir is "ours," they say, just as *Krym nash* (Crimea is ours).

In 2014 Putin, upon annexing Crimea, justified Russia's claims to the peninsula in his address to the State Duma:

> We are not simply close neighbors but, as I have said many times already, we are one people. Kiev is the mother of Russian cities. Ancient Rus is our common source and we cannot live without each other. . . . Crimea is our common historical legacy and a very important factor in regional stability. And this strategic territory should be part of a strong and stable sovereignty, which today can only be Russian.[3]

From this and similar declarations one may extrapolate the Kremlin's reasoning: as the European Union supported the Euromaidan—and Germany, once the country of Nazism that the Soviets defeated, is the most powerful state in the Union—Russia and its historical space are essentially under assault from the West, from those bent on destroying Russian supranational identity.

Because Kiev had lurched westward with its protest movement,

Putin argued that Ukrainians had betrayed their cultural roots and endangered Russia's security. After all, a westward-looking Ukraine might join NATO; the alliance's promise of eventual membership (made in the Bucharest Declaration of 2008) figured in his thinking.

In 2016 Putin, who happens to be Prince Vladimir's namesake, had his own statue of Vladimir the Great built in Borovitskaya Square, just outside the Kremlin's western corner walls. In doing so, he was implicitly calling for Russian national unity and the defiance of enemies at home and abroad, just as the prince did a millennium ago. This move dismayed Ukrainians commemorating the millennial of St. Vladimir's death in 1015. They complained that Russia has misappropriated a key element of their spiritual heritage. After all, Vladimir the Great had no relation to Moscow.

The new monument in Moscow was originally to stand more than seventy feet higher than its prototype in Kiev. The authorities planned to locate it on the Russian capital's most elevated terrain—Sparrow Hills (formerly Lenin Hills), similar to Vladimir overlooking Kiev. But ecological protests broke out, which prompted municipal authorities to move it to a more prominent—if lower—space a mere hundred yards from the Kremlin.

Another Vladimir, Lenin, is also now separating Russia and Ukraine. Ukraine once had the greatest number of Lenin statues in the former Soviet Union—more than five thousand, according to one count.[4] For the past twenty years it has struggled to take them down. During the Euromaidan protests, *Leninopady*, or "falling Lenins"—as the demolitions of Lenin statues came to be popularly known—proliferated. Often, Lenins that remained standing were "Ukrainianized"—that is, dressed up in *vyshivanki*, traditional Ukrainian embroidered blouses. For many Ukrainians, tearing down their granite-and-bronze Lenins symbolized their country's right to determine its own future. Others opposed the demolitions—especially

those who were aging and conservative and valued Russia's close historical ties to Ukraine—and, most of all, pined for the more stable,
if less free, Soviet decades.

Both of us had been to Kiev numerous times before. Jeff first visited
in 1985 and kept going back to see his friends and relatives of his
wife there. Most notably, though, he sojourned in Kiev after the Orange Revolution and witnessed the deep disillusionment that followed, as President Yushchenko and his prime minister Tymoshenko
ignored Ukraine's pressing problems and became adversaries. At
least the Orange Revolution never lost its ability to inspire hope; for
a time, people were able to confront Russian pressure and liberate
themselves from it.

For Nina, the connection goes even deeper—all the way back to
her great-grandfather, Nikita Khrushchev. Born in 1894 in the
Russian village of Kalinovka on the Ukrainian border, he moved at
age sixteen to the Ukrainian mining town of Yuzovka, which is now
Donetsk, a hotbed of pro-Novorossiya sentiment following the ouster
of Yanukovych and Russia's annexation of Crimea. In 1938, Stalin
appointed Khrushchev, known for his expertise in agriculture, to be
Communist Party Secretary in Kiev and tasked him with returning the republic to normalcy after the devastations of Holodomor.
This man-made famine of 1932–1933 had taken between six million and seven million lives and involved state confiscation of
grain from Ukrainian and Russian peasants for export, in return
for heavy machinery needed for Stalin's industrialization drive.
Khrushchev argued against the Soviet Union's reliance on Ukraine
for a large part of its agricultural production and stressed the need
to develop more effective farming elsewhere in the country.

During the Great Patriotic War, Khrushchev served at the Ukrainian front, but once the war ended, he took up his old job again—running the Communist Party in Kiev. In 1956, having assumed control of the Soviet Union, he denounced Stalin's crimes and the Cult of Personality in his now-famous "Secret Speech" at the Twentieth Party Congress and began de-Stalinization and the reform policy known as the Thaw. Ukraine celebrated the resulting lessening of repression more than any other Soviet republic.

After Khrushchev's removal from power and Brezhnev's ascension, the former fell into disfavor in Moscow, but his name has largely enjoyed respect in Ukraine. Of course, some Ukrainians consider him, despite his revelation of Stalin's crimes, no less a Soviet oppressor than any other Communist Party leader. But more often than not, people's faces light up at his mention; they remember that, although he was ethnically Russian, at home he often said that "in his soul" he "wanted to be Ukrainian"; he respected Ukrainians for their work ethic and independent spirit. They recount glowingly how Khrushchev tried to improve life in their republic and at times even confronted Stalin about his neglect and abuse of Ukraine's agricultural potential. With its relatively warm climate and fertile land, Ukraine had historically been known as the "bread basket" of the empire, Russian or Soviet, but Khrushchev argued it should not be the only one.

When in 1954 he transferred Crimea from Russia to Ukraine, he hoped only to improve the peninsula's governance. At the time, Ukrainians hardly noticed. (Even Khrushchev's older daughter Rada, who traveled with her father surveying the area before the transfer, remembered, after the Crimea annexation in 2014, that "At the time they didn't even want Crimea. Apart from historians, few Ukrainians cared about it as the possible original baptismal place of Kievan

Rus or considered it to be theirs.") Over decades, however, the peninsula did come to represent Ukraine's competitive spirit with the Russians.

Although for the past fifteen years Kiev has been undergoing something of a Westernizing renovation with loans from the European Union to help, at least for the past few years, the sum effect is still less café cappuccino than café *vareniki* (Ukrainian dumplings). Andreyevsky Descent, where Bulgakov once lived, has slowly become a bustling market street on which one can buy locally sewn *vyshivanki* (in sizes promoted as large enough to fit Lenin statues), artisanal pottery, and traditional Ukrainian dresses and blouses superior in quality to if not always as fashionable as, say, Ivanka Trump's made-in-China brand. A large banner stretched across the road proudly announced, in Ukrainian, that *Andriivskii uzviz—tse Monmartr abo Grenich Villidzh Kiiva* (Andreyevsky Descent neighborhood is the Montmartre or the Greenwich Village of Kiev).

Down in the city center, we would later walk around Kiev Passage, a pedestrian street off Khreshchatyk. There, high-end designer boutiques—Max Mara, Gucci, Louis Vuitton—give off an air of European chic.

Kiev may be the capital of a country aspiring to join the West, but much about it retains whiffs of the provincial Soviet midsize town. The pedestrian underpasses running beneath major thoroughfares in the center, like the labyrinthine tunnels leading to the subway entrances, recall scenes from the Moscow underground of the 1990s—kiosks of various shapes and sizes sell everything from milk to pastries, stockings and local Ukrainian handicrafts. Patriotically emblazoned in the yellow-and-blue colors of the Ukrainian flag, T-shirts and even kitchen towels also feature portraits of poet Taras Shevchenko, the nineteenth-century anti-Russian nationalist.

We chose to stay in the Hotel Dnipro, which once welcomed Com-

munist Party apparatchiks from Moscow; a convivial and convenient temporary abode, it nevertheless remains unmistakably Soviet.
The downstairs bar asks patrons to purchase cocktail nuts from a
nearby store; the top floor breakfast room features a black grand piano
on which, at seven o'clock in the morning, a musician played
Beethoven's Fifth Symphony in C-Minor; the elegant waiters served
food that surely came straight from tin cans. Outside, though, an almost Swiss-style orderliness prevailed and public transport ran on
time.

The next day, in *Budinok Kavi* (House of Coffee), an upscale café
tucked away on a placid pedestrian street off Independence Square,
we met Bohdan Yaremenko, a Ukrainian diplomat in his mid-forties
who had served as his country's general consul in Edinburgh and as
its ambassador in Istanbul. These days, he directs a foreign-policy
think tank, the Maidan of Foreign Affairs. Bushy-haired, with a bon
vivant's corpulence and an easy smile, Yaremenko told us that he sees
the vestiges of a bygone decade as evidence not of failed modernization, but as characteristics typical of a small country, one whose
capital was not striving after the imperial grandeur of Moscow. The
recent noise about whose Vladimir statue—that of Kiev or the Russian capital—is bigger and better stirs nationalist pride here.

"But Ukraine," he went on to say, "should concentrate on genuine European integration, a desire for which was at the center of the
Euromaidan revolution, rather than make remodeling Kiev the goal
of reforms. The symbolism of Europe is attractive, but the country
needs to do a lot before it gets there. Ukraine's power system needs
to change and function not so Kiev can look like Europe but because
a bankrupt and corrupt society cannot form a part of Europe."

In Yaremenko's view, an inversion of goals has allowed Ukraine's
post-Maidan president Petro Poroshenko to consolidate power in
preparation for the presidential and parliamentary elections of 2019.

Yaremenko worried that although Poroshenko, the wealthy owner of the Roshen candy company, is the opposite of Putin, a former KGB colonel, he has augmented the role of the SBU, Ukraine's Security Service. Some reforms—those concerning the judicial system, the pension fund, and the state bureaucracy—are slowly making their way through the Verkhovna Rada, Ukraine's often tumultuous parliament. Others, including those dealing with public health care and land reform, have stalled. Moreover, the government's unwillingness to tackle corruption—the principal obstacle to the country's westernization—has proved a major matter of contention between Kiev and the European Union.

"I am very unpopular in some quarters," Yaremenko declared, "because I don't cheer for the European Union granting us visa-free travel and approving the full implementation of the European Union–Ukraine Association Agreement." (Yanukovych's refusal to sign this accord sparked the Euromaidan revolt.) "The government here," he added, "thinks that the West won't abandon Ukraine, because of the wounds Russia has inflicted on us. But before elections it will be even slower in pushing through austerity measures to improve the economy and curb corruption."

Yet Yaremenko saw reasons for cautious optimism.

"Ukraine should be able to do better," he said. "Even though the Ukrainian Soviet Socialist Republic had more Lenin statues than Russia, Ukrainians do not believe state power is sacred, as they do in Russia. There the Kremlin is the center of the state that people serve. Here those on top of the political ladder are just the hired hands of the people."

This difference in how leaders are perceived, in his view, accounted for the relative restiveness of Ukrainians. "One of the reasons for our revolutions, the Orange Revolution of 2004 and the Euromaidan revolt of 2013," Yaremenko explained to us, "is that the authorities here upset people by thinking they can do anything with no accountability. Yanukovych managed to make a lot of people angry. Here the rich are upset about things that Russian oligarchs tend to tolerate. Yanukovych, like Putin, thought that he was the only one with any rights."

Yaremenko added that during the Euromaidan even his usually apolitical mother was angry at how the authorities dealt with protesters and spent nights preparing Molotov cocktails for them in her apartment in central Kiev. These days, however, such revolutionary fervor has given way to apathy. Just as what happened following the Orange Revolution, politicians at the top are now squabbling with one another, leaving the people's priorities unattended.

Two opportunities for fundamental change in ten years wasted! It all sounded hopeless. We asked Yaremenko what could be done.

"Snap elections," he replied. "Change at the top could come though frequent snap elections. In one election, you can't replace all the politicians from the past," but frequent elections, called without warning, would prevent the "ossification of power" and keep everyone on their toes.

What did he think of Ukraine's giant neighbor to the north?

"Relations with Russia will only get worse," he said matter-of-factly. "But more than just diplomacy will come to an end. The sense of Slavic brotherhood we once shared will disappear, too. Before, of course, Moscow called the shots, and Ukraine grudgingly accepted it, and still considered the Russians 'brothers.'" No longer.

If Ukraine ever did join the European Union, Yaremenko insisted, it would present no threat to Russia, even if it became a member of NATO. (A Kremlin strategist might beg to differ. After all, having elements of the world's most powerful military alliance just five hundred miles from Moscow would change Russia's strategic situation in an unprecedented way.)

The real threat, said Yaremenko, came from the example an enlightened, democratic government in Kiev would set for Russians living under the Putin model of a semiauthoritarian corporate state unfriendly to the West. For the occupants of the Kremlin, it is a matter of life and death that their former communist neighbor never present Russian citizens with an alternate, more attractive model of governance. If Ukraine successfully manages to join Europe, it may well end up sounding the death knell for Putinism—the political mythology that casts Putin as successor to all the imperial autocrats peopling Russian history, including Nicholas I and Stalin.

"Moscow," Yaremenko added, "has more to lose with its Byzantine fantasy. If Russia doesn't develop, it will lead to China, the new global superpower, swallowing whole the Far East and Siberia. A vastly weakened Russia will then also lose the Northern Caucasus and the Volga region to their growing Muslim populations. Kaliningrad may again become German."

Fresh from Kaliningrad, we smiled. "There is no evidence of that."

"Either way," Yaremenko continued, "if Russia loses some of its eleven time zones, it would then no longer be able to position itself as the 'Great Russia.' The remaining lands might have no choice but to attach themselves to Ukraine. Moscow might return to its historical origins as a remote northern principality, shorn of territories to its south or east of the Urals."

Ukraine supplanting Russia, Kiev replacing Moscow as the nexus of power for the East Slavic peoples? This, however improbable, was something to think about.

These days, Kiev functions as a hub of exile for some in the Russian opposition, who carry on their business in Ukraine without the surveillance and constraints that would bedevil them at home. One such opposition member is forty-two-year-old Ilya Ponomarev, formerly a State Duma deputy of the social democratic party *Spravedlivaya Rossiya* (Just Russia) and a member of the Left Front. The son of longtime Communist Party functionaries, Ponomarev hails from the Novosibirsk Oblast—arguably the most advanced part of Siberia, owing to the world-class scientific community it has in Akademgorodok, a town specifically dedicated to advanced research. A charismatic communist with a spotty reputation in opposition circles, he alone among the State Duma's 450 deputies voted against the annexation of Crimea in March 2014. After this, he sojourned in the United States for two years, and then moved to Kiev, where he was enjoying a lifestyle free of the responsibilities with which his former position in the Duma saddled him.

We met Ponomarev in a café by our hotel, taking seats before picture windows offering unobstructed views of the ever-busy Khreshchatyk. His neat beard and red cardigan added maturity to his youthful looks. As a Duma deputy in Moscow he earned the nickname "butcher of the internet" among his critics—in 2012 Ponomarev controversially voted for strengthening state control of the web to prevent the dissemination of "content that may harm children's development."[5] That law gave way to the following year's ban on "propaganda of non-traditional sexual relations around minors"—colloquially known as the "gay propaganda" law,[6] the Kremlin's socially conservative project meant to endear it to the Orthodox Church. This time Ponomarev abstained from the vote, but the damage to his reputation had been done.

However, in Kiev Ponomarev insisted that with access to information comes democracy. Despite being, as it were, a declared enemy of the Russia-wide popular annexation of Crimea, he was at ease. He objected, he said, because the annexation would bring animosity, even bloodshed (he was right, as the war in eastern Ukraine had demonstrated), and eventually dislodge Ukraine from Russia's sphere of influence (as indeed it has). It would give the West a reason to ceaselessly criticize Russia and, moreover, justify plans to expand NATO further eastward.

"Before Crimea," Ponomarev stated grandly, "our country was an example to the world. Now Russia acts just like the United States—aggressively interfering in other countries' affairs when they disagree with those countries' politics." In his criticism of the United States he differed dramatically from views espoused by most in Ukraine and the majority of the Russian opposition.

In philosophical terms, he argued that Russia's "problem is one of an ideological construct—an undiversified, large-scale vertical economy." Unlike Yaremenko, however, Ponomarev told us that geography is not Russia's handicap.

"Isn't Russia too big to function coherently?" we asked.

"Obviously," Ponomarev replied with a laugh, "Russia has two afflictions: *plokhiye dorogi i duraki*"—bad roads and morons. He was reprising an apocryphal saying (often attributed to Nicholas I and Russian writer Nikolai Gogol) that is routinely used to lament Russia's poor highways and infamously capricious bureaucrats. "But even though its regions are not well connected to each other, it does not change the reality that a country can be both big and prosperous."

He went on. Russia's borders would disintegrate not because of the country's size, but because the *vertikal vlasti*, or "power vertical"—the highly centralized system of government Putin managed to institute—robs the country of its potential. Disintegration would originate not with those opposing Putin, but from Putin himself, because he does not allow politicians to develop.

"If you have the right technological 'know-how,' you can make Russia work," he stated, tossing in a bit of English. "Surely, it's tough to govern a country with territory stretched out all the way to Kamchatka, but if the setup is horizontal with local governments working to full capacity, then the problem of communication between the regions could be resolved." Something similar to America's electoral college might help people in sparsely populated outlying regions— and in Russia, these are many—defend their rights against the center.

We told Ponomarev that, for our book, we were looking at Russia through the prism of its geography. "Does Russia need to give up its empire to develop further?" we asked. In such a gigantic, sprawling country effective local governance has rarely been possible, whether under the Soviets or post-1991, because of the strongly centralized nature of the state.

According to Ponomarev, this centralization developed from the way Russia took shape, with cities, especially in Siberia, beginning as military and trade outposts of the empire. Then under Stalin they became industrial centers, with forced labor through the detention camps system, the Gulag, making up for a shortage of manpower. Russia's hinterland regions are sparsely populated and ill served by transport; picture a spiderweb, with almost all threads leading to the Kremlin.

Even today one gets a sense of this while traveling around the land. From the Ural Mountains to the Far East, relatively few population centers spot the vast, often unvarying landscape of forest, rivers, and steppe. After the Soviet collapse, Russia's regions acquired a good deal of autonomy, taking it at President Boris Yeltsin's urging, but Putin has managed to reimpose a degree of centralization. He divided the country into eight federal districts and eighty-five smaller federal subjects, with the local authorities once again primarily serving the center and loyalty to Putin a necessary attribute for regional leaders.

To help put an end to this centralization, Ponomarev suggested designating cities in remoter areas as regional capitals. For example, West Siberia's de facto capital could be switched from Tyumen to the much smaller city of Khanty-Mansiysk. Both are oil boomtowns, but the undersize Khanty-Mansiysk needs more state support to draw visitors and capital. That's one way, said Ponomarev, for a big country such as Russia to democratize its expanses and make people feel at home there, with a stake in their development. Better roads and communications would follow.

Well, yes. But Ponomarev's ideas sounded somewhat Leninist; his communist predecessors have already tried them. It was Bolshevik policy to populate as much Soviet territory as possible. Just as in a classless "dictatorship of proletariat," no one group of people would enjoy privileges others did not, and in theory all regions of the country would be equal. By this logic, living in Tyumen should be as wonderful as living in Moscow. But the problem with such grand theoretical visions is that they rarely survive real-life implementation.

"And what about Crimea?" we asked. "Should it be Russian?"

"Yes," he replied, "even though it was annexed illegally."

So, even the one State Duma deputy who voted against Crimea's becoming a part of Russia believes it should be Russian!

Before we left Kiev, we visited the city's main memorial to the Holodomor. For decades, the Great Famine, in part a result of the forced collectivization of agriculture, was a state secret; estimates of its death toll—from starvation, mostly, but also from cannibalism—have ranged from three million to ten million lives. What's known is that in 1932, at the start of the Holodomor, Ukraine's population stood at about 33 million, but just before Khrushchev took over in 1938, the number of inhabitants had dropped to 28 million—a decrease of more than 10 percent—a literal "decimation."[7] Of course, Stalin's infamous purges also contributed to the fatalities.

Ukraine's Rada in 2006 passed a law recognizing the Holodomor as an act of genocide against the Ukrainian people. In 2008 Kiev raised a commanding monument in Pechersk Hills, near the eleventh-century Monastery of the Pechersk Caves. The whole Holodomor complex—its park, its subterranean Hall of Memory—stands just a few yards away from another memorial—to World War II—that is filled with fresh flowers and people paying their respects. Contrary to post-Crimea nationalistic Russian assertions that the Euromaidan protests were intended to bring German rule to Ukraine and defy the victory won in the Great Patriotic War, Ukrainians do appreciate what the country, among other countries, suffered in World War II. They just no longer want to be Russian vassals.

We stood in front of the Holodomor memorial, built to resemble a church steeple with, at the top, an eternal flame fashioned out of bronze, and listened to its somber, solitary chimes—one chime for each life lost. Near its base, golden storks—rustic symbols of prosperity (Khrushchev used to say that a stork nest on your home's roof meant good luck) spread their wings atop cast-iron grids representing prison bars. This magnificent architectural monument to the famine is perhaps the truest indicator of Ukraine's desire to define its past and control its future—a tall order, even according to Bohdan Yaremenko, but the most laudable one imaginable.

3

ARKHANGELSK, SOLOVETSKY ISLANDS, SAINT PETERSBURG, AND MOSCOW

KREMLIN TIME, OR RUSSIA'S CLOCK OF CLOCKS

TIME ZONE: MSK; UTC+3

> Those who doubt Putin's vital role in the victory of the Great Patriotic War, simply do not understand his essential role in the Baptism of Russia.
>
> —A contemporary Russian joke

Kiev may be the *mat gorodov russkih*, mother of Russian cities, but Moscow is the mother of cities in Russia. It is the principal metropolis of the former Russian Empire, then of the Soviet Empire, and now of the Russian Federation—the (Third) Rome to which all roads lead.

The Moscow time zone, the Greenwich Meridian for Russia, stretches, in the south, from the border with Ukraine north to the oft-frozen shores of the White Sea in Arkhangelsk, and beyond, all the way to the Barents Sea of the Arctic Ocean.

Arkhangelsk and Solovetsky Islands: Russia's Utopian Dystopia

Some 760 miles from Moscow, Arkhangelsk, a city on the White Sea that owes its origins to the czar Ivan IV, popularly known as *Grozny*, the Terrible (better translated as Formidable or Fierce). In the 1500s, Ivan concluded the "gathering of Russian lands"—the de facto reconquest—from their local Russian rulers and Tatar-Mongolian overlords. He created the czardom of Muscovy and initiated Russia's expansion eastward, into the Urals and Siberia. In the next century, under Peter the Great, the first Russian emperor, Arkhangelsk became Russia's first and, at the time, only naval port. Although icebound for most of the year, it served as a key outpost against the Norwegians and Swedes competing for influence in this remote northern region. It also bestowed upon Russia Mikhail Lomonosov, who would become one of Russia's preeminent scientists and men of letters, the founder of Moscow University in 1755. Lomonosov came from a relatively modest background, born to a family of *pomory* (local sea fishermen) and farmers in a village in Arkhangelsk's vicinity.

Today Arkhangelsk is a depressed industrial city with a port that fell into disuse when Peter the Great began restricting trade along Russia's Arctic coast to boost that of the Baltic Sea, following his construction of Saint Petersburg. In recent years, Arkhangelsk has been losing out to the Crimea's Sevastopol, the warm-water port on the Black Sea.

Strangely enough, for a city so far-flung and beset with inclement weather, Arkhangelsk has managed to develop a modest tourist industry by touting its polar nights (and aurora borealis) in winter and its white nights in summer, and its rich historical heritage. At the time of our visit, we found a shaggy, pensive two-humped Bactrian camel welcoming tourists to an exhibition of ice sculptures celebrating the town's five-hundred-year history on Lenin Square. (Only in ever-paradoxical, geographically distended Russia would one discover a Central Asian ungulate overseeing parka-clad visitors to the extreme north.) Moreover, right across the street sits the regional government headquarters, where a billboard recounts the establishment, in the 1920s, of the first labor camps in the Gulag.

The first and most infamous of these camps—the "Mother of the Gulag," as Solzhenitsyn put it—was located on the Solovetsky Islands, colloquially called Solovki, a short forty-minute flight northeast of Arkhangelsk. Solovki soon became a byword for incarceration in brutal conditions—"go to Solovki!" meant "go to hell!" But there is much more to Solovki's history than hell. Indeed, as with so much in Russia, the tale of Solovki's existence consists of a paradox blending wrenching tragedy with almost otherworldly holiness.

In the fifteenth century, an Orthodox Christian monk, and now saint, named Zosima arrived on Solovki seeking refuge from persecution in Moscow, then ruled by the tyrannical Ivan the Terrible. He and two other monks settled down for good and founded a monastery—Solovetsky Monastery—that soon morphed into an influential center of Orthodox Christianity. With its large landholdings—the islands cover 134 square miles—and its varied sources of income, from fishing to algae extraction to salt gathering, Solovetsky Monastery flourished.

The harsh subarctic winter climate—windy and humid, with temperatures below zero—and trying summers during which thirty types of ferocious mosquitos emerge from bogs to torment man and beast, plus three hundred species of fauna, many of which do not fear people even today, all serve to augment the islands' legendary aura of mysticism, of being outside this world. A curious fox entered the house where we stayed to spy on us; a deer calmly paused to let our snowmobile past, which brought to mind notions of paradise before the fall of man. These, of course, quickly fade when you recall how many humans killed one another here. Local lore has it that only the devout could survive Solovki's arduous conditions; hence, before the fifteenth century, the islands had no permanent inhabitants. Settlers proved able to defend their autonomy for several hundred years and even welcomed exiled opponents of autocracy but eventually found they had to surrender to pressures from the state, with monks eventually almost officially serving as jail guards of political opponents deemed guilty in the eyes of the czars. They began turning their monastery's cellars into prison dungeons, some of which were so small that one could barely sit. Under Peter the Great, Russia further encroached on Solovki's monastic vocation, conscripting monks to serve as the jail guards of political criminals. The twenty-foot-thick walls of the monastery and the surrounding sea began to entrap rather than protect, and the island transmogrified into a Hades—utopia turned dystopia.

Following the October Revolution in 1917, the monks served the new regime as vigorously as they did the old. They eagerly accepted political prisoners sent to them by the new communist state, only to soon become prisoners themselves. The Soviet atheists had little use for Christian guards, and the priests were declared "enemies of the people." The Bolsheviks closed the monastery as a religious institution, enhanced its prisons, and established the Specialized Solovetsky Camp, or SLON. The acronym, which means "elephant" in Russian, was the topic of many grim jokes about the incongruities of Soviet life, which situated an elephant in Russia's far north. But after seeing a camel on the shores of the White Sea we hardly found the idea of an African beast here absurd. Many viewed the monks' fall from the Lord's favor as divine punishment. After all, they had betrayed their heavenly master to help found a version of human hell.

Yury Brodsky, a photographer and Solovki historian who took an iconic picture of one of the cathedrals—the photo, shot through one of the monastery's barbwire windows, showed the darkened cupola topped with a red star in place of a gilt cross—suggested to us that the island's saga is nothing less than a microcosm of Russia's broader history. The monastery ultimately devolved into an unholy trinity consisting of the state, its religious faith, and its *karatelnye organy* (punitive organs).[1] Post-Soviet Russia has sanctioned this sacrilege by adorning the current five-hundred-ruble banknote with a depiction of long-suffering Solovetsky Monastery on its obverse. What sort of holy man would come up with such an idea?

Large gray and black stones—those from which the monastery was built—cover the shores of the White Sea here. A black boulder now commemorates all the political prisoners who perished on the island. The spot on which it stands, appropriately, turned out to be an old unmarked mass grave, and the adjacent street now carries the name of a Solovetsky detainee, Pavel Florensky, an inventor and religious philosopher who lost his life here in 1937, at the height of the Terror. Since then, members of many religious denominations and nationalities (including Muslims, Catholics, and Poles) who suffered in the purges have had their own stone monuments erected on Florensky Street. In the 1990s one such rock, dubbed the Solovetsky Stone, was transported to Moscow and placed in front of Lubyanka, the FSB headquarters, to honor the Gulag's victims. (A Soviet bust commemorating Stalin continues to stand half a mile away, by the Kremlin's wall.) In the summer months these days, however, as state-fanned xenophobia rises, tourists often deface the memorials with nationalist graffiti.

The islands have turned into a quasiofficial sanctuary for the Russian Orthodox Church and the Russian state. People we met jokingly called it the *funktuary*, a mashup of "sanctuary" and "functionary," and laugh about the visits of supposedly repentant Kremlin apparatchiks. Many locals would enjoy running them up and down the steps leading up to the 250-foot-high Sekirnaya (Flagellation) Hill—a trial said to absolve sins. (Flagellation Hill is where the angels supposedly killed the fisherman's wife in the 1400s.) "Look at all those sins those Muscovites are guilty of!" they exclaim.

Palatial Petersburg

Four hundred miles southwest of the Solovetsky Islands lies Saint Petersburg, which long rivaled Moscow for domination of Russia. Saint Petersburg, founded in 1703, is the creation of Peter the Great, who enacted westernizing reforms on the thitherto Byzantine country that effectively brought about its split personality syndrome. Yet, better than any other Russian ruler, he managed to foment Russian nationalism and instill a desire to modernize. Putin, a native of Saint Petersburg (once Soviet Leningrad), has seen himself following in Peter the Great's footsteps—to merge the old and the new across all of Russia.

As part of his westernization program, the first Russian emperor moved the capital from tradition-bound Moscow to Saint Petersburg, Russia's "window to Europe." Saint Petersburg would become the only Western-style metropolis in Orthodox Russia. Not all were pleased with Czar Peter's efforts to bring Russia into the modern world. Russophile writer Fyodor Dostoyevsky acknowledged this when he reportedly said, "We may be backwards, but we have soul."

Tens of thousands of serfs died of disease and hunger draining the gloomy swamps along the Gulf of Finland, on the Baltic Sea, to build Saint Petersburg and fulfill the dream of Peter the Great, a task they accomplished in fewer than ten years. The emperor was determined to convert mostly landlocked Russia into a naval empire on a par with Holland, which he had visited on his embassy to Europe. Saint Petersburg boasts marble embankments along the Neva River, imitating the "first" Rome, and other top-tier European cities— Amsterdam, Venice, and Paris. The Russian tricolor is even modeled after the Dutch. Luxurious palaces, designed by Italian and French architects, dot the downtown area and the suburbs. Celebrating Western-style modernity with its factories, military academies, shipyards, and plenty of German tradesmen hard at work, the city represented everything that the rest of backward, sleepy Russia was not.

The proximity of Saint Petersburg (eventually renamed Petrograd, and then Leningrad following Lenin's death in 1924) to the West, however, became risky after the Bolshevik Revolution. Then independent Finland and Estonia lay only twenty five miles away, which meant the Soviets would have little buffer space to fight back an army invading from either country. Moscow, on the other hand, stood more than four hundred miles from the nearest border. After Lenin reclaimed Moscow as the capital in 1917, the clock on the Kremlin's Spassky Tower became the measure of all things temporal in Russia—the country's "standard time," as it were.

Byzantine Moscow

Moscow's almost nine-hundred-year history has witnessed the transformation of the once-remote northern village of the twelfth century into the truly Byzantine capital of the Putin era. (The Byzantine Empire fell in 1453, but one might not know this in Russia today, where

Putin has often acted as though he were the direct descendant of a Byzantine emperor.) Founded, according to most legends, by the prince Yury Dolgorukiy amid bog and forest along the Moskva River, Moscow arose as Kiev began to lose its influence in the 1100s. The name Moskva, meaning "the place of marches" or "gnats," is said to come from the area's Finno-Ugric tribes.

At times you can't help feeling that Moscow *is* Byzantium, its modernized version, with Mercedes and gourmet supermarkets. As did Byzantine emperors of centuries past, Putin and his supporters talk about Russia today as if it were a divinely ordained power, destined to withstand the moral corruption and decay supposedly emanating from the West. Hence, the Byzantine double-headed eagle emblem now not only graces government buildings but pops up everywhere, even on milk cartons and cell phone covers, produced outside Russia by wily foreigners. Byzantium and its leaders and symbols are discussed on talk shows, their imperial grandeur cited as an example for Russia's own future glory. Orthodox priests with distinguished beards preach, in their sermons, about how Russia, if it is to regain its greatness, must look to its Christian predecessor's past. The television station *Spas* (Salvation) not only reports on the history of Orthodox Christianity but also comments on foreign and domestic affairs. *Spas* has repeatedly shown a feature-length 2008 documentary called *The Demise of the Empire: A Byzantine Lesson*, with other major Russian networks following suit. The not-so-subtle idea behind all this nostalgia for Byzantium is that Russia can, and even should, exist only in opposition to the West, which supposedly hated Byzantium in the past just as much as it despises its spiritual heir, Russia, today.

Yet this is fanciful thinking. The old ideas and symbols that Putin has used to strengthen Russia's self-image no longer correspond to today's global realities, nor do they reflect Russia's present capacities. And even though the double-headed eagle once again purportedly signifies imperial power, in reality it incarnates the country's split personality, appearing to be a desperate attempt to mask a deep sense of insecurity—the anxiety of a former superpower torn between the old and the new.

During his first decade in power, Putin, financed by high oil prices, did indeed manage to transform Russia from the bankrupt, desperate loser of the Cold War into a wealthy country with an independent foreign policy often running counter to the interests of the West. But in 2011, Putin—prime minister from 2008, when Dmitry Medvedev formally (and temporarily) occupied Russia's top post—faced presidential elections as the global financial crisis wrought havoc on Russia and oil prices collapsed. He thus announced that he needed to return to the Kremlin to "steer Russia in the right direction"[2] and unite the country. (It is worth noting that Putin had chosen not to become a traditional autocrat by amending the constitution so that he could run again in 2008, but allowed at least the appearance of democracy by stepping down from the presidency to assume the post of head of government.) This went down poorly, with a Russian electorate insulted by the Kremlin's assumption that the people did not deserve to choose their leader. The 2012 presidential elections, as a result, did not go smoothly, with nationwide protests gathering hundreds of thousands at a time rocking Russia. Putin still took the Kremlin, his victory aided by the industrial regions of Siberia and Far East, but in view of uncertainty, Putin clearly decided that the path to future reelection lay through presenting Russia as threatened by an enemy abroad—as usual, the West.

He did take to heart his imperial project. In 2010, the Kremlin, then under President Dmitry Medvedev, declared modernization by reducing Russia to only nine time zones to streamline business relations with Moscow. But when Putin returned as Russia's president, larger size began to loom anew. He swiftly canceled the time-savings calendar, reverting the country to its eleven-time-zone geography.

Since then, Putin further surrendered to the traditionally xenophobic, inward-looking approach of what we might call "Byzantinism"—the attitude of "us versus them," with the Third Rome better than the First, and so on. Few Russian leaders have managed to escape such a pattern of interaction with the outside world. Stalin's obsession with the grandiosities of power is perhaps the most relevant to understand Putin.

With Moscow as the capital of the (atheist) Soviet empire, Stalin could not, of course, declare it a holy city, yet the style and structure of the buildings he had erected was often nothing short of Byzantine. His imperial ambitions found expression in reinventing the palatial architecture of Saint Petersburg, though deriving a more modern inspiration from the 1914 Municipal Building on Center Street in New York City. After all, New York's nickname was, Stalin knew, the Empire State. Victory in the Great Patriotic War required a victorious style of urban renewal. At home, Khrushchev recalled Stalin's thinking of the time: "We won the war.... Foreigners will come to Moscow, walk around, and there are no skyscrapers. If they compare Moscow to capitalist cities, it will be a mortal blow to us."

During the decade starting in 1947, the Soviet government oversaw the construction, on Moscow's seven hills, of *Stalinskie vysotki* (Stalin's high-rises), as the wedding-cake buildings came to be known, and a new eight-hundred-foot-tall headquarters for Lomonosov Moscow State University on Lenin Hills (Vorobyevy Hills before and after the Soviet era). The architects planned to grace the building's central tower with a statue of the university founder Mikhail Lomonosov. Lomonosov, or so the plan envisioned, was to resemble the victorious Stalin. In 1953, thousands of Gulag inmates completed the construction of the headquarters, which remained the tallest building of its kind in Europe until 1990. The statue of Lomonosov, however, was never mounted atop the tower, since Stalin died that year and soon fell into disgrace, following Khrushchev's de-Stalinization.

Some of the seven buildings provided spacious living quarters for the *nomenklatura*—the officials, artists, and scientists the Kremlin considered vital for the success of the regime. Most other Muscovites huddled by the dozens in communal apartments. Figuring among the high-rises was, and remains, the grandiose Ministry of Foreign Affairs in Smolensk Square, from which Sergei Lavrov, Putin's seasoned foreign minister, often fires his salvos toward the United States and conducts diplomacy across the globe.

The constructed high-rises were audacious and stunning, but an eighth one, the Palace of Soviets, was to top them all, with a truly gigantic statue of Lenin as its principal feature. Stalin had intended to be buried beneath it, but following his death and denunciation, the Soviet government abandoned the project, and it was never built.

With Khrushchev's policy of de-Stalinization came a "humanization," as it were, and the much-celebrated (and much-cursed) era of the *khrushchevki*. On Khrushchev's order, Soviet builders raised some eight thousand five-story apartment complexes all over the Soviet Union. These simple buildings that provided families with private lodgings came to be known as *khrushchevki* or *khrushcheby* (from *trushcheby*, slums) because of their stark contrast to extravagant Stalinist architecture. Khrushchev hoped to foster, inexpensively and on a broad scale, personal privacy at a time when individualism was considered something of a secular sin.

Stalinist urban planners made people share old multiroom dwellings or built apartment blocks in which as many as thirty inhabitants per unit shared a bathroom, and a kitchen. The housing reforms of the 1950s gave families their own kitchens and bathrooms in modest, low-ceiling units located in blocs built according to little-varying plans across the country. For those taking up residence in the new *khrushchevki*, this meant no prying apartment-mates and thus a reduced likelihood that someone might listen in on your private conversation and report you to the KGB. The threat of being packed off to a Gulag labor camp for something said at home, at least, all but vanished. Labor camps, too, were formally halted in 1960, though some individual camps exist even today.

For half a century, these five-story buildings symbolized a freer Russia. Khrushchev believed that the Soviet Union would become communist by the 1980s and wanted his modest buildings to tide people over until the onset of true "proletarian" luxury in the coming "workers' paradise." Instead, however, the Soviet Union collapsed (along with the communist dream, of course), but the *khrushchevki* remained, having patiently withstood political disaster and the often harsh Russian climate.

Today, with notions of Moscow's and Russia's "Byzantinization," the Kremlin is set to enact plans to demolish the modest constructions and replace them with upscale apartment complexes, giant hotels, and slick business centers—all with the aim, as in the Stalin era, of benefiting the state and its functionaries more than the people. Some *khrushchevki* are, indeed, more decrepit than others and should be replaced, but others require nothing more than a renovation (which would save the government time and money). In the summer of 2017 tens of thousands protested against plans to demolish the 1960s-era homes in Moscow, as did many more thousands of people across Russia.

Such "urban renewal" plans followed Moscow mayor Sergei Sobyanin's revolutionary—and highly unpopular—gentrification of much of Moscow. The building of roads and the replacement of asphalt sidewalks with cobblestones keep the capital, and other cities, in conditions of eternal, disruptive *remont*—the endless "renovation"

Russians learned to live with in Soviet times. Sobyanin's endeavors also just happen to enrich those involved on the construction side. His apparent motive: to turn Moscow into a *gorod progulki* (a city for strolling). And of course to impress those arriving for the summer 2018 FIFA World Cup soccer tournament; visitors did enjoy impromptu fan parties on the broad sidewalks. Still, the fifteen-yard-wide pavements, outfitted with benches and the occasional tree, even though meant to encourage cycling and scootering, instead have further congested traffic in a city long beset by terrible jams. Their grand dimensions seem to mimic the reality of Stalinist-era construction that aimed to create a city that would inspire admiration but not actually provide comfort for those living there.

In 2015 many in Moscow also shivered in disbelief when Sadovoe Koltso (Garden Ring Road), a major avenue circling central Moscow, boasted a new addition to the old Stalin *vysotki*, an Oruzheiny (Weapon) high-rise. Made of glass and steel, it is a skeleton of what the state in the 1950s used to build with bricks, an eerie ghost of the Stalin past in the Putin present.

Whether it is headed by Stalin or Putin, the country's leadership is always imitating what it sees abroad—in this case, Western-style living conditions. Russia, despite its civilizational claims, models its greatness on what others, namely the West, have already achieved. Now, the authorities seek to re-create, in a Russian nouveau imperial style, the luxury of Western cities. However, ambitions to build the Russian equivalent of Via Condotti in Rome or Avenue des Champs-Élysées in Paris derive from a desire to serve the needs of the Russian state, not the Russian people. No longer the ascetic revolutionaries of prerevolutionary Russia or the badly dressed Soviet apparatchiks of the 1960s, the men and women of Putin's ruling elite emit an air of sophistication. Russia, after all, has been open to the world for more than a quarter of a century. Putin himself, who began his first presidential term in pitch-black badly tailored suits with sleeves too long for his short stature, is now dressed impeccably in navy blue. Sobyanin's gray suits are, too, beyond reproach. Medvedev is known for his fancy ties and expensive watches—his presidential and prime-ministerial corruption became a subject of a YouTube documentary produced by the Kremlin chief nemesis, Alexey Navalny, the anticorruption lawyer and blogger. Released in March 2017, the video helped galvanize tens of thousands of protesters in cities across Russia. It was the first large grassroots rally in the country since a series of demonstrations preceding Putin's third term.

Stoleshnikov Lane (Moscow's version of Via Condotti), which winds its way just behind the Bolshoi Theater, has always been a street for shoppers. Today the luxury on display rivals that of, say, Madison Avenue on the Upper East Side in Manhattan. On Stoleshnikov now stand branches of Gucci, Prada, Christian Louboutin, and even Santa Maria Novella, the oldest and the highest-class pharmacy in the world. The latter store hails from Florence and is located on the grounds of an eponymous cathedral where monks once concocted perfumes. "Everything is great in Russia," an Italian friend once told us sarcastically. "The only thing missing is Santa Maria Novella." No longer.

One rainy spring afternoon when Moscow was buzzing with preparations for the May 9 Victory Day Parade on Red Square, we walked into that brand-new Santa Maria Novella in Stoleshnikov. Glass tables brimming with perfumes; wall displays of soaps, candles, and home fragrances; antique mahogany chairs under the Roman-like columns; and Leonardo da Vinci's prints on the walls— Italy indeed. Immediately smothering us in world-class customer care, a leggy blond attendant ("Anastasia, the curator," according to her name tag) showered us with an array of the finest coffees, chocolates, and sample scents. We asked her what would make the best gift. She informed us that Sergei Shoigu, Russia's minister of defense, just had bought an eau de cologne here.

"For the Victory Day Parade," she added. "We are proud that he will be wearing our fragrance when receiving the troops."

The immensity of Soviet victory in the Great Patriotic War, which cost 26 million citizens their lives, merited, and of course got, in Soviet times, magnificent pageantry. But already in the Khrushchev era such parades were losing their splendor—even their raison d'être.

"Whom are we planning to invade?" Khrushchev wondered aloud as he inspected a military base outside Moscow in September 1964. "Nobody! Yet we have all these weapons, and because of the exuberant cost of our military people are losing their pants." Brezhnev, however, returned the parades to their Stalinesque glory. Proud of his past as a war hero, and expanding the Soviet military and acquiring the rank of marshal long after the war ended, Brezhnev, in white parade uniform, enjoyed the spectacle of thousands of troops marching in front of him on Red Square.

After the collapse of the Soviet Union, and with Russia no longer a superpower, Yeltsin discontinued such costly ceremonies altogether. Yet in 2005 Putin started them up again for the sixtieth anniversary of World War II. Then, with the leaders of the United States, Great Britain, and other Western countries sharing the podium with Putin at the parade, Russia still seemed to have a global future.

With the international community much less on Russia's side now, the Victory Day parades are becoming ever more breathtaking in their grandiosity. Last May Red Square witnessed more than ten thousand troops and 114 units of tanks, missile defense systems, and armored vehicles, including the new monstrous, white-camouflaged Arctic defense machines, with polar bears painted on their sides, that are able to operate in minus-fifty-degree weather.[5] Led by Shoigu, the troops and tanks passed before President Putin to the loud cheers of the crowds. Such military might be, at least theoretically, deployed against European powers and the United States. According to curator Anastasia, Defense Minister Shoigu's tastes in perfume from that very Europe, which Russia is potentially planning to attack, should inspire the admiration in the rest of us.

As we looked over the wares on offer, we chitchatted with Anastasia about Russia's heroic past. She asked if, the previous week, we had gone to the Patriot Park on the outskirts of Moscow in Kubinka to watch as two thousand people dressed as Soviet soldiers reenacted the 1945 storming of a mock-up of the Reichstag by the Red Army. Part of the Magic World of Russia site, this patriotic Disneyland of sorts, appropriately designed by a Hollywood firm, had Shoigu along with five thousands spectators watching period tanks and weaponry, explosions, gunfire, and men dressed as Nazis falling to the ground in flames.

Anastasia said that she was "excited" when she watched the event on television. Today officials like Shoigu and even more so Putin himself are not just leaders, they are celebrities. Shoigu won national popularity the previous decade while running the Ministry of Emergency Situations and has since been prominently featured in media coverage as a savior in military garb. Russia suffers from aging infrastructure, illegal construction, and professional negligence—movie theaters burn, retirement homes collapse, trains derail. But who doesn't like a man in uniform!

And we do not need to remind anyone that the world can't get enough of Putin's own James Bond exploits: his 007-ish flying planes, diving in submarines, and riding horses bare-chested. For the Russians, he is their national hero; for the West he is an equally entertaining anti–James Bond villain.

Despite all his chastising of the West for its supposedly hegemonic objectives, Putin surely understands that there is no other choice than for Russia to join it. Does Russia's current animosity toward the West stem from a desire to re-create a militaristic state along Soviet lines, or is it truly a quest for the renewed role in the world as a superpower? Or is it simply a call for respect and recognition—for "imperial status," so to speak, if nothing else? Russia's behavior vis-à-vis Europe and the United States may amount to less a sign of aggressive intent and more a defensive reaction to the fear of encirclement. After all, NATO has expanded to Russia's borders and plans to one day induct Ukraine and even Georgia, another former Soviet republic, the Western aspirations of which the Kremlin tried to suppress in 2008. Such fears of "Europeanization" run counter to Russia's imitation of Europe since Byzantine times. Of course, they have been borne out by history with, three times in the past 210 years alone, the country having suffered invasion from the West.

Putin, however, surely would like to enter the history books not as a dictator, but as the leader of a country he has guided out of impoverished backward chaos into modernity and relative wealth. Modern Russia, he must know, cannot afford isolation, with one aspiring satellite, Serbia, and one alliance of convenience with China, along with a number of unsavory clients in Central Asia, the Middle East, and Latin America. If Russia does become a monolithic imperial state, it will betray its true ambition—to fulfill its European aspirations of finally joining the modern world and becoming a part of the West.

4

ULYANOVSK (SIMBIRSK) AND
SAMARA (KUIBYSHEV)

CITIES OF THE MIGHTY VOLGA

TIME ZONE: MSK+1; UTC+4

In Russia, there is a thousand-year-old tradition—the same
dream is transferred from generation to generation, from father
to son, from one political system to the next—that in the country
so rich with natural resources people will live well one day.

—A contemporary Russian joke

Whence Greatness Comes—Ulyanovsk

In Ulyanovsk, a medium-size town of 600,000 inhabitants on the
Volga River about five hundred miles southeast of Moscow, one
senses, in a primal way, Russia's might. As Kiev is the mother of all
Russian cities, the Volga is the mother—*matushka*—of all Russian
rivers. More than two thousand miles in length, the Volga is the
grandest river in Europe—it has come to be dubbed *Bogynya* (the
Goddess). It is celebrated in Russian literature and art both for its un-
fathomable might and the role it has played throughout the country's history.

From Ilya Repin's famous nineteenth-century painting *Barge Haulers on the Volga* (depicting exhausted, disheveled laborers on shore dragging a floating barge by means of ropes tied round their torsos) to Alexander Ostrovsky's 1859 play *The Storm* (which foretold the Russian Revolution of 1917), the river has inspired the imagination and held a preeminent position in local lore. Wide and mostly tranquil, the Volga turns dangerous during floods and changes in the seasons. It is also a lifeline—a *kormilitsa*, or one who feeds—connecting the towns and villages along its shores, in part because of Russia's notoriously bad roads.

Residents of Ulyanovsk maintain that their position just downstream from the confluence of the Volga and the much-smaller Sviyaga tributary subjects their city to powerful magnetic currents that mysteriously influence the area's climate, population, and culture. The Volga, not surprisingly, figures prominently in how the people of Ulyanovsk see themselves: their city is, as they would say, the "Aristocrat on the Volga," because of the many literary and noble families in the Russian empire hailing from here. It is perhaps no coincidence that the center of town, which sits on a hill overlooking the river, is called, with an allusion to royalty, Venets (crown). Therein lies a contradiction of a distinctly Russian sort. The city's original name, Simbirsk, was changed to Ulyanovsk in 1924, to commemorate Vladimir Lenin after his death. Lenin, whose original last name was Ulyanov, was born here in 1870. His family was one of minor aristocrats but not royal. And the regime he led to power ultimately rested on regicide.

Long before Lenin there were other greats from Ulyanovsk. Simbirsk was the birthplace of Nikolai Karamzin, who became known as the father of modern Russian letters under Catherine the Great and Alexander I. The town also boasts of Ivan Goncharov, the renowned nineteenth-century novelist. A major nineteenth-century poet, Nikolai Yazykov, came from here. And so did the Slavophile writer Sergei Glinka, a relative of the famed Russian composer Mikhail Glinka, author of "The Patriotic Song"—the Russian anthem of the 1990s. The Tolstoy and the Vyazemsky families have roots in the region as well.

In the late 1700s Catherine the Great, understanding the town to be a crucial trade and military outpost on the Volga protecting European Russia from invasion from the east, designated it capital of the Ulyanovsk *Guberniya* (a political entity akin to a state or province) and handed out vast plots of land in the region to loyal aristocrats. The two most infamous peasant rebellions of the 1600s and 1700s (led by Stepan Razin and Yemelyan Pugachev, respectively) played out in and around Simbirsk. In 1833 Alexander Pushkin visited, searching for stories about Pugachev, who had aspired to replace Catherine the Great as ruler on the Russian throne.

Then came the Decembrists—the Russian nobles who formed a movement against the czar's absolute monarchy. Their 1825 uprising drew in many officers and was brutally suppressed—some were hanged; others exiled internally, dispatched to the Simbirsk *pochtovyi i katorzhnyi trakt* (postal and penal servitude throughway), to trudge for months in rain and snow to their Siberian abodes of involuntary residence.

As we strolled down Ulyanovsk's Goncharov Street on a sunny May morning, Sergei Petrov, an elderly historian, professor, and local celebrity, led us, root and branch, through the family trees of locally born Russian and Soviet luminaries, speaking rapidly and passionately. With his impish eyes, circle beard, and silvery aristocratic coif, Petrov, a voluble raconteur enamored of meandering discourse, seemed to have stepped from the pages of a nineteenth-century Russian play. His gray checkered suit looked too dressy for our morning tour and ill befitted his blue-red cardigan or his tattered brown loafers.

As we progressed down the street, passing by pastel-hued shops with fin-de-siècle facades, every fifteen minutes or so somebody recognized him and stopped us for a chat. Each time we expected Petrov to run out of words, or stories, or even breath itself, he surprised us by producing more facts about the town he so loved. Peasant rebel leader Stepan Razin, he said, was wounded during his assault on Simbirsk; he survived only to be captured and drawn and quartered on Bolotnaya Square in Moscow. The Volga Germans had always held leadership positions in town, as the drab, redbrick Lutheran Cathedral of Saint Mary he pointed out would attest. With these Germans often in charge, Simbirsk prospered, which augured ill for it after the 1917 Revolution. "One out of nine people here belonged to the gentry. Imagine what this meant when the Bolsheviks took over!" He paused. "People were burning their title deeds, they were so afraid! Most of them just fled to other parts of Russia."

We stopped in front of the Simbirsk Classical Lyceum Number 1, where Lenin had studied and where, near the entrance, a plaque showed, in stark Social-Realist style, the iconic revolutionary with Alexander Kerensky, who was also born here and would head the provisional Russian government after the czar had abdicated in 1917.

"Lenin let him live," Petrov told us. "I believe they may have shared Christmas goose together when they were growing up. Did he do so because both were born here, in this special town on the Volga? Could Lenin have showed him some compassion for this? I can't prove it, but I think so. Now you see them together on the same plaque! You will find nothing like this anywhere else in Russia!" Kerensky eventually immigrated to the United States, where he died in 1970.

Petrov conjured up a lost world of landowners, high culture, and even cosmopolitanism—imagine, German gentry dwelling on the banks of Russia's mighty Volga! That almost no trace remains of any of this mattered not to Petrov, who could verbally resuscitate the lost souls of the world the Bolsheviks destroyed—a world, we sensed, he would have been happy to inhabit.

The next day, alone, we visited the Lenin *dom musei* (house museum), located on—what else—Lenin Street, in central Ulyanovsk. A modest, two-story graying wooden house with a few bedrooms, a dining room, and a study was the greatest attraction for the seventy-five years of Soviet rule. And it was not just Lenin—other members of his family were revered, too, as studious and serious, the pinnacles of communist morality. His father, Ilya, was an inspector of public schools; his older brother, Alexander, a revolutionary radical, was executed in 1887 for trying to assassinate Czar Alexander III; his younger brother, Dmitry, was a doctor and a writer; his sister, Maria, another revolutionary who studied at the Sorbonne. Millions of people from all over the world had come here to admire Lenin's childhood home and see the environs in which he came of age.

After the fall of the Soviet Union and the death of communism as a promising ideology, interest in Lenin almost disappeared. The authorities in Ulyanovsk, nevertheless, converted his neighborhood into a historical sanctuary, the Birthplace of Lenin, which encompasses all the landmarks connected to his era. At first glance, this might seem strange. Even the November 2017 centenary celebrations of the Bolshevik Revolution in Russia barely featured Lenin. Instead, festivities focused on centuries of heroism in Russian history and, of course, on the Soviet victory in the Great Patriotic War. Why? We can only surmise that Putin, approaching two decades in power, is concerned with preserving it, and therefore is not particularly fond of revolutions. Yet the Lenin sanctuary found unexpected saviors in hordes of Chinese visitors. It now forms part of their "Red Tour"—visits to the landmarks of the revolution's history. Lenin did not direct the revolution from here, of course, but his sanctuary gives a good idea of what the world he destroyed looked like.

But, as we discovered, even the guides at the Lenin house museum no longer talk much about communism and revolution. They showed us the modest family bedrooms, a dining room that doubled as a game parlor and study, Ilya's dark office with the dauntingly progressive books on the shelves, including Nikolai Chernyshevsky's nineteenth-century guide to socialism, *What Is to Be Done?* As had Petrov, they spoke at length about the intellects the Volga region had produced, among whom just happened to be the intellects of the Ulyanov family. Their home impressed us with its unremarkable, bourgeois interior—a reminder that the man who led the revolution of prole-tarians and peasants was, by birth and upbringing, neither.

To learn more about Lenin in the town of his birth, we toured the Lenin museum on the eponymous square in the central Venets district. Typically Soviet in its mammoth dimensions, built of pink-red Soviet-era marble, the museum exudes grandeur of a sort and de-picts Lenin in historical perspective that began with the role of Simbirsk in the Russian Empire. This perspective now emphasizes imperial coherency—centuries of Russian history peopled by firm, formidable leaders from the bygone times of Peter the Great to Cath-erine the Great (who gave Simbirsk its first coat of arms consisting of a crowned Greek column) to our day, the Putin era. From the double-headed eagle to the hammer and sickle to the double-headed eagle again. Coherency—and elision of all the wild and destructive detours Russia has made to end up where it is today.

The museum's current account of Russia's history almost grants Stalin a role as prominent as that of Lenin—something impossible from the time of Khrushchev's Secret Speech to the beginning of the Putin era. Today it highlights Stalin's program of crash industrial-ization (carried out in the 1930s) and the Soviet victory, under his command, in the Great Patriotic War. *Velikiy vozhd i uchitel* (the great leader and teacher) announces, without a hint of irony, the caption under one Stalin portrait. This is just what cult-of-personality propaganda called the dictator during his almost thirty years in power. The murderous Holodomor accompanying the industrialization, the devastating political purges, and the Gulag camps merit only brief mentions and are explained away by *raisons d'état*: to make a country great one needs to take tough—even brutal—measures.

Examining the museum's exhibits, for the first time we realized that only four leaders have remained in Russia's recent, and well-curated, official historical memory. First, Lenin, almost devoid of political value now, who has become more a monument than a personage. He serves as a symbol of continuity, if no longer of communism. He represents that important, almost century-long time when Russia was a great country, even a superpower, that made the world tremble. Stalin comes second, after being partly rehabilitated in the mid-2000s when Moscow decided to emblazon his name in gold letters on the ceiling of the Kurskaya subway station and school textbooks began lauding him as a "wise manager of his people" who, instituting the forced-labor camps, acted out of necessity to compensate for a shortage of manpower. In fact, in the last decade Stalin has become more "alive" than Lenin, who was also once lauded as *zhiveye vsekh zhivykh* (more alive than all the living). The continuous celebrations of the Soviet victory in the war against Nazi Germany render him almost as contemporary as Putin himself.

Leonid Brezhnev is the third leader on record and serves as a convenient bridge between the Stalin and Putin eras. (Putin is the fourth, of course.) Brezhnev can even boast of his own anniversary wing, opened to the public in 2016 to commemorate his 110th birthday. This section displays official gifts, such as his portraits made from grain in Belorussia or knit on a carpet by weavers in Tajikistan.

Originally, the museum managers had intended that the exhibit be temporary, but visitors liked it, the young docent explained, so it has become permanent.

And what of the "reformers"—Nikita Khrushchev, Mikhail Gorbachev, and Boris Yeltsin? They have almost completely dropped out of history, at least as the Russian state now presents it. The museum had dedicated a small corner—"Reformers and Their Reforms"—but addressed them nowhere else.

"What about Khrushchev?" we asked a guide.

She shrugged her shoulders.

"There was no administrative order issued to set up such an exhibit," she replied.

"Did you ask why?" we pressed.

She walked away, unwilling to answer uncomfortable questions. The reformers have largely disappeared from history in Russia because they don't accord with the black-and-white view of Russian grandeur, as personified in firm leaders who must always appear unrepentant, despite the scale of the suffering they oversaw or caused. These three leaders showed humane concern for their citizens, which set them apart. As imperfect as their reforms were, they tried to democratize the imperial monolith. Khrushchev denounced Stalin, thus making the Russians doubt their communist czar. As part of his Perestroika, Gorbachev introduced *glasnost*—a wider dissemination of information, which allowed people to ask questions and hold the state to account. Yeltsin proclaimed Russia a democratic state that should join the world instead of fighting it. Nonetheless, they were products of the same authoritarian culture as the authoritarians preceding, and also following, them, and therefore they never fully succeeded.

Once retired, Khrushchev often reflected on the lack of Russia's political progress forward. "Russia is like a tub full of dough," he used to say. "You push your hand through and you reach the bottom. You pull out your hand, and then right in front of your eyes, it is, again, a tub full of dough, without a trace of your hand. Perhaps Russia does need a strong hand to make change happen." A depressing yet apparently accurate observation.

Some are still striving after change these days. During our visit, Alexey Navalny, at the time a potential rival to Putin in the upcoming presidential elections, arrived to open up his campaign headquarters. In making his quixotic yet laudable bid for the anti-Putin vote, Navalny managed to gather supporters all across Russia, organizing at least fifty regional teams—unprecedented opposition outreach in a country where most political activity of note takes place in Moscow. Ulyanovsk was one of those towns he found most receptive—perhaps because of their affinity with another young radical, born in this little town, railing against the autocratic regime a century ago. It did not matter: the Putin electoral authorities eventually refused to let him register his candidacy on account of alleged crimes of embezzlement and a criminal conviction that many believe was fabricated to keep him out of politics.

Ulyanovsk benefited greatly from the bicentennial celebration, in 2012, of the birth of the novelist Ivan Goncharov, one of Russia's most famous domestically, though perhaps lesser known abroad. The Goncharov home museum, once the family estate, aims to document how Goncharov helped characterize Russian identity through his 1859 masterpiece, *Oblomov*. Its eponymous protagonist—kindhearted, perpetually lazy, languidly aristocratic—remains one of the most endearing and enduring literary embodiments of the Russian predicament so often typified by statements Russians make about the "Russian soul," namely, "we may be backwards but we"—unlike other peoples, the implication is—"have *soul*."

Goncharov Square, next to the museum, features not only a Soviet-era bronze statue of the writer pensively taking notes, but also more recent additions: Oblomov's "philosophical sofa" (commissioned, a plaque incongruously informs us, by the local firm Commercial Real-estate) and a pair of bronze slippers. (Oblomov rarely changed out of his robe or ventured outside the house.) Both seem to symbolize an often all-encompassing stagnation ever present in Russia and the deep fear of change that underlies it. A quote from the novel encompasses this kind of thinking: "When you don't know what you're living for, you don't care how you live from one day to the next."[1] The home's builders, however, seemed to have feared little in designing luxury: the three-story corner brick building, situated a few blocks west of the Volga, stands elegantly trimmed in white granite, with its own clock tower.

Few aspects of life in Russia are divorced from politics: in the museum's entrance hall hangs a photograph, taken in 2012, of Putin and Sergei Morozov, the governor of Ulyanovsk Oblast, as the former grants the city and the museum an order to celebrate Goncharov's bicentennial. There is also a certificate announcing Goncharov's post-humously awarded title, Honorary Citizen of Ulyanovsk. As if the literary titan, a citizen of Russia almost a century and a half before either leader was born, would have cared! The writer lived and died in Simbirsk quite well without this honorific, but Russians cannot step away from the Soviet tradition of showering Russian figures, both historical and contemporary, with ceremonial medals and awards.

Goncharov's museum showcases what is both marvelous and ma-levolent about Putin's country. There are wonderful exhibits—Goncharov's wainscoted study, pages from a draft of *Oblomov*, and copies of the novel's first editions, in addition to the writer's letters to Mikhail Volkonsky, son of the famous Decembrist revolutionary Sergei—that elevate your spirit and help you appreciate the richness of Russia's history and arts, the true manifestations of the Russian soul, as it were.

Yet the grumpy museum attendants suspiciously followed us everywhere and barked at us for attempting to explore on our own, without their vigilant supervision. Instead of answering our polite questions about what we were looking at, they gruffly instructed us to read the information sheets beneath the exhibits and visit the rooms in *strictly* clockwise order. *"Nelzya! Vam tuda!"* (It is forbidden to go this way. You have to go that way!)

Never mind. Overwhelmed by the richness of Goncharov's life and work and by Ulyanovsk's literary heritage—the town was also a place where Pushkin and the Decembrists resided—we wanted to buy Goncharov's books, and *Oblomov* most of all. So we approached a table strewn with souvenirs at the exit.

There was no one there. The guard barked at us, confirming the obvious: "The ticket lady has stepped away." When she would return he would not or could not say.

If we learned anything visiting museums across Russia, it was that those who sell tickets or souvenirs are often absent from their stations when you need them most. Sometimes a lack of visitors might be to blame, but there is a deeper problem: even after two and a half decades of capitalism, customer service, at least outside Moscow, is not a priority. The Goncharov museum might stand as a monument to Russian high culture, but the recently renovated restrooms lacked toilet paper, paper towels, and soap, even as its clean white tile walls bore illustrations of blue swans and pink flamingos. After examining for hours the stately home of one of Russia's literary giants, one wonders why one's tour must end on a note of exasperation and personal humiliation. Perhaps, however, this humiliation has a point in a country where people are subordinate to the state. If the authorities don't believe citizens deserve rights, citizens, accordingly, don't believe they have a right to civilized comfort. The Soviet Union, it must be remembered, was notorious for its deficit in toilet paper, and citizens resorted to using yesterday's *Pravda* newspaper pages instead. Incidentally, in Stalin's times this was a grave crime, which made the use of the restrooms a truly trying experience.

Wet hands or not, we were nevertheless determined to buy a Goncharov souvenir. The souvenir stand lady returned. We asked for a copy of *Oblomov*.

"We don't have one."

"Why not?"

"They are not available."

"Why not?"

She shrugged her shoulders. "The municipal authorities have not issued the relevant order for us to sell such books here."

Selling postcards of Ulyanovsk was one thing, but the classics of Russian literature, presumably for lack of demand, quite another. The saleslady sent us to the bookstore nearby. We followed a muddied path to a sign reading BUKINIST (secondhand bookseller). We entered the dilapidated, disorderly shop, with tomes old and new strewn on a table, stacked on the floor, and piled on the stools—a bibliophile's dream, one would think. But before long, the disheveled shopkeeper was apologizing to us. No, he had no copies of Goncharov's works, either.

"Try the basement," he suggested. "They have school textbooks down there."

Downstairs we found no Goncharov. However, pasted to the door under a sign reading ADMINISTRATION was a portrait of Putin, cut out of a calendar. Along the wall stood stacks of the *Criminal Code of the Russian Federation*. We finally asked the female shopkeeper how we were to obtain a copy of *Oblomov*.

"Try online," she said, barely lifting her gaze from a computer screen.

The next morning was cold and gray, unusually so for a May day. We ventured down to the Volga embankment to take a tour along the river. The port was open, yet empty, with no boats scheduled to run. Vendors still peddled (to whom, we wondered) the souvenirs of the area—tiny magnetic portraits of Lenin, Karamzin, Goncharov, and even Stalin (even though the dictator had no relation to Ulyanovsk), and, of course, Putin.

We approached the ticket office inside the dock building.

"Two tickets for a boat tour, please," we asked the woman behind the window. She shook her head: there were no boats running.

"The weather is bad," she added, in a friendly but basically indifferent way, "but if you want to rent the whole vessel for six thousand rubles [about $100] for yourselves, you can." We decided to do just that and were quickly ushered aboard an old cruise ship meant to take as many as 120 passengers.

Our cruise ship was a remnant from the Soviet days. The remaining craft are half a century old, but many have been modernized and refurbished. In 2011 one sank near Kazan, another Volga town, and more than sixty people lost their lives. The ships have been better managed since then. We hoped ours would be.

Under leaden skies, chilled by a wind ruffling the pewter-hued surface of the water, we pulled out from the port, passing a gloomy junkyard—or, rather, docked passenger ships, including the former giants of Soviet waterways, ones with hydrofoils that lifted the hulls out of the water, allowing them to reach speeds as high as a hundred miles an hour. Now they sit as rusting behemoths. It was painful to remember that during Soviet times and even as late as the 1990s, these winged craft circulated among all the Volga's major towns, including Kazan, Samara, and Nizhny Novgorod.

Denizens of the Volga, of course, have always used the river to get about. But in 1956 the river became Khrushchev's special project—as anticapitalist as he was, he was also searching for ways to improve people's lives after the harsh Stalin decades. At the time over three thousand hydrofoil vessels coursed the country's major waterways at high speed, ferrying people quickly and easily to their destinations. Inspired by the Soviet state space program, the craft were emblazoned with names like "Rocket" or "Meteor." But then came the collapse of the Soviet Union. The Yeltsin government abandoned industrial projects and public services in favor of privatization. That killed the shipyards producing the hydrofoils and left the speedy craft known as meteors to rust away in their nautical graveyards.

A mechanic on our boat told us that he used to pilot the meteors from the Khrushchev era, but then, he said, they were declared cost-ineffective, so he was compelled to switch to excursion craft running at more leisurely speeds. His eyes dreamy with nostalgia, he listed at least seven routes those meteors used to run in the region.

"Now people smarter than us own them," he declared sarcastically. "Our speedboats are being used as far away as Vietnam and China. You can find some still gliding down rivers in Canada, Greece, Yugoslavia, Netherlands, Thailand, and Turkey." He paused. "I rue for what we had and stupidly destroyed."

The mighty *matushka* Volga, spreading away on both sides of us, should have been breathtaking, yet what struck us was the shambolic, neglected shoreline that has only recently begun reviving. Still, for an hour and a half we had a large, majestic Volga liner on the river all to ourselves—something impossible to imagine anywhere else, at any other time, and at so little cost.

The sun finally appeared, right after we sailed under Ulyanovsk's recently built President Bridge—one of the longest in Europe, the mechanic told us. It is one of the two bridges in Ulyanovsk, and with a typically Russian story behind it. By 2009, work on the structure had been stalled for over two decades, but then Putin came to town and voiced his displeasure at the delay. In quick order, the bridge was completed. Another, older bridge we passed beneath bore the name Imperial. It dated from the 1910s, when Emperor Nicholas II visited Ulyanovsk.

In Russia, where the welfare of the state takes precedence over the needs of the citizenry, public works are often enacted to meet the exigencies of the bureaucracy rather than to help people live more comfortably. The President Bridge, indeed, has been a necessary improvement, lessening traffic bottlenecks in the region, but functioning waterways would be an even bigger improvement. A demand for them has yet to reach Putin's desk, it seems.

Even though we were the only two passengers aboard, the barwoman in her middle years, Lyudmila, stood at her post ready to serve us and to talk. Fixing the scarf covering her henna-red hair, she offered us peanuts, instant coffee, and bottled water. She marveled at our foreignness. She had seen foreigners before but never really talked to one. She had never ventured beyond the Volga region but did enjoy traveling along the river. She told us that while working as a janitor at the train station, she liked to watch the trains arriving from or heading out to distant, enigmatic destinations—Moscow, Minsk, Saint Petersburg. But "the Volga pulls me in, and I had to come here," she said, displaying a mouth filled with gold teeth. In the old days, such teeth were a manifestation of an achieved or an aspired-to status, mostly found in men and mostly those men coming from the Caucasus, Siberia, and the Russian Far East. She had a son, who was about to graduate from the Suvorovsky Military Academy in Moscow. She worried that he would be sent to war in Ukraine or, even worse, in Syria. "The curse of war," she sighed.

In Russia where wars—fighting, winning, or preparing for

them—are a big part of the Kremlin propaganda of the country's superior heroism, Lyudmila's sad comment showed how the horrors of war scar society despite the upbeat patriotic message.

Lyudmila was upset about how life along the river had changed. She could no longer walk around the port, she said. "It's all very strict now, all fenced up. The area became private property after a rich guy bought it to make money, but it turned out to be too much trouble for him to do anything."

After the Soviet Union collapsed, markets became a priority, and the state abandoned publicly funded river transportation in almost all Volga towns and elsewhere in Russia. Businessmen bought ports and the crafts berthed in them, but all this required investment, and the new owners, unsure of quick returns, proved unwilling to provide any.

We checked with Lyudmila if there was a way to get by water from Ulyanovsk to Samara, our next destination. A boat trip theoretically would last only a couple of hours, while by car it would take at least five on a crowded, potholed two-lane road, stretches of which were under construction.

"No such luck," Lyudmila said. "You have to travel by taxi or bus." She went on to recount to us how she used to run to the piers to buy the world-famous black caviar from Volga sturgeon. "Now there are few boats and no black caviar."

As the boat trip drew to a close, we tried to tip our chatty bar host, but she refused to take any money. "We were told not to take bribes," she explained. In a country where so many state employees do take bribes, from the plumber to the president, Lyudmila was the best the country has to offer—kind, cordial, hardworking—and uncorrupted. The kind of Russian Goncharov described in *Oblomov*:

His heart has never struck a single false note; there is no stain on his character. No well-dressed-up lie has ever deceived him and nothing will lure him from the true path. A regular ocean of evil and baseless may be surging around him, the entire world may be poisoned and turned upside down—Oblomov will never bow down to the idol of falsehood, and his soul will always be pure, noble, honest . . . Such people are rare; there aren't many of them; they are like pearls in a crowd![2]

Ever keen to tout Ulyanovsk's status, our local historian Petrov had grudgingly admitted to us that their part of Povolzhye (as the territories adjacent to the Volga have been historically called) had been transferred to the Samara time zone down the river. As he reminded us, Simbirsk was once the capital of a *guberniya* that prestigiously shared the Moscow time, but now clocks in Ulyanovsk run in synch with those of downscale Samara further east.

Stalin in Samara

The next day, after a hot, bruising five-hour car ride (to cover a mere 150 miles!) instead of the pleasant two-hour boat trip we would have enjoyed in previous decades, we pulled into Samara. With a population of 1.2 million and known in Soviet times as Kuibyshev, Samara, with its traffic jams, high-rises, and busy shopping malls resembles something like a Moscow-on-the-Volga. The old wooden huts, some almost fallen to the ground, still abound—something Moscow has not seen in decades—but the local offices of Gazprom banks affiliated with it, and the giant state-owned Sberbank look formidable and palatial. They are second only to buildings that belong to the municipal administrations and the security agencies. Such structures, despite what they symbolize—the Russian state's dependence for its survival on its bounty of natural resources and the unceasing labors of its police force, both covert and overt—do rescue the city from anything resembling a provincial air.

Indeed this has always been so, and thus Soviet planners selected Samara for a unique honor, as we would see.

Upon arrival, we stopped by the city's museum of ethnography. In contrast to the Ulyanovsk museums, the Samara display is not supposed to be political, but exhibits about the history and customs of local peoples quickly give way to yet another tribute to Russia's imperial grandeur. The museum is mostly dedicated to Stalin and his victory in World War II, with due coverage awarded to Lenin and the czars—Peter the Great and Catherine the Great, Nicholas I and II, Alexanders II and III, and so on. And then there was Czar Putin, promoter of the double-headed eagle and all it stood for.

In the far corner, next to an exhibit of the region's prehistoric era and mock dinosaurs, we found a small section devoted to Stalin's purges. Yet if you didn't know the history of all the bloodshed and imprisonment in his day, you might come away with the impression that the bosses of the People's Commissariat for Internal Affairs (NKVD, the precursor agency of the KGB), not the dictator himself, were to blame. One cannot understand Russia's history without comprehending the atrocities of the Stalin era and how they inevitably grew out of unbridled one-man rule and the need to eliminate—*physically*—any possible contender to the throne.

In Samara stands a far more impressive relic of Stalin's era and that of the war he prosecuted victoriously: the famed Stalin Bunker.

As Nazi troops rapidly advanced toward Moscow in 1941, most of the USSR's ministries, foreign diplomatic missions, and political families (including those of Stalin and Khrushchev) departed for Samara (Kuibyshev in those days), which was to serve as a makeshift reserve national capital in the early war years. The city also hosted facilities critical for the Soviet military—aviation and engineering plants and higher education institutions, including a relocated Moscow University. A massive riverbank bunker was built for Stalin just in case he had to be evacuated, too.

Though open to groups, visiting it as individuals would be, it turned out, no easy task. First, we tried to book a tour from Moscow. The website urged us to reserve tickets by phone, but when we called, we were rudely informed that we could not get in unless we were part of a group.

"Leave your names and call the day of your arrival. Maybe you'll get in," we were told.

We did as advised. That morning, Nina made the calls.

When she finally got through, a man's crackling voice answered.

"Deistvuyshyi obyekt gosudarstvennoi oborony. Dezhurnyi po obyektu" (Active facility of state defense. Facility officer on duty speaking.)

"I am Nina Khrushcheva, and I've called a few times before. We want to make sure we are let in to the bunker."

"I remember your name. That Khrushchev, I'm no fan of his."

"Why?"

"I'm sick of him. He wrecked too many things (*mnogo ponatvoril*). Just take Crimea. Your name, Nina, is even the same as his wife's, *blyad*," he cursed, using the Russian word for "whore." "But fine, come on over."

The man never even asked if Nina was related to the former Soviet premier. It took nothing more than hearing the name to set him off.

We took a cab to the bunker, located at 167 Frunze Street and concealed beneath a nondescript apartment building. At a nondescript plain back door, a crowd of some forty eager visitors stood waiting for admission, some, no doubt, worried as we were that they would be refused entry if they were not part of a group. But ultimately the guards let everyone in. They still operated according to the tried-and-true Soviet precept of managing public places: even if they have to let you pass, you will have to suffer for it.

An almost cubist stained-glass portrait of Stalin puffing on his pipe welcomed us in. We climbed twelve stories down a steep staircase to the Generalissimo's quarters: a conference room with a large map of Russia, and a wooden oval table surrounded by twelve chairs; and a living room office with a white sofa, a desk covered with a musty piece of green felt, and a red emergency phone line, all watched over by an austere portrait of Alexander Suvorov, one of czarist Russia's greatest military heroes. The last Generalissimo of the Russian Empire, Suvorov inspired the first Soviet one.

The cheerful guide, a blond woman in her forties, couldn't hide her excitement about how roughly Stalin treated all those who were tasked with defending the Motherland. "One of the local factories," she said, "which was producing munitions during the war, at first made less than required." Stalin reprimanded them. "You can't make just one bomb a day," he bellowed. "You have to make hundreds, thousands a day!" Fearing for their lives, they did just that.

She finally delivered the punch line—"Stalin actually never stepped foot in the bunker, remaining in Moscow all through the war"—but mentioned nothing about Stalin's key role in starting the war. Fearful of being undermined by capitalist France and Great Britain, and even more afraid of Hitler's invasion of the Soviet Union, Stalin was eager to sign the Molotov–Ribbentrop Pact, the nonaggression treaty with Nazi Germany, in 1939. This, in effect, permitted the Third Reich to take over Europe without worrying about a Russian response. After the Nazi invasion of the western areas of the Soviet Union, Stalin, in the early stages of the war, blamed massive Russian defeats on his countrymen's unpatriotic behavior. But the military failures owed much to inexperienced officers who assumed their duties after the NKVD had wiped out the gifted old officer corps, accusing them of being "enemies of the people."

The bunker, our guide told us, was built in nine months and cost 19 million rubles ($324,000 in 1942)—more than $5 million today. We overheard two men, perhaps father and son, walking in front of us down the clean, cold spiral staircase.

"Imagine that, they built it so quickly, but nobody stole anything!" said the young one.

"Of course not," the older man replied. "You would not steal under Stalin."

"But with Khrushchev, you could!"

"Oh, that Khrushchev!"

After much climbing up and down claustrophobic stairs and passing through innumerable steel doors resembling those aboard a submarine, the tour ended and we reemerged at street level. We went over to introduce ourselves to the two duty officers. Both looked to be in their eighties—still too young to have fought in the war but, judging by their bearing and mannerisms, quite likely former police or KGB officers. They were also clearly devoted Stalinists and were exited to meet Jeff, the American.

"Trump has sent you to see what power Russians have!" said one. "Tell him that we are peaceful people, but we won't be pushed around!"

We asked which of them had been so rude to Nina on the phone earlier that morning. Both denied having spoken to her, alleging, oddly and irrelevantly, that their German was better than their English, so there must have been some misunderstanding. This statement made no sense, as she had spoken to him in Russian. Whatever. Since Jeff had introduced himself as an American journalist, we could only conclude that they feared he would report on how angry

Stalinists had mistreated his "minder," and they wanted to avoid any scandals.

We walked back out into the glorious spring day. After listening to our guide expound on the heroic nature of the Soviet Union's most infamous mass murderer, we needed some air and a drink. The bunker lies just a couple of blocks from the Volga's shore. Samara sits on the river's left bank. The rocky Zhigulevsky Mountains on the right bank dominated the view from the bench on which we sat.

Pleased with such stunning scenery, we nevertheless recoiled at the bunker guide's de facto glorification of totalitarianism and repression, which, in the twenty-first century, run counter to everything Europe stands for. Russia is not Europe, many would say. Yet Europe is and always has been Russia's main point of reference, the standard against which, willingly or not, it both judges itself and finds itself judged. This held true even deep inside the Stalin Bunker. There, our guide had proudly informed us that it was Europe's deepest (121 feet); which is more than twice as deep as Adolf Hitler's bunker in Berlin and, of course, far deeper than Winston Churchill's piddling dugout in London.

We spoke English as we sat drinking the cans of Zhigulev beer we had just acquired from the centuries-old famous local brewery of the same name. The brewery's on-site store offers numerous varieties of beer on tap and salted-fish treats to go with them, all traditionally much beloved in Russia, but long gone from Moscow's posh environs.

Soon we found ourselves the object of curiosity of high school students sitting on a nearby bench. This was, it turned out, their graduation day; their cohorts strolled past us, dressed in stylized Soviet-era school uniforms—plain brown dresses and laced white aprons for girls, dark blue woolen suits for boys. Those were the uniforms that Lenin's unfashionable wife, Nadezhda Krupskaya, had adopted for schoolchildren in the 1920s. Hated for their dullness in Soviet days, they have made a comeback as a festive school outfit for special occasions such as graduation and evoke nostalgia in those pining after the now-defunct communist superpower.

Hearing us speaking English, the young Russians on the next bench were curious about the foreigners visiting their town: "Do you need help?" they asked in good enough English. "Would you like to have something translated or explained?"

Switching to Russian, we expressed our pleasure at seeing how well kept the Volga's embankment was here—families strolling, one of which appeared to be same-sex, children running, teenagers skateboarding. Crowded even on a weekday, the embankment stood in contrast to the neglected wasteland along the river in Ulyanovsk, and we told the students this. They proudly explained, "Ours is the longest river embankment in Europe!"

"Is Russia Europe?" we asked.

"Well, no," one of the boys answered. "But Samara, as the country's reserve capital during the war, is now the capital of the oblast and needs to look the part. Even though Nizhny Novgorod [another Volga town] has taken over as the unofficial capital of the Povolzhye, we are going to catch up." The others voiced their agreement.

Samara had languished in disarray for decades, but in recent years it has been trying to revive its riverine transportation business. From here speedboats—the meteors that we saw rotting away in Ulyanovsk—run to the larger industrial cities on the Volga, including Kazan, Tolyatti, and Syzran.

Our new friends described how the river loops around the hills, creating a peninsula encompassing a reserve of tens of thousands of acres of national forest that, before the Revolution, used to be farmland. In the decade preceding the Great Patriotic War, factories began encroaching on it as the Soviet Union, fearing attack from the West, prepared for potential evacuation eastward of industries in European Russia.

In Soviet times Kuibyshev was, like Kaliningrad, a "closed city" owing to its defense-related industries. It also became, eventually, the "space capital" of the USSR, producing rockets and much else the country's space program required. (The city was also famed as the producer of the *Pobeda* (Victory) timepieces—a Soviet Rolex of sorts.) Our young interlocutors complained that these days the Russian space industry relies on foreign-made equipment and is being neglected.

Yet the space museum remains one of the city's prominent landmarks, featuring, as it does, exhibits of the war. It was Khrushchev who presided over the Soviet Union's space program, long after Stalin's death. The Sputnik satellite circled the globe for the first time in 1957, twelve years after the war ended. Yury Gagarin made mankind's first journey into space, when Stalin was thoroughly expunged from the Soviet pantheon. And yet here he is again, the dictator rehabilitated. The museum presents the momentous achievements of the Space Age—some of the Soviet Union's most momentous—as the direct consequence of Stalin's era.

"What is Samara really good at?" we asked the new graduates.

"Industries, of course," they replied.

"But you say factories are being neglected here."

"Well, Samara is more a trade town these days. As a major river town, we've been always good at trade, too."

After saying good-bye, we walked back up toward Kuibyshev Square, breathtaking in its size. "It's the largest in Europe!" said a passerby, noticing our fascination.

"Are we in Europe?" we asked him.

"Well, not exactly," he replied, chagrined.

The square's ever-mutable name reflected the historical epochs through which it, and Russia, had passed. In czarist Orthodox Christian Russia, it was called Sobornaya (Cathedral) Square, for the huge house of worship that once graced its northern reaches. The Soviets dynamited the cathedral and designated the square Kommunalnaya (Communal) but eventually changed that to Kuibyshev, in honor of Valerian Kuibyshev, who ran the planned economy under Stalin. In 2010, a municipal commission recommended switching the square's appellation back to Sobornaya, but the mayor nixed the move. The young people we had spoken to on the riverbank didn't know who Kuibyshev was, but, in any case, they insisted that "At thirty-seven acres ours is the largest square in Europe." Again, Europe. Where we were not. But to which Russia looks.

Trapped between the double-headed eagle and the hammer and the sickle, Samara straddles the old and the new, the traditional and the modern, the communist and the capitalist.

Ramshackle, centuries-old wooden buildings decorated with intricately carved eighteenth-century latticework stand next to high-rises of glass and steel. Samara is a city of contrasts that even in Russia one rarely sees.

On our way back to the hotel, as we sped past the wooden houses, we asked a friendly cabdriver named Nikolai, "What are you going to do with the old huts, renovate them with contemporary amenities? Only a few, we saw, have been redone that way."

"No," he laughed. "The city got 26 million rubles [at the time $500,000] to drape painted tarps over walls facing the street. Just like the old Potemkin villages! Two hundred years later, Russia still has not changed!"

The Potemkin reference goes back to the summer of 1787, when Catherine the Great set out to inspect the recent additions to her vast empire, including the Crimean Peninsula, annexed from the Ottomans four years earlier. Catherine's lover, Prince Grigory Potemkin, the governor-general of her new southern provinces, knew shabby land- and cityscapes would displease the Germanic empress, who set high standards for order. So he saw to it that roadside buildings along her route would be lined with cheerful, prosperous facades, to hide the reigning squalor of rural poverty. On her return to Saint Petersburg, Catherine announced she was pleased with her new territory's bucolic riches.

Centuries later, the authorities still carry out renovations to impress visitors, be they czars or presidents. The current Potemkin program in Samara owed its origins to the 2018 World Cup, because along with ten other cities in Russia, it was picked to host a number of the tournament's matches. This time, the local government has decided to hide Samara's unseemly side not from the president, but from foreigners.

"At least in the USSR the authorities knew how to make life better. We made rockets and watches, we had boat rides on the Volga," Nikolai said.

We were curious: Kuibyshev was the reserve capital during the war, and the Soviet space industry capital after that. Yet the authorities have not managed to change the look in many downtown spots.

Just a few feet away from the wooden shacks on Vilonovskaya Street stands a fancy yellow building showing elements of Classical Stalinist style. There dwelled the Khrushchevs, the Stalins (his children, that is), and other political families evacuated from Moscow. Nina grew up hearing stories about the privileged wartime abodes within.

Nikolai had no answer as to why even the city center seventy years later still falls short of the "second capital" designation, except to note that Putin was working on it. Which did not mean that he was necessarily a fan of Russia's current ruler.

"With capitalism," said Nikolai, "there is no money for anything good for the people. And our governor is almost a communist," he announced, referring to the regional chief Nikolai Merkushkin. Officially a member of the dominant *Yedinaya Rossiya* (United Russia) party, Merkushkin has racked up a notoriously long list of complaints among his electorate, all the while making strident statements about the West's plot to destroy Russia. "Of course, things take a long time," our cabdriver said. He was speaking before Putin's elections in March 2018. "We'll see who will replace the governor."

"But didn't you say communists did everything well before Merkushkin, who was also a communist?" we asked.

"Those were good *Soviet* communists, but now they are bad *capitalist* communists," Nikolai replied.

Before the presidential elections, a sort of "musical chairs" was taking place across Russia, with mayors and governors being dismissed and others nominated in their stead to assure that Putin's de facto party, United Russia, would fill all the most important positions with the most reliable—that is, loyal—people. Just a few months after our visit, in September 2017, Merkushkin resigned "voluntarily" and was replaced by Dmitry Azarov, a local politician with a better economic pedigree.

For comparison, the Kremlin powers that be spared Ulyanovsk's governor Morozov such a fate in his Lenin-famous hometown. His good standing with the Kremlin has helped assure the longevity of his position. Even though Ulyanovsk could certainly use more sprucing up, Morozov has done well navigating local and national political, social, and cultural currents.

The farther east we would travel, the more we would see the well-being of a city, a whole region even, relying on the local government for its prosperity, while that prosperity was dependent on the regional authorities' cordial relationship with the Kremlin.

5

PERM, YEKATERINBURG, AND TYUMEN

THE URALS' HOLY TRINITY

TIME ZONE: MSK+2; UCT+5

> When you are Putin, the Russia you see
> around you is flourishing.
> —A contemporary Russian joke

Europe's Final Frontier

Three towns in the time zone that is second past Moscow—Perm, Yekaterinburg, and Tyumen—are major stopovers on the Siberian Throughway (in Russian, Sibirsky Trakt, also known as the Moskovskiy Trakt, or the Moscow Throughway). The throughway was the longest road in the world and for centuries connected Moscow and the Far East, passing through China. The three towns are also main junctions on the Trans-Siberian Railway, forming the trinity of the Urals—the mountain range dividing Europe and Asia.

Perm is the Urals' culture capital—the "first city in Europe," we would be told, and the setting for Anton Chekhov's *Three Sisters* and

Boris Pasternak's *Doctor Zhivago*. Named in honor of Peter the Great's wife, Catherine the Great, Yekaterinburg—known as Sverdlovsk in the Soviet days—is the regional political center and the capital of the vast Ural region. Boris Yeltsin was born in a village nearby. Tyumen is the hub for the region's oil industry, the industry supporting the Russian state and enmeshed in its politics.

The Perm Paradox

Lewis Carroll, in *Alice in Wonderland*, offers us a charming précis of how diet affects character. "Pepper . . . makes people hot-tempered . . . vinegar . . . makes them sour . . . chamomile . . . makes them bitter . . . and barley-sugar and such things . . . make children sweet-tempered."

Hard candy confected from barley sugar was for the prim Victorian Brits, of course. For the doughy Russians, Carroll's Russian translator Nina Demurova's pronouncement is apt: "*ot sdoby dobreyut*" (they grow kinder from eating buns). In Russian *sdoba* (yeast dough buns) and *dobryi* (kind) share a root.

Perm impresses with its buns and its decorative gingerbreads—Russia's most famous—and kindness. The city's bakeries brim with a variety of pastries sweet and savory, with fillings of cheese, fish, meat, cream, and potatoes and coming in various shapes and sizes. The vendors, smiling, make suggestions and offer samples of flavors you have never imagined. Say, an intricately decorated multilayered calf-liver cake with fresh herbs—amazing. Or a salmon turnover with cheese—even better.

After the lean, dour Soviet decades with their empty shelves and shortages, baking has been making a comeback all over Russia. One can buy fine baked goods even in subway stations—but in Perm they are even finer. The Russian soul, they say, dwells in its pastries and pies. Long before Lewis Carroll came on the scene, Russians had their own saying: "A home is not nice because of its decor, but because of its pies."

Maybe that is why Chekhov and Pasternak chose to memorialize Perm in their work. Chekhov's *Three Sisters* tried to salvage their intellectual lives in a "regional garrison town" where they eagerly dreamed of moving to the more refined Moscow. *Doctor Zhivago*—Pasternak's novel about a Russian poet-physician in love with another man's wife—is set in the fictional town of Yuryatin, based on Perm, amid the upheaval of the Bolshevik Revolution. There love blossoms between Yury Zhivago and Lara. Their meeting place—the nineteenth-century caryatid-decorated house in gorgeous Prussian blue, now on Lenin Street, that once belonged to the wealthy local trader Gribushin—is as important a character as the lovers themselves. They call it the "house with figures" here. In a double literary twist, Yuryatin's doctor learns that Chekhov's *Three Sisters* was, too, set in Perm.

The last city before the Urals, Perm, according to its residents, is "where Europe begins." Others view it as the last European city— the end of the world, even. The Perm Paradox.

The intoxicating smell of lindens, so rare elsewhere in Russia, wafts over the house from where these trees stand on the nearby Komsomolsky Prospect, adding to the house's fin-de-siècle charm. Next to it stands a more recent, commercialized sign of the times: a posh *Doctor Zhivago* restaurant, named in the post-Soviet tradition of pilfering literary texts for marketing memes. Have its customers read Pasternak's novel? Doubtful—the story is popular in Russia, the book itself much less so. Popular, because the novel's history is a political ordeal that many Soviet artists had gone through. After Khrushchev's Secret Speech Pasternak wrote a Zhivago romance set at the time of the Revolution, like Bulgakov exploring political themes of Stalinism and religion. The manuscript, forbidden in the

Soviet Union—de-Stalinization notwithstanding—was secretly published in Italy in 1957. Pasternak received the Nobel Prize in Literature, but the Soviets forbade him to travel abroad to receive the honor. Later in life, Khrushchev was embarrassed by this decision he called "despotic."

Having passed by the house with figures, we continued on Lenin Street, which we assumed would lead to the city's Lenin statue. We asked two young women for directions, but they didn't know the Soviet leader's location. Luckily, we came upon an older man who kindly explained that in Perm, a city of culture, the local Lenin monument was associated not with his eponymous street but with a park, where he stands in front of the stately pale blue Tchaikovsky Opera and Ballet Theater.

Music and ballet have always been cultivated here. Sergei Diaghilev, a native of Perm, founded in Paris in 1905 the *Ballets Russes*—the most famous twentieth-century Russian contribution to European high culture.

A hundred years later, in the summer of 2017, the city continued those cultural traditions. The Tchaikovsky Theater's orchestra, MusicAeterna, conducted by the Greek (and current Perm resident) Teodor Currentzis, opened the Salzburg Festival with its performance of Mozart's *Requiem*, the first time such an honor was bestowed on a non-Austrian company. Many do wonder how this town so off-center can attract world-class artists such as Currentzis. His explanation was that he chose to move to Perm because there he found "the spiritual depth he had been craving."[1]

Currentzis is not the only one who believes that Perm offers an atmosphere conducive to the creative life. The prominent art entrepreneur Marat Gelman, another native of Perm but known throughout Russia, launched many projects in town, including the Perm Museum of Contemporary Art, PERMM.

In the mid-2000s, the young governor of the Perm region, Oleg Chirkunov, had an idea to follow in the footsteps of Diaghilev, Chekhov, and Pasternak, and to turn Perm into the new capital of Russian culture. He was encouraged by Putin's then pro-European statements, including his BBC interview that "Russia is part of the European culture." "I cannot imagine my own country in isolation from Europe and what we often call the civilized world. It is hard for me to visualize NATO as an enemy,"[2] Putin said.

Chirkunov indeed made Perm's culture prosper, but by 2012 the political atmosphere changed and the governor resigned, effectively ending the period of the Perm "cultural revolution."

After Putin's third term as president began in 2012, the Russian government showed itself increasingly intolerant of diverse viewpoints—including in art—and the Kremlin decided Gelman's creation enjoyed too much popularity among the political opposition. In 2013, the government, or so Gelman contends, deprived him of control of the gallery, though it remains open and still plays an important role in the city's cultural life, albeit operating under the tighter supervision of the authorities.

Perm's spirit of the post-Soviet cultural revolt finds expression in the city's bus stops even today. Famous in his own right as a hip internet designer and a founder of a Moscow-based urban design firm, Artemy Lebedev, son of the writer Tatyana Tolstaya, in the late 2000s designed each stop to creatively reflect themes in Perm's past. Unfortunately, by the time we visited in July 2017, many of these stops had, in a way, shared Gelman's fate, and been damaged or defaced with graffiti.

Despite today's reigning conservatism, Perm hasn't completely lost its magic. Construction sites are ugly everywhere. In Russia, they amount to pathological eyesores, lasting ages, blocked from public view by gray hulks of concrete or drab canvas curtains, casting a pall of gloom over towns. But not in Perm. Since 2011 construction sites have enjoyed the ministrations of artists from a street art festival who paint the surrounding fences according to themes they chose. First, they selected "Perm—a European City," of course. The year of our visit it was "Perm's Lengthy History," in reference to the Permian Period of the Paleozoic Era.

We walked alongside a multicolored construction site fence admiring the artists' work, then asked a young bearded man painting there what else there was to see nearby. He hopped down from his ladder and, wiping a smudge of green color from his forehead, pointed to the linden-lined Komsomolsky Prospect, with its Central Exhibition Hall and its Art Gallery.

"They have a tribute to Marc Chagall and the Bible, a rarity," he responded. "And the Art Gallery, which is in a cathedral, has an exhibit showing eighteenth-century wooden sculptures. There you'll see Christ and Saint Nicholas looking more like pagan monuments, with flat cheekbones and slanted, widely spaced eyes."

Inspired by his detailed recommendations, we rushed to the Chagall exhibition of biblical lithographs. As we bought our tickets, the vendor said, "*He*"—Chagall—"*is a Jew!* But even he painted God Russian."

"He didn't," we interjected. "These are not Russian but *biblical* characters."

"Doesn't matter, a Jew portrays Christian religion!"

The Russian Orthodox Church, effectively an institution of the Russian state, was rank with xenophobia and anti-Semitism. Distrust of anything perceived as foreign, or at least not Christian—or specifically Orthodox Christian—fueled both the pogroms of the czarist era and discrimination against Jews during the Soviet decades. Thankfully, the bane of anti-Semitism has largely disappeared in modern Russia.

"You're not from here?" the vendor asked amicably.

"No, from Moscow and New York."

"From far away, then! Thank you for stopping by. How do you find us comparing to New York and Moscow?"

"Very cordial," we replied.

The woman could not have smiled more broadly.

Perm's claims to European civilization buttress its identity and define its history. A banner over the Heroes of Khasan Street, once the Sibirsky Trakt, proudly announces Perm to be the sister city of Oxford.

Never mind that Perm, rather un-Oxford-like, is a nightmare to reach from any of the nearby cities. A two-lane highway, potholed and narrow, serves as the main road into and out of town. On the way to the center, a mess of jewelry and fur stores line the unevenly paved lanes, heralding the Urals and Siberia, where hunters and gold miners once dominated towns. There is a reason for this. In times past, the state dispatched convicts to the region in the hopes that they might hunt for sable to supply the western areas of the Russian Empire with its precious fur. They also dug for gold.

The cobblestone streets and lawns on Perm's squares may have seen better days, but, we discovered, repairs are under way. Oxford, Perm is not; yet there is an orderliness to this place. Once the village of Yagoshikha—but founded as a city in 1781 under the patronage of Catherine the Great—Perm was strategically planned, which is unusual for a Russian town. A German and an Anglophile, Catherine wanted it to reflect her penchant for order, productivity, and civic awareness (or at least as much as would be permissible in an autocracy).

She may have succeeded. Perm's European status allows it to evade, to an extent, Moscow's control and still exude a feeling of a progressive cultural environment.

Many Russian towns, we noticed on our travels, present themselves as the center of something. Which makes sense. When the "power vertical" (as Putin once termed the Kremlin-dominant power structure he was set to reestablish in Russia) dominates all, each place creates its own raison d'être, at least for the purposes of public relations. Ulyanovsk showcases the aristocratic lifestyle and Lenin; Samara, its status as Russia's wartime reserve capital and the hub of the space industry. Kaliningrad, of course, takes pride in being the sprawling country's westernmost territory. And Perm, in the midst of the Ural Mountains, geographically, at least, is indeed the easternmost border of Europe.

Oppressed societies often express themselves through humor. In Russia, engaging in satire has enabled people to overcome their fear of the government and feel free of it. "If we can make fun of the Kremlin," Russians have reasoned, "the Kremlin can't have complete power over us." The city of Perm has taken a humorous approach to naming its tourist walkways, for example. A one-ton bronze bear stands in front of the giant, Soviet-era Ural Hotel as the terminus of the Green Line, the town's main historic route. Russians have never appreciated having the fearsome bear as their informal national mascot. When we asked Permyaks—those living in Perm—about their bear statue, they responded with a cheerful *"Stesnyatsya nechego!"* (nothing to be ashamed of). The bear stands not only for Perm, they explained, but also represents a subtle, ironic dig at foreigners, who, Russians believe, imagine bears walk around the streets of the country. The Red Line arrows show the way to sites associated with *Doctor Zhivago*, a love story.

Perm's pride is the Kama River and its splendidly renovated embankment. The Kama has always figured in the past and present of the city. To the west, it flows into the Volga and is its longest tributary; in the east it connects with the great Siberian rivers, the Ob and the Irtysh. In Catherine the Great's time, the Kama was famed as a supplier of salt, which was exported west at a great profit. Muscovites even developed a nickname for Perm traders, *solyenye ushi* (salty ears).

Amber-adorned souvenirs on sale in Kaliningrad's airport. *(Courtesy of Nina Khrushcheva)*

Above the banks of Ukraine's Dnepr River arises Saint Vladimir, the baptizer of Kievan Rus. *(Courtesy of Nina Khrushcheva)*

On Bolshoy Solovetsky Island, an onion-domed chapel stands in front of the tiny local airport building, a wooden structure painted azure. *(Courtesy of Nina Khrushcheva)*

Dusted with fresh snow, the fifteenth-century Solovetsky Monastery served as a prison during the early Soviet years. *(Courtesy of Nina Khrushcheva)*

Only in Russia: a bactrian camel hailing from the Central Asian realms of the czarist and Soviet empires offers tourists rides through snowy Arkhangelsk, in Russia's far north. *(Courtesy of Nina Khrushcheva)*

In Ulyanovsk, home-land of Vladimir Lenin, the drab architecture of the Lenin Memorial calls to mind the Soviet era. *(Courtesy of Nina Khrushcheva)*

In Perm, the Gribushin House, where novelist Boris Pasternak set scenes from his masterpiece, *Doctor Zhivago*. *(Courtesy of Nina Khrushcheva)*

The timeless rural landscape around Perm bespeaks peace and a slow pace of life. *(Courtesy of Nina Khrushcheva)*

On Lake Baikal's Olkhon Island, shaman Gennady Tugulov wears the traditional garb of his spiritual vocation. *(Courtesy of Jeffrey Tayler)*

A lone protestor takes a stand beneath Novosibirsk's monument to Lenin. *(Courtesy of Nina Khrushcheva)*

Outside the Buryat capital of Ulan-Ude rises the ornately adorned main temple of Ivolginsky Datsan, Russia's main Buddhist sanctuary. *(Courtesy of Nina Khrushcheva)*

Dusk descends on the embankment of the Amur River dividing Blagoveshchensk and the Chinese town of Heihe. *(Courtesy of Nina Khrushcheva)*

A flower market graces Yakutsk's Ordzhonikidze Square, to the delight of locals. *(Courtesy of Nina Khrushcheva)*

In the outskirts of Magadan, Russia's "Gulag capital," the stark Mask of Sorrow monument calls to mind the victims of Stalin's Great Terror. *(Courtesy of Nina Khrushcheva)*

On land once occupied by Magadan's House of Soviets now stands the Holy Trinity Cathedral. *(Courtesy of Jeffrey Tayler)*

Veering northeast into Gulag land, the Kolyma Route (once a dirt track trod by Stalin's condemned) has been paved and is now officially known as the R504 Kolyma Highway. *(Courtesy of Nina Khrushcheva)*

In the rubble of Kolyma's Butugychag labor camp, where prisoners mined uranium unprotected, abandoned shoes recall the perished. *(Courtesy of Nina Khrushcheva)*

On the way into Vladivostok, the Just Russia party has emblazoned a cement wall with the patriotic catchwords "Crimea is Russian!" *(Courtesy of Nina Khrushcheva)*

In Vladivostok, the soaring twin suspension towers of the Golden Bridge, along with much else, evoke San Francisco. *(Courtesy of Jeffrey Tayler)*

The fog-shrouded stony redoubts of the Kamchatka Peninsula loom over the Pacific Ocean. *(Courtesy of Nina Khrushcheva)*

Ignoring the condescension, the Permyaks, proud of their roots, erected a monument to that, too.

Of course, "Europeanism" here has a decidedly local tinge. The fashion store *Comme Il Faut* brims not with *haut de gamme* threads, but with giant displays of plastic flower arrangements; signs for the festival mini-Avignon display photos of the Kremlin in Moscow; and the Wonder Woman Pizza shop—where we stopped for a bite—was eerily empty, its servers busier with their phones than with us. We were almost the only customers. Nevertheless, the pizza shop's owner was at least gender-aware, choosing for its theme a female superhero, and not Superman or Spider-Man or some overtly masculine figure. This was unusual in patriarchal Russia. Though we saw signs saying *Administratsiya po Blagoustroistvu* (administration for civic renovation), streets and squares have been under construction for years, we were told. Perm's airport was one of the worst we saw during our journeying— jammed with disgruntled passengers and their screaming babies, with little flight information available, and a waiting lounge area resembling those of bus stations in provincial Soviet cities. Yet, unusually for Russia and very socially consciously—which is also unusual—many billboards here denounce the wearing of fur. This in the fur-producing Urals and despite all the fur shops lining the Heroes of Khasan Street.

When it underwent a cultural awakening of sorts in recent decades, Perm also began to champion the values of civil society, at least for a while. Hence, on a sunny July morning, we rode out to Perm-36, once a Gulag labor camp but now a museum, just outside the village of Kuchino, some sixty miles northeast of the city. The countryside through which we passed, with its undulant green hills empty of human habitation, recalled the Scottish Highlands, if under a cloudless azure sky.

In Perm-36, hapless prisoners engaged in logging—one of the most brutal forms of hard labor. Among them, struggling to survive the inhumane conditions for which the camps eventually earned worldwide infamy, were prominent dissidents, including the long-suffering writer Vladimir Bukovsky and Gleb Yakunin, the late priest and member of the Moscow Helsinki Group.

The fate of the Perm-36 museum is, unfortunately, typically Russian. Opened in the 1990s when Boris Yeltsin was eager to expose the horrors of Soviet totalitarianism, the establishment for two decades was affiliated with Memorial, a human-rights organization dedicated to keeping alive Russia's history of political repression. At the time, Perm-36 was more than just a museum; its mission was to inspire social consciousness. The site was a special one—it survived Khrushchev's Thaw and was operational as a political prison into Brezhnev's 1970s. The expositions contextualize how Perm-36's inmates lived with displays found in its white-walled barracks, a hall used for meetings and showing films, a forge, a sawmill, and a repair shop. A green watchtower overlooks its rusting barbwire perimeter, beyond which stretch empty fields and scraggly forest.

After Russia's 2014 annexation of Crimea, the connections between Soviet repression and the modern Russian state's current aggressive nationalism became too obvious to ignore. The museum was almost closed; its annual gathering devoted to human rights, *Pilorama* (Sawmill), ceased to convene after complaints of dubious sincerity from former prison guards and nationalistic Stalinists about its supposedly "antipatriotic" stance. The Kremlin, however, decided that closing the Gulag site would only give ammunition to Putin's critics. So, instead the government took over Perm-36 as a historical project under the auspices of the Russian Ministry of Culture and replaced the museum's Memorial founders with new state appointees.

To control the message, the institution is now less about this site as a once horrible camp; it has become about the Gulag as a whole. It focuses less on political prisoners, the purges of Stalin's Great Terror, or Stalin himself. It nevertheless continues to display the details of the prisoners' stark life, their bare barracks and their plank beds, and a chillingly simple interrogation room furnished with only two chairs, a table, and single lamp—all presented in the context of the Stalin regime's efforts to industrialize Russia. The message is curated: traveling to the faraway region of Perm to see all this isn't even necessary; the museum's website offers a virtual tour.

Eager to see Perm-36 in person, we took a tour led by a flaxen-haired woman in her thirties with a businesslike demeanor. She instructed visitors on how to think about the inmates' life of misery and deprivation: it is just a part of Russia's great history. Sacrifices must be made, she told us. This broadly means that while undertaking the creation of a mighty country with a new social order, you should expect a few negative, unintended consequences. By this logic, our marvelous, if somewhat flawed, leaders had the state's best interest in mind. "The great utopia when all was possible," one display poster declares, with no hint of irony. Moreover, "enemies of the people"—including religious objectors who gouged out the eyes from portraits of Stalin and Vyacheslav Molotov, the Soviet signatory of the 1939 nonaggression treaty—were driven by their "primitive" private interests with no understanding of the state's mission for the good of all. That was our guide's party line, also delivering the ultimate Kremlin message: embracing our past makes Russia great.

A jolly older man in a sailor's striped shirt and a blue-and-white sailor's cap soon joined our group.

"Aren't you lucky that this man, who used to be here, can tell you all about the camp?!" the guide exclaimed.

We assumed him to be a former *zek* (labor camp inmate). But no, it turned out that he served as one of the guards and now works as a mechanic at the museum. He bemoaned the hardships of his job now in the same breath as he regaled us with tales of the prisoners' plight. He was bearing out the words of Anna Akhmatova, one of the Soviet era's most famous poets. Akhmatova, after Stalin's death and the beginning of Khrushchev's Thaw, mused that the two Russias—"*odna, kotoraya sazhala, i drugaya, kotoraya sidela*" (one that was putting people in prison and the other that was sitting in those prisons)—were finally "going to look into each other's eyes." That was almost happening around us—almost, because the members of our group were far too young to know how the Stalinist labor camps came about. No one objected or showed discomfort about the way the story of mass incarceration was being told.

In this, the Putin state was successful in diverting attention from the horrors of the repressions by presenting them as one of the tools for creating a great country.

"How have things changed here since the museum became part of the state?" we asked.

"They haven't," the docent replied with a strangely perky smile. "We have the same exhibits. We just put them in the proper historical context."

That's the genius of the Putin regime—opposing or controversial views are not always forbidden, but their "context" is manipulated for the benefit of the Kremlin.

Even though Perm-36 tells the story of the Gulag, it fails to present Stalin as the Kremlin's chief murderer. And, as we had seen elsewhere, Khrushchev does not figure into the story told; his post-1956 mass rehabilitation of Stalin's prisoners is absent. In the prisoners' movie hall, a wall displays a long array of official portraits of high-level Soviet political figures, but the out-of-favor premier is nowhere among them.

"How come?" we asked. The woman replied, "Oh, right, I never noticed. Perhaps it's because our museum is not political."

The Gulag system was *not political*? How could this be, given that the greater part of those who did time here were political prisoners?

Khrushchev's omission told us a lot about Russia. As our tour finished and we boarded our taxi to leave for Perm, we concluded that in Russia, despots are understood better and admired more than reformers; their harshness is justified as having served the good of the state. Reformers, on the other hand, are considered weak. When despots kill, they do so to save the country; when reformers try to bring justice, it must be because they have ulterior motives, and patriotism is not among them. At the start of Gorbachev's Perestroika the ailing Molotov explained this state of mind: "With Stalin we followed the directions of a strong hand; when the hand got weaker, each started to sing his own song."[3] More than two and a half decades after the fall of the Soviet Union, this mentality still holds. "Singing one's own song" remains dangerous insubordination to the state's "power vertical."

Our next stop east was Yekaterinburg—the Ural's capital and throbbing heart and the onetime stomping ground of Putin's predecessor, Boris Yeltsin. Traveling by car, a dozen or so miles out of Perm, the "first city in Europe," we noticed something we had missed on our way to the labor camp: an artfully designed bus stop bearing a sprawling, faded banner: "Glory to Dear Stalin for the 70th Anniversary of Our Great Victory 1945–2015."

We were glad to be on our way.

Yeltsin's Yekaterinburg

Approaching Yekaterinburg by the Moscow Thoroughfare, we drove by another memorial erected in honor of victims of Soviet political repression, a giant diptych in bronze authored by the artist Ernst

Neizvestny. The monument displayed two faces—one, a mask of suffering with closed eyes; the other, a visage encased in what seemed to be concrete blocks. The message was indicative of Russia's split-personality disorder: one half of the country was imprisoned, with the other half guarding it. Russia still cannot decide what it wants to honor. It cannot decide what it is: a European nation or a country that glorifies its despots.

Yekaterinburg is the only city in Russia that fondly memorializes Boris Yeltsin, the bearlike, reform-minded Czar of Russian Democracy—he sought to embrace the aura of czarlike power on the top of a postcommunist system. Born in 1931 in the local village of Butka, Yeltsin attended the Ural Polytechnic Institute, preparing to lead Russia's industrial heartland. That he did, in the mid-1970s becoming the regional Communist Party Secretary. He moved to Moscow to become its mayor in the 1980s and to join the Politburo—a Soviet parliament of sorts. Rising from the regions Yeltsin became a powerful figure in the collapse of the Soviet Union and led the Kremlin afterward.

Posthumously, this son of the Urals serves as Yekaterinburg's main attraction, with the Yeltsin Center rivaling in majesty any American presidential library. The center is a giant, ultramodern cubist complex that lauds the defunct head of state as—oddly, or perhaps not—a new Lenin of sorts, presenting to its visitors a version of the former president no less mythologized than a Bolshevik revolutionary. While visitors swarm throughout the glass and steel complex, television crews are at work filming the displays.

We were to meet with the center's deputy director, Lyudmila Telen, but she was away in the capital during our visit. In her place, she had kindly arranged a tour for us with the center's director of archives, Dmitry Pushnin, a tall, balding fellow in his forties. From the complex's central circular hall (reminiscent of New York's Guggenheim), where a bronze Yeltsin sits ruminating on a bench, our eloquent guide led us to the first exhibit: an exposition of the future president's early job as the First Secretary of the Communist Party's Central Committee for the Sverdlovsk region, a position that put him in control of one of the most important industrial zones of the Soviet Union. Thanks to Yeltsin, Pushnin told us, the mighty, highly industrialized Soviet-era Sverdlovsk (named after Yakov Sverdlov, a Bolshevik revolutionary) retained its glory as the new Yekaterinburg. Now with almost a million and a half inhabitants, Yekaterinburg is the fourth largest city in Russia after Moscow, Saint Petersburg, and Novosibirsk.

"This seems a bit like Ulyanovsk and Lenin. When the Kremlin leader is from a certain place, the place gets a lot of mileage from it," we remarked.

Pushnin bristled at such a comparison, saying that Yekaterinburg was much more exciting than Ulyanovsk and had always been.

"It is," he explained, "the *real* center, Russia's window into Asia," occupying, as it does, a crucial spot in the Urals, with territory both in Europe and Asia.

Established in 1723 under Peter the Great to process metals mined from the nearby mountains, the city bears the name of the towering emperor's wife, Yekaterina, or Catherine I (not to be confused with the later empress, Catherine II, the Great). Yekaterinburg came into being more than 150 years before Novosibirsk, the current unofficial capital of Siberia. On orders from Catherine II, in the eighteenth century Yekaterinburg joined the Perm *guberniya*. In the Soviet era, Yekaterinburg became Sverdlovsk (with the surrounding territory renamed the Sverdlovsk Oblast, a designation it has retained). Message intended by the administrative move: Sverdlovsk was becoming more important than Perm, far surpassing it in both size and in the number of vital industries based there. Once the Soviet Union fell, Sverdlovsk became Yekaterinburg once again.

Pushnin pointed out a display showing black-and-white photographs of Ipatiev House, in the basement of which Czar Nicholas II and his family were murdered by the Soviets in 1918. The Bolsheviks' brutal act and how Yeltsin responded to it would mar the future president's legacy. In the 1970s, the Ipatiev estate was supposed to be transformed into a museum. Instead, in 1977, Yeltsin, then the region's Communist boss, quietly ordered its demolition. By the late Brezhnev era, as the myth of soon-to-arrive communism was fading, the Ipatiev House became a destination for pilgrims wishing to honor the murdered czar's memory. Yet the Yeltsin Center presents Yeltsin not as a seasoned Soviet apparatchik conducting the Party's business but as an unwilling political "executioner" of Moscow's will.

Few who know Soviet history would argue with this assessment. But Pushnin's subsequent comment—"we displayed the controversy as accurately as we could"—also suggested a savvy public relations move to control the key message: Yeltsin was different from other Soviet leaders, who played up their successes and never admitted making mistakes. In tearing down the Ipatiev House Yeltsin betrayed himself as a true Soviet indeed. But he was different, too—as president of the new Russia he allowed the rehabilitation of the czar's family to happen on his watch. Was it an act of repentance, a feeling of guilt? Did he succumb to the social pressure from the public? Fed up with atheist communism the country was ready to love their czars again.

Pushnin didn't say.

The next exposition detailed the return of the remains of the czar and his family from Yekaterinburg, where they had been discovered in a shallow grave in a nearby forest, to Saint Petersburg in 1998. It displayed photographs of the construction, on the spot where the Ipatiev House had once stood, of the Church on Blood of All Saints Resplendent in the Russian Land. Work on the house of worship began during Yeltsin's terms in office but was completed only in 2003, with Putin taking credit for the return of the last czar.

As did so many former communist leaders, Yeltsin went from advocating Soviet policies that resulted in the destruction of churches and the persecution of religion to the post-Soviet building of cathedrals almost everywhere imaginable. A new chapel even rose on the premises of Moscow's School for the Ministry of the Interior—perhaps the most ungodly institution of the Russian state, with a history of punishing opponents dating back to 1802, to the reign of the authoritarian Alexander I.

After the Soviet collapse, the rehabilitation of the Russian Orthodox Church has allowed it to play an outsize—and growing—role in the country's political life. For instance, Patriarch Kirill instilled himself in politics by telling Russians, just before the bitterly contested presidential elections of 2012, that Putin revived Russia after the disastrous 1990s through a "miracle of God."[4] Russia's main problem is its propensity for veering from one extreme to the other. In this case, the swinging pendulum—from fervent Orthodox faith to virulent, anti-theistic communism—of Russians' allegiance has destroyed millions of lives. First it was a justification of serfdom, then of purges and forced labor camps. Yet for all the Putin government's stridently expressed views, at times embodied in legislation that seems intended to mollify the church, including a law prohibiting the "gay propaganda" of the "corrupt West," the state has, by and large, persecuted relatively few. A sager approach to governance in Russia shows that the ruling elite has learned at least some lessons in moderation.

We stopped by a trolleybus on display. In many Russian cities, trolleybuses still play a major role in local transport. But this was *the* trolleybus Yeltsin took to work in 1985. After becoming the head of the Communist Party of Moscow (which essentially made him the capital's mayor) Yeltsin, famous for his fight against privileges accruing to those in power, rode it to show that Politburo members should live no better than did ordinary Soviet citizens. His fight, we might add, did not last long. After he became president, the number of privileges he enjoyed skyrocketed; those with access to power would become richer, those without, poorer.

We then came upon an exhibit devoted to a wildly popular television show of political satire, *Kukly* (Puppets), showing Yeltsin and Gennady Zyuganov, the post-Soviet Communist Party leader. The display was meant to showcase Yeltsin's open-mindedness. Unlike his chosen successor, Putin, Yeltsin did tolerate his critics on the airwaves. They found in him an easy target: by the time he resigned, on New Year's Eve of 2000, his popularity had sunk to 2 percent. *Kukly* didn't last long after Yeltsin's departure. The Kremlin's new master did not like his puppet, fashioned after E. T. A. Hoffmann's 1819 character Zinnober, from "Little Zaches, Great Zinnober." Seemingly more insecure, and a former KGB operative, Putin apparently thought it inappropriate that the Russian public should watch a televised mocking of his person. Hoffmann's description was not exactly flattering: "An unobservant eye would discover little about the face, but if you look more closely, you discover a . . . a pair of small, darkly flashing eyes."[5] Moreover, Hoffmann's character had questionable credentials, just as Putin did, many thought. And yet, as Hoffmann has it, Putin's puppet, "for most people," was "a perfect gentleman, poet, scholar, diplomat, and lover."

We had serious questions for the chief archivist about Yeltsin's term in office. What about his 1993 shelling of the Russian parliament, then called the Supreme Soviet, which is housed in a building known as the White House in Moscow? What about the constitutional crisis it had provoked by abolishing the legislative body? At the time,

Yeltsin was locked in combat with a government accusing him of the corrupt and incompetent management of the economy that had given rise to the oligarchs and had drained the country's coffers. Yeltsin dissolved the parliament, arguing that the communists, who held a majority, would bring back the Soviet Union. The dissolution was illegal, as was the shelling of the parliament, of course. But in the 1990s, the words "the threat of communism" were magic and excused all excesses. And here at the Yeltsin Center, we learned, they still do, at least according to our guide.

Pushnin both lamented and celebrated the fact that many pro-Putin public figures—including the highly educated and fervently Orthodox Christian Oscar-winning film director Nikita Mikhalkov and the retrograde Minister of Culture Vladimir Medinsky—have declared the center a "*rassadnik inakomysliya*" (a hotbed of dissident thinking).

"Such attacks on us are good," Pushnin stated, "for our reputation in other circles. And let's face it. The Kremlin needs us to create the impression that it's allowing freedom. Just by our existence, the center upholds the constitution, which guarantees freedom of thought and expression and prohibits censorship."

Once again, the Perm-36 phenomenon—the Kremlin's appropriation of the opposing views to promote its nonautocratic reputation. But whereas Perm is no longer a mass destination for the liberal luminaries who used to attend the annual *Pilorama*, the Yeltsin Center is still a must-visit for prominent artists, journalist, writers, and European diplomats. Perm-36 and the Yeltsin Center are, in short, the last holdouts of Russian democracy.

Although the Yeltsin Center denounces Stalinism and lauds Khrushchev's Thaw in its historical displays—in contrast to the Lenin museum in Ulyanovsk—the exhibitions do not dwell on the questionable acts of Yeltsin's reign. Still, when viewed in retrospect from the Putin era, the hardships and errors of Yeltsin's presidency appear more acceptable than they were at the time.

One of the most glaring of these errors was the 1994 invasion of Chechnya—in what would become known as the First Chechen War—when Yeltsin rejected the demands of the Chechen Republic for a separate state. In the 1990s, as the Soviet empire was crumbling, Russia unequivocally pronounced itself pro-Western and democratic, for free markets and free choice. The Chechens, not surprisingly, declared independence in 1993, under the leadership of their president, Dzhokhar Dudayev, a former air force general. In January 1994 Yeltsin responded by sending Russia's armed forces to besiege the Chechen capital of Grozny. In doing so, he was following in the footsteps of his Russian imperial predecessors.

Chechnya, a tiny Muslim republic in the mountains of the North Caucasus, has posed a problem for Russia for centuries. In 1810, under Czar Alexander I, Chechnya's leadership "voluntarily" joined the Russian Empire. That immediately triggered a guerrilla war as locals sought to regain the independence their leaders had supposedly surrendered willingly.

During the decades of conflict that followed—with the Chechens continuously oppressed by the Russian state—a succession of Russian writers ventured into the mountains to write about the war, winning fame through the literary brilliance they manifested. From Pushkin's poem "A Prisoner of the Caucasus" (1821) to Leo Tolstoy's depiction of the conflict in his novella *Hadji Murat* (1912), these works of literature romantically acknowledged that the Chechens, hotblooded warriors that they were, could not be fully conquered.

The twentieth century was hardly kinder to them: Stalin, fearing that ethnic minorities might rebel against the Russian majority following the Nazi invasion, initiated a policy of "population transfer," a Soviet version of ethnic cleansing. Through operations conducted by his murderous secret police chief Lavrenty Beria in 1944, the Chechens, and other peoples of the Caucasus, were deported to Central Asia and Siberia in unheated cattle cars in the dead of winter. About a quarter of them died. The Chechens' doomed struggle, in particular, was commemorated in Anatoly Pristavkin's *The Inseparable Twins* (1981), a powerful narrative about two boys, a Russian and a Chechen, who became brothers of a sort in the crucible of forced national relocation. The main message of Pristavkin's tale: the Chechens cannot be conquered; hence, they must be freed.

No one can understand Russia without understanding its literature, yet Russian leaders often fail to contemplate its lessons. Yeltsin and now Putin, who launched the Second Chechen War of 1999–2009—by then a battle with militants of various Islamist groups—learned that Chechnya may be pacified for a while but not vanquished. Putin has resolved this dilemma for now by allying with Chechnya's current strongman, Ramzan Kadyrov: in return for remaining within the Russian Federation, Chechnya receives generous state subsidies, with Kadyrov allowed to run his republic as his own private estate—an outwardly Islamic state, in fact.

The Yeltsin Center tackles none of these political questions. A skillfully laid out display of the First Chechen War letters from Chechens and Russians makes clear the terror overhanging the bloody conflict. Its message, not exactly controversial: war is a curse on everyone.

"How do you reconcile Yeltsin's involvement in the war with his democratic aspirations?" we asked our guide. He evaded the question and instead stressed the emotion expressed in the letters, and how "so very openly" the center decided to display them without taking sides.

Pushnin then led us to a stunning, sun-drenched hall—the Hall of Democracy. There ceiling-high windows opened onto the city, bathing in light a sky-blue mural entitled *Svoboda* (Freedom) painted by a well-known dissident, the Yekaterinburg-born artist Erik Bulatov. The word "freedom" emblazons not only the mural, but also the hall's mirrored columns. Freedom—the aspiration of the new, liberal Russia Yeltsin helped birth.

For a moment, we felt carried back in time, to the era when Yeltsin's Russia—chaotic, corrupt, and fearful—was still heading toward a freer future, a future in which Russia would, at some point, become part of Europe rather than what it is, de facto, today: a world of its own. Leading their tour groups, upbeat guides in their early twenties reminded us of the promise of the 1990s, when Russia's talented, hardworking citizens were going to transform the post-Soviet space from Kaliningrad to Kamchatka.

Anatoly Chubais, Yeltsin's deputy prime minister, also known as the "father of Russian privatization," once planned to accomplish this glorious transformation "in three 'shock' years," following the dictates of neoliberalism laid out by mostly American advisors. This was a transformation "the rest of the world spent three hundred years achieving," as Chubais said in a television interview back in 1994.

Pursuing such a utopian goal did not bring about the desired results of capitalism and democracy; instead it sowed disillusionment and mistrust. That feeling of both high hope and bitter disappointments was, perhaps, best captured by one exhibit, an orange sweater, a birthday gift from the late Boris Nemtsov, Yeltsin's onetime prime minister and, later, a leading member of the opposition to Putin. The orange color, Nemtsov's undated note says, is "a reference to what Russia is missing today," that is, freedom, a nod to the prodemocracy movement in Ukraine that brought about the Orange Revolution of 2004.

No doubt, the center, as do presidential libraries, aims at highlighting its namesake's victories and downplaying his defeats. A replica of his Kremlin office, complete with a decorated Christmas tree, does take one back to December 31, 1999. Then, Russia's first-ever president, at age sixty-eight, looking exhausted and slurring his words, addressed the country and announced he was resigning and ceding power to Putin, whom he had handpicked to replace him. Yeltsin had reason to do so: he needed to ensure that his family's riches remained intact following the presidential elections, scheduled for 2000, which he surely would have lost. His less than laudable motives notwithstanding, Yeltsin became the only Soviet-era leader who voluntarily left office. The now sixty-six-year-old yet ever-youthful Putin is staying in power at least until 2024. In 2000 Russians complained that Yeltsin's riches were calculated at fifteen million dollars, a meager amount compared to Putin's projected worth, counting palaces, yachts, watches, cars. The total has come to some 40 to 70 billion dollars,[6] although his annual Kremlin salary is about 8.9 million rubles ($137,000).[7]

"This is a lesson in civics—giving up power when it's time," our guide told us, having mentioned nothing of the complicated circumstances surrounding Yeltsin's resignation. "We teach kids who come here to learn about democracy, societal responsibility, political literacy, and so on." The young guides listening in ardently nodded, their eyes shining with a conviction rarely seen elsewhere nowadays. They seemed to belong to the hopeful 1990s, when Russia, by leaps and bounds, was advancing toward something better. What a contrast they presented to the museum guides in Ulyanovsk—tired, scolding elderly ladies with beehive hairdos who seem to have stepped out of the Soviet past. The Yeltsin Center's young people were indeed guides to the future.

In a way, despite its remote location, Yekaterinburg has been progressive. It gave birth to Russian hard rock. Now iconic bands—Nautilus Pompilius, Chaif, and Agata Kristi—with their revolutionary

Ural Rock style and philosophical lyrics—first reflected the hopes and struggles of Soviet-era Perestroika and then of the disorderly, yet free, 1990s. In front of one of the city's business centers stands a statue of Vladimir Vysotsky, the Soviet bard known for his brutally honest, wry depictions of Soviet life. A local skyscraper—"the most northern sky-scraper in the world," locals say, is even named after him. Vysotsky, a James Dean of sorts, died in 1980 and is celebrated all over Russia as "the heart of the nation." He sang about the hardships and heroism of the everyday people in lyrics delivered in his signature raspy voice. His simple heartfelt words provided an alternative to dry socialist realism—the officially approved artistic style of the Soviet Union. Vysotsky was a Muscovite, yet the people of Yekaterinburg, and else-where in Russia, recognize his spirit as akin to their own.

The sculptor Ernst Neizvestny was also from Yekaterinburg. In his work, Neizvestny, approaching his craft by following his indi-vidualistic, original inclinations, challenged the artwork borne of so-cialist realism, with its themes always relevant to the workers' state and that state's politics. In 1962 at the Manezh exhibition he heatedly disagreed with Khrushchev's criticism of avant-garde art. Yet in recognition of the achievements of the Thaw, Neizvestny made his most recognized creation, the former premier's grave memorial in Moscow's Novodevichy cemetery: Khrushchev's bronze head between two jagged pieces of white marble and black granite—he is both the anti-Stalin reformer and the Soviet reactionary.

After saying good-bye to Pushnin, we spent the rest of the day walking around this well-kept city, which has a cool, Chicago feel-ing about it. It is a mighty manufacturing metropolis with skyscrap-ers, diverse outdoor exhibits of art, its own music, and a lively nightlife. It even passed our café culture test with flying colors. Not only are coffee shops many, they are lively and open late into the night, welcoming curious and hungry passersby.

Though with Putin having scored a record-breaking win in the presidential elections of 2018, the Kremlin has apparently decided to disregard effective governance as a crucial factor in maintaining control over some of Russia's cities and oblasts. Now in his nineteenth year in office, Putin expects Russia to surrender to him. The more homogeneous and devoid of any potential discontent the country is, the longer he may stay in power. If the public begins to demand a renewal of political blood, obedient governors and mayors should be prepared to suppress any related discontent. Such logic runs counter to the Kremlin's own long-standing argument that the economically better developed regions should offset the less developed ones.

Until recently Yekaterinburg had skillfully managed to balance serving both its people and Moscow—an increasing rarity in Putinland. In 2014 Yevgeny Roizman, a charismatic politician of the Just Russia party beat a candidate from the ruling United Russia, and has been, since then, resisting Kremlin-backed contenders for regional power. At the beginning of Putin's fourth term, however, he resigned in protest against the new rules aimed to cancel direct local elections.[8] Stifling changes to the vibrant city are probably to come, but during our visit in July 2017 the pulsating energy of the metropolis that never sleeps was still manifest.

The new café Makers, on Malyshev Street, off Moskovskiy Throughway, sits just a few blocks from Yekaterinburg's Lenin Square. Its bright pink refrigerators and green-jungle-leaves wallpaper make it look as though it could have been a hip destination in Brooklyn. Typewriters sit on each table offering visitors a chance to pound out their views and suggestions; pencil cases are meant to hold your coffee bill, and once paid, your banknotes; pencil cups serving as tip jars—all are fun and clever, but not pretentious. Plus, their espresso is out of this world.

Not all shops around town, however, cater to modern tastes. Two streets, Chelyuskintsev and Sverdlov, are lined with fur stores emblazoned with a potpourri of names, from the banal to the patriotic—Squirrel Furs, Czar's Fur, Russian Furs, Furs of Siberia, World of Fur, and so on—selling mink and shearling, beaver and chinchilla. Fur coats, the ultimate apparel of status and achievement, have always enjoyed primal popularity among Russians, even during the socialist decades. Here, too, they unite Europe and Asia; from the Urals and Siberia, fur has been traded west from time immemorial.

After perusing them, we readied ourselves to depart for our next destination, further east. On our minds would weigh, with a certain degree of sadness, the lost promise of the Yeltsin years—a time when in Russia almost anything seemed possible, as the soaring glass ceilings of the Yeltsin Center reminded us.

Tyumen, Capital of Russia's Klondike

On a warm, clear July morning after a five-hour journey by rail through ragged deciduous forest and marshy clearings, our train slowed and stopped by the platform. The brilliant afternoon sun reflected off the metal-and-glass station festooned with a sign proudly announcing, WELCOME TO TYUMEN. The building, one of the major stops on the Trans-Siberian railroad, had been recently renovated, as was apparent in its ever-changing electronic tableaux announcing arrivals and departures, its spotless, mostly white modern interior. The Russian Railways have become a billion-dollar business with competitive prices; clean and comfortable cars; efficient services; and modern, well-kept stations. The station and service to Tyumen were no exception.

Founded in 1586, Tyumen, the current hub of the Russian oil industry, has had an even shinier look than most. After all, 64 percent of the region's oil reserves, as well as nine-tenths of its natural gas, lie nearby. The Antipinsky Refinery alone, for example, processed almost eight thousand tons of oil in 2016. Moreover, Tyumen, population 750,000, is the capital of the vast Tyumen Oblast stretching from the border with Kazakhstan to the north, all the way to the Arctic Ocean. Compared with much of the world's vision of oil in the deserts, Russia is different once again—its oil country is nestled in the mountains and steppes of western Siberia.

Some of the largest international oil companies maintain offices in Tyumen, and Tyumen residents enjoy commensurately higher incomes—in fact, they have the highest standard of living in the Russian Federation.

No matter how sleek Tyumen's train station was inside, though, upon debarking we confronted a motley crowd selling everything from furs to meat and cabbage pies to ice cream and pungently salted fish—a scene familiar along many stops on the Trans-Siberian. In Soviet days when consumer goods were available in limited supply, travelers loved jumping down onto the platform and perusing the creams or cakes or flowers on offer. In the Yeltsin era, when the economy collapsed, many in the outback found the only way to survive was to trade just about anything of value they could cart onto the platforms—from cups of tea and pastries to family heirlooms. Today, despite the much-improved economy, private trading of this sort persists, as prosperity is still a distant dream for many.

The origins of Tyumen's name remain obscure, though it probably derives from the Tatar *tumen* ("ten-thousand-strong army"), which makes sense for a settlement that in the Middle Ages was a military stronghold—an ancient, prominent town belonging to the Tyumen Khanate of the Golden Horde, Khingi-Tura, on the Tura River. Tyumen stood on the old caravan route connecting the Povolzhye (lands along the Volga) with Central Asia. In 1580, Cossacks, pushing eastward to win territory for the czar, wrested control of the town from the Tatars. A few years later, Russians established their own fort there, the first Moscow outpost on the eastern side of the Urals. Tyumen found its status augmented when, as the nineteenth century drew to a close, the government decided to build the Trans-Siberian Railroad through Tyumen. For political reasons it bypassed the more elegant town of Tobolsk, a famed place of exile for the Decembrist revolutionaries, the crème de la crème of the Russian aristocracy. During the Russian Civil War, the last czar's family hid out here for a while, sheltered by the troops of Admiral Kolchak, until the Reds overtook them in January of 1918. During the Great Patriotic War, Lenin's body was moved from the Red Square mausoleum to the blue-and-white nineteenth-century college building here that now holds the State Agrarian Academy. In the 1950s, government prospectors discovered major oil fields all around the Tyumen Oblast, which transformed this region into an industrial hub. Tyumen quickly became an administrative and educational center, with its renowned Tyumen State Oil and Gas University being founded in 1956.

Its history and prosperity notwithstanding, this town with its oil-boom ambiance resembles a Russian hybrid of the Klondike and Las Vegas, populated with modern-day prospectors and those who service them. People visit jewelry stores more than cafés; café culture is not Tyumen's forte, yet garish restaurants abound. *Zolotaya Lavina* (Gold Avalanche) jeweler serves double duty as both a workshop for gold and diamond goods and, of all things, a bridal salon. Its large windows feature Siberian belles gracefully modeling wedding gowns. Nothing looks permanent; everything has something of the flashy, slapdash about it.

We couldn't help wondering, where did Tyumen's four-hundred-year history go? The new has obliterated the old. Even though it boasts the highest standard of living, the city revolves around oil revenues and buying things—furniture or fur or jewelry—not around enjoying life's comforts, such as, say, having a cup of coffee or a relaxing meal.

Yet in this Vegas-cum-Klondike we discovered incipient signs of change to come. Although some of the restaurants serve reindeer meat and sour cream–smothered pelmeni, the Double B Coffee and Tea (a café from a Moscow franchise) employs a barista sporting a fashionably scruffy beard and a man-bun; he deployed the panache of a true artisan in making us an espresso, taking a full twenty minutes to do so. "How cool am I, creating this real European drink in this real coffeehouse that has its headquarters in the Russian capital!" his mien seemed to tell us. Outside, fashionably dressed young men and women strode down clean, well-paved sidewalks, glancing at their reflections in store windows. Tyumen folk project a cool, tough demeanor: they live in an oil-rich town and take pride in being Siberians; one may even say they have created what amounts to "Siberian chic." The display of toughness, though, seems too ostentatious to be real. Perhaps it is no wonder that Grigory Rasputin was born in a nearby village. A notorious fraud, Rasputin wielded tremendous influence over Russia's last empress, Alexandra, the wife of Nicholas II, for his seeming ability to alleviate her son's hemophilia.

Souped-up motorbikes with oversize tires roar about Tyumen, showcasing their owners' excess of testosterone and spare cash, and muscle cars shoot by with their camouflage paint-overs, perhaps signaling a readiness to fight for the country. Many display both the red flags and Russian imperial Saint George ribbons, which in the Putin years have come to represent Russian nationalism. They became especially popular after Russia's lightning takeover of Crimea. Some of Tyumen's store windows display huge posters, inviting tourists to "Crimea, the Holy Origins of Russia," in reference to Vladimir the

Great's 988 baptism of Kievan Rus, which according to some sources took place in Korsun, present-day Chersonesus, in Crimea.

During the Stalin decades of Soviet classicism, the government built grand statues, opulent parks, and elaborately designed subway stations—"people's palaces," as it were—to compensate, at least in part, for the austere nature of life. Even now, in Tyumen, public displays of state wealth spent on the "needs of the people" seem to matter more than encouraging the private investment that would flourish in the café culture we saw developing elsewhere in Russia. Here the cafés were almost empty. We detected further evidence of this in the city's large pedestrian zone in the center, along Tsvetnoy Boulevard (named after a famous street in Moscow); there, those out for a stroll wander across several squares with fountains and pose for photos beside the jets of water, line up to enter museums, and visit the circus.

Public displays of state wealth lavished on the people also lend an official imprimatur to individuals the state selects as convenient for its image. On Tsvetnoy Boulevard stands a tribute, sculpted in bronze—a helmet and motorcycle gloves—to the local bikers' band, Siberian Hawks. When we visited, it was surrounded by admirers. Tyumen Oblast governor Vladimir Yakushev has been a vocal supporter of the Hawks. Yet he is not entirely original in this. Putin, famously, has been riding with the right-wing nationalist group, the Night Wolves. These biker gangs became synonymous with Russia's intense displays of militant patriotism and machismo in the wake of Moscow's confrontation with Ukraine.

Of course, influence can travel both from the capital to the provinces and from the provinces to the capital. Moscow's mayor Sergei Sobyanin was once governor here. Since assuming office in 2010, he has been busy transforming Moscow into a grander, if more congested, version of Tyumen. (As one might imagine, this has not gone down well with urbane Muscovites.) In particular, he has broadened many sidewalks downtown to, in places, forty-six feet across, which has constricted roadways and worsened Moscow's already horrific traffic jams: an example of Sobyanin's know-how gleaned from his years in provincial Tyumen, where he also broadened sidewalks. If it is unclear why a provincial city like Tyumen would need outsize sidewalks, it is even less comprehensible in Moscow, which is, after all, first and foremost a city of cars—small sporty Italian cars, glistening black Audis and Volvos, boxlike Mercedes SUVs. Besides, frequently inclement weather discourages pedestrians, in both cities.

Famously partial to cobblestones or, to be exact, their cement equivalents, Sobyanin is rumored to have once declared, "Asphalt is not native to Russia." He has, thus, been turning Moscow upside down every summer, tearing up thousands of miles of asphalt walkways (1.5 million square miles at the summer 2017 count) and laying down chunky concrete cobblestone look-alikes—at great inconvenience to residents—under the pretext of beautifying the city, just as he once did in Tyumen.[9] Few Russia watchers would be surprised to learn that his (now former) wife Irina and her firm *Aerodromstroi* (Airport Construction) were involved in installing such faux-cobblestones in Moscow and elsewhere. In her native Tyumen, Irina was known informally as Irina *Bordyur* (Curbstone Irina). Cobblestones, if laid poorly, can become a menace to pedestrians, and are, after all, at least as foreign to Russia as asphalt is. No matter: during the eight years of Sobyanin's tenure, the city has refurbished walkways with Curbstone Irina's bricks. Imagine the wealth flowing into *Aerodromstroi*'s coffers!

Nevertheless, the slickness, artificial though it may be, that Sobyanin has brought to Moscow (and once to Tyumen) seems to be going down well with the Kremlin. In fact, just as Stalin's favorite architectural style, socialist classicism—exemplified by wedding-cake skyscrapers with intricate facades—found itself replicated in major Soviet cities today, Sobyanin's broad sidewalks have become commonplace all over Russia. A political message lies within these walkways: down their broad expanses a content, imperial, and patriotic citizenry is expected to stroll, grateful for the largesse of their government in making their time on the pavement more pleasant.

Tyumen residents, as far as we could tell, take pride in their proliferating array of Russian Orthodox churches. In recent decades and partly during Sobyanin's tenure as governor, the city, as a taxi driver named Mikhail admiringly (and with some degree of exaggeration) joked to us, "exceeded the Kremlin plan by erecting twenty thousand new places of worship, churches, chapels, and so on." A macho fellow in a sleeveless T-shirt exposing his biceps, tattooed with images of the Kremlin, Mikhail explained while driving us around town: "Putin is good because he represents *power*! He uses his office as head of state—a sacred office—to show Russia's greatness. Russia will be saved through *pravoslavie, samoderzhavie, narodnost*"—the Orthodox faith, state power, and the people, those pillars of Russianness introduced by Nicholas I. "It will flourish through the expansion of its empire, its messianic, civilizing influence over other cultures. We would be nothing without our size."

"What about other empires? Do they also have a civilizing influence?" we asked.

"Ha, they are truly evil. Those European settlers, when encountering Native American tribes early on in North America, gave them smallpox-ridden blankets to eliminate them, using illness as a means of biological warfare. That's how they conquered North America, through death. What kind of empire is that?!" He contrasted how Russia spread east across Siberia. "We're tough and strategic here. The Russian people expanded to the east for freedom and to spread its influence, and that's how our national character was built," Mikhail exclaimed proudly, though his toughness seemed a little too much on display, as though he had to strike a patriotic note in speaking to outsiders.

He was not entirely wrong about the Americans, but he was also not quite right about the Russians—their expansion was not benevolent, either. In fact, he confirmed just one truth: all imperial conquests are problematic.

In the center of Tyumen next to the City Administration on Lenin Street stands *Patron* ("cartridge," as in ammunition), a store catering to hunters and outdoorsmen. In addition to guns and fishing tackle, *Patron* also displays a dark green cannon on wheels. Manly hunters, one presumes, are also patriotic and ready to defend the Motherland. A block away, next to the imposing local affiliate of the Ministry of Internal Affairs, across from the Lenin statue in Central Square, we spotted yet another hunting store, Bagira—as in Bagheera, Mowgli's panther protector, from Rudyard Kipling's *Jungle Book*, still immensely popular in Russia. Through its tinted windows we saw posters lauding "Military Tourism in Crimea"—here is Crimea again, nowadays the pinnacle of all things Russian. Patriotism, firearms, and guns, all amalgamated into flashy advertisements displayed as much for the money they would generate for tour companies as for the increase in revenues the state has hoped to generate for its newest region, reliant, since czarist days, on summertime visitors for much of its annual income.

Yet not only hunting shops manifest fervent patriotism here in Tyumen; local cats are enlisted in this noble task, too. Tyumen may be the only city on earth boasting a Siberian Cat Park (*Skver Sibirskikh Koshek*), laid out to honor feline service during the Great Patriotic War. Then, local authorities rounded up two hundred tough Siberian cats and dispatched them westward, to save Leningrad's Hermitage Museum, in which marauding rats were damaging priceless works of art.

Even fashion here is of a distinct Tyumen style we had not encountered elsewhere in Russia (in recent years, at least; such attire was
common in summertime Moscow in the early 1990s). Young women
strolled down their city's wide sidewalks draped in flower-print
dresses—rather common, yes, but they reach to the ankle, resembling
a mixture of a ball gown meeting casual Friday threads. In a coffee
shop, we couldn't hide our curiosity and complimented a young woman
on her dress, which was festooned with prints of large red roses.

She replied, "We in Tyumen like to wear nice clothes. To dress
up, if you will."

"What kind of fashion is it?"

"*Siberian* fashion!" she answered combatively.

No patronizing Muscovite visitors were going to impugn her taste,
motivated, at least in part, by the pride Siberians take in their home
region. During the chaotic Yeltsin years, Siberians often referred to
European Russia as "the continent"—implying that the turmoil in
Moscow belonged to another land.

Impressed with such conviction, we smiled and got our coffee.

After passing through the Urals and entering Siberia, we recalled
a line from Nikolai Gogol's famous play *The Government Inspector*:
"From here you can ride for three years and won't reach another
country." It took the exiled Decembrists over a year to march to this
province. Nowadays, Tyumen is only a thirty-hour train ride (not
much, by Russian standards) from Moscow, but here, for the first time,
we began to ponder, "What happens when you cross into another time
zone? Does more than scenery change? Do people change?"

Almost imperceptibly, we felt Russia's spirit changing—into
something more expansive, infused with the grandeur of a land
whose geographic boundaries, as well as the human cruelty they have
witnessed, exceed our capacity to comprehend.

6

OMSK

....

A MIXED METAPHOR OF PUTIN'S EMPIRE

TIME ZONE: MSK+3; UTC+6

> If you write the word "Navalny" on a snowbank, it will be cleared in
> an hour; if you write "Putin," it will stay on for the fourth term.
> —A contemporary Russian joke

It is eight in the morning and guests in one of the city's leading ultramodern hotels awaken to a persistent rapping on their doors.

"Housekeeping!"

"Too early! Please come back later!"

"No, I can only make up your room now!" Two stocky, glum middle-age ladies are determined to clean the rooms that very moment. "Wait down in the lobby!" they bark.

What's the point in holding out? guests wonder, subjected to such harassment. Their morning sleep has been ruined anyway. Not fully ready to face the day, they obediently depart their rooms and settle into the Knoll-style leather chairs in the spacious lobby, well appointed and flooded with brilliant Siberian summer sunshine. Next to them stands a spotless glass table on which lies a glossy Cartier catalog, a brochure advertising luxury cars, and a leather-bound tome on skiing in the Swiss Alps.

Slowly turning the pages that display tidy chalets, and still grumpy about being forced from their rooms, they say hello to another middle-age woman entering with a vacuum cleaner. She flicks the "on" switch and her machine roars into action. The guests' conversation dies in the racket as she vacuums around their feet, under the table in front of them, and beneath their chairs, meticulously and for a long, long time. The lobby is empty, and she has plenty of places she could be cleaning apart from their corner. But surely, she is following the routine dictated by the hotel's administration; the presence of hotel guests is not about to deter her.

Welcome to the four-star *Hotel Mayak* (Lighthouse), so picturesquely situated at the confluence of two mighty Siberian rivers, the Om and the Irtysh. Welcome, in fact, to Omsk, capital of Omsk Oblast, after more than twenty-five years of capitalism.

On the southern steppes of Siberia, only some seventy-five miles north of the border with Kazakhstan, Omsk has a population exceeding a million people, and a three-hundred-year-old history dating from when the Cossacks were pushing east over the Eurasian landmass and attempting to secure trade routes back to cities in Russia's west. A perfect metaphor of the Putin empire—a fine, double-headed eagle almost smack in the middle (2,500 miles to Kaliningrad, 3,125 miles to Kamchatka) of outback Russia—Omsk, despite its potential and aspirations, comes up short.

In Russia, Omsk enjoys a bad reputation, ranking extremely low in quality of life. Even though it is one of the country's top industrial cities (though long "closed," owing to its space-program-related industrial plants), its municipal budget is just over ten billion rubles (about $200 million), which is almost three times less than that of Novosibirsk, the next major city to the east on the Trans-Siberian rail line. The federal government takes most of Omsk's revenues from oil and heavy industry central to the city's economy, leaving little left over for local use.

Omsk, with its large population and revenue-generating potential, should be one of the most attractive places for investment in Russia. But its inhabitants lack the requisite purchasing power. And as the service economy leaves much to be desired—as the maids in our hotel so clearly demonstrated—in recent years Omsk has lost around ten thousand people, most of them with higher education. In the late 1980s and early 1990s the city was an infamous hub of Russian racketeering, with political and economic clans fighting one another to the death; even the city's mayors and the oblast governors couldn't get along. To this day, it has a reputation for crime. The best one can do in Omsk, it seems, is leave.

In the 2000s the Russian internet was buzzing with images of the Omsk Bird—aka, ominously, the Winged Doom—a shimmering black raven draped in a red cape with a Venetian hood that originally came from a painting by the German artist Heiko Müller. With the anonymously added caption "Welcome to Omsk!" the symbol came to stand for addiction to narcotics and gambling. The idea of living in Omsk, at least for those not from here, eventually became as frightening as inhabiting a real-life Hieronymus Bosch grotesque. Though it really had little to do with the city, the image of the Omsk Bird nonetheless came to represent it, perhaps because so few people from elsewhere in Russia actually visit the place.

It hardly helped that in 2014 even a local monument—a giant sphere of wood and metal named *Derzhava* (Fatherland)—decided to escape from one of the main squares, and the square named after Ivan Bukholts, Omsk's founder, at that. Lashed by a violent thunderstorm, the Fatherland rolled off its perch—incidentally in front of our hotel—into the Irtysh. This prompted the Omichis (inhabitants of

Omsk) to concoct another meme, *Ne pytaytes pokinut Omsk!* (don't you try to leave Omsk). *Derzhava* failed to heed the injunction and tried to abscond yet again, though less successfully.

Otherwise, Omsk has done little to help better its image. Its metro system has just one station, going nowhere. Its "new" airport has been under construction for forty years. And despite the availability of funding, plans to build two four-star hotels, the Park Hills and the Hilton, came to naught.

The new young mayor, Oksana Fadina, with a doctorate in economics from the Agrarian Academy, now promises to reverse the fortunes of this major industrial city that seems to have never caught a break.

Its university is named after Fyodor Dostoyevsky, who in the 1850s was imprisoned here for plotting against the monarchical regime. His grim novel about the horrible conditions in the Siberian labor camps under the czars, *Notes from a Dead House*, was set in Omsk, which he described as "a despicable little town. Almost no trees. In the summer it is hot, and sandy winds blow; in the winter, storms come. There is almost no scenery to speak of. The little town is dirty, military and debased to a great degree. . . . If I didn't find people here I would have perished completely."[1]

Given that Dostoyevsky so passionately hated the town, the decision to dedicate the university to the writer seems surprising. Dostoyevsky's criticism notwithstanding, Omsk was once a place that mattered. Established in 1716, it was the imperial capital of Eastern Siberia, the seat of a steppe-and-forest *guberniya* that included parts of what is now Kazakhstan. Eastward still, its Altai region served to connect the Russian and Kazakh steppes. In its flatness, the landscape of this colossal province resembles much of the rest of Siberian Russia as it gives way to Central Asia and its deserts.

Like Samara, which touts its status as Russia's wartime reserve capital, Omsk takes pride in having been, if only briefly, Russia's "third capital"—the so-called White Capital, after Moscow and Saint Petersburg fell to the Reds in 1917. In 1918 Admiral Alexander Kolchak, a man of many talents—he was a polar explorer and a writer, in addition to being a warrior—became the head of the czarist Russian government as opposed to that of the Bolsheviks, and ruled what remained of "White" Russia from here. But not for long. The Bolsheviks caught up with him and executed him in 1920.

In the post-communist era the Kolchak legacy contributed to the city's image of itself as vital to the course of Russian history. The Admiral Kolchak House, located in an estate he once occupied, is dedicated to the history of the Civil War. We paid it a visit. Two studious-looking young men—one a monarchist with a shaggy beard, the other a clean-shaven technocrat—mesmerized the few visitors with their tale of Omsk as Russia's third capital. We learned that it was not selected for this honor just because it was far from Moscow and Saint Petersburg. No, many officers abandoned by the czar's government after World War I traveled here to better their lives, thereby making the city a natural seat of governance. Their large number drew Kolchak's forces here as well. Under his command, these officers banded together to protect the monarchy and fight the Reds to their last breath. Here the short-lived commander of White Russia remains as big as Lenin once was. A few steps away from the museum stands an elaborate four-story restaurant named Kolchak. A garish collection of many styles—an old wooden house decorated with the admiral's portraits set against more recently added gilt onion domes as from an Orthodox cathedral—the Kolchak offers diverse dishes from a variety of cuisines, including French and Japanese, just as the more Europeanized elite of czarist days would have liked. A banner stretching across the street in front announces that the Kolchak Restaurant offers a "taste of true Russian democracy," presumably in the variety of plates on offer.

In fact, though, the admiral believed not in democracy, but in a military dictatorship for Russia. A century later, however, local legends (and advertising exploiting them) based on his time in town have given rise to a Kolchak-related craze: scores of people digging in nearby forests for the elusive Kolchak gold, riches supposedly hidden from the Reds during the Civil War. Fads aside, life in Omsk does owe something to its martial past. Its Cadet School, founded in 1813 and originally the Omsk Military Cossack School, is the oldest such establishment in Siberia and now offers some of the best war training in Russia. And locals laud the Saint Nicholas Cossack Cathedral across the street, Lenin Street, as an outstanding landmark evocative of the lost glory of the old czarist army.

The loss of its imperial glory sealed Omsk's fate in the new communist country. When in 1920 the Red Army pushed out the Whites, the Kremlin made sure that the city would lose its prominence. Most state institutions moved four hundred miles east to the small town of Novonikolayevsk (now Novosibirsk, the third largest Russian city and the capital of the neighboring oblast). Omsk has been left fighting to regain its lost status ever since.

As Dostoyevsky observed (and we confirmed), dust has been one of the town's most notable features. In the 1950s, the Omsk authorities planted hundreds of trees to clean up and "green" the climate. The Soviets promoted the idea of *podchineniye prirody cheloveku* (submission of nature to man) as a means of demonstrating progress that, presumably, only devoted communists could bring about. A famous song of the 1920s promised in the new Soviet Russia "to make fairy tales a reality"—and Omsk was to become a *Gorod-Sad* (Orchard City)—evidence that communists could force nature to submit to their will, tame vast steppes, and bring even dust storms under control.

After the Soviet collapse in 1991, these much-touted strivings turned out to have produced little. Trees were cut to free land for private construction, with the result that the long-suffering town found itself with a new, and ugly, moniker: the City of Trunks. Today, it is dirty and dusty indeed, even though in recent years another "green" policy has favored the planting of trees and the creation of parks.

This policy, too, has largely failed. By the end of a day of walking around, our shoes were caked with dust, and our clothes felt as though they bore a patina of week-old grime. After rains, roads widened in Sobyanin-esque style were unusually muddy. In 2016, during Putin's annual national press conference (usually an event with questions screened in advance), one Omsk woman was able to sneak in a complaint about her town's miserable roads. The president, always eager to act as a caring "father of the nation," intervened, and in fact did thus foster some improvement to Omsk's infrastructure.

Environment shapes character. The people of Omsk seemed reserved, even gruff; was it because of the dust, crime, the perpetually unbuilt metro, the reigning air of futility? Or does inhabiting a closed city for so many years sap the spirit? Could Omsk's militaristic history have rubbed off on its citizens? Surprising for a city so dusty, Omsk, we discovered, is fitness oriented, at least along the newly renovated Irtysh river embankment, where people were out biking, jogging, and stretching.

Omsk was the only town in Russia in which we felt uncomfortable speaking English. When we did so, people eyed us with suspicion. As we took cell phone pictures of the local Ministry of the Interior building—an impressive structure with an adjacent monument consisting of an obelisk with a double eagle on the front honoring the "Heroes of Security Forces"—a group of police officers approached us.

"You can't take pictures here."

"Why not?"

"This is a security installation."

"But this is a public space."

"Please leave."

A mother passing by with two small children overheard the conversation and cast us a suspicious glance, as if to say, "Why do you take pictures of Omsk's landmarks? For what nefarious purpose?"

Omsk's Lenin statue and its surroundings reflect the city's purely Russian essence—that is, its "neither Europe nor Asia" quintessence. The onetime leader of the planet's proletariat, standing in bronze, occupies a small park in the middle of a traffic circle with no crosswalk leading to it. A diminutive Orthodox chapel hides behind him. Across the road is yet another park, one celebrating those who fell fighting with Kolchak's army. Diners in the adjacent Kolchak Restaurant may contemplate Lenin, the chapel, and those who perished for Old Russia as they sample their French or Japanese delicacies. In what other country on earth does one encounter such jarring, seemingly casual, juxtapositions?

Yet Omsk's contradictions have a charm of their own. Religion and Old Russia and the czars versus Lenin surely feed into an obsessive desire to put the adjective "European" on signs advertising seemingly every type of business, from those selling furniture to clothes to wallpaper and even medicines. As if the word "European" is going to produce a different, more coherent, *better* reality. A European Wallpaper store nestles oxymoronically in a concrete Soviet-style highrise. Geneva Watches sells anything but. And a nearby log shack announces itself as the Rome Clothes Salon, offering selections that surely come straight from the looms of China. To be fair, though,

across Russia a mania for things Italian—Rome, and particularly
Venice—prevails. We noted the Pizzeria Venezia in Ulyanovsk; a
Venezia dance hall in Tyumen, and plenty of Venezia cafés and restaurants in places too numerous to mention. But Omsk offers a glaring oxymoron: *Russky Dom Mody Venezia*, that is, the Russian
Fashion House of Venice. There is such a thing as Russian fashion—
think of Valentin Yudashkin, for example—but its reach is, well, less
than global.

The birthplace of one of the most mystical Russian painters, the
symbolist Mikhail Vrubel, lies just outside the portals of Omsk's
Vrubel Museum of Art: a grand mansion with a pale green facade and
cream trim that resembles a baroque train station standing on—of
course—Lenin Street in the center of town. Announced years ago as a
Siberian affiliate of Saint Petersburg's Hermitage, it remains an affiliate of that institution in name only. Nevertheless, it presents its
contents with curious verve, displaying pieces of prerevolutionary
furniture from the upper classes as an exhibit centered around the
much-beloved Soviet-era, yet deeply anti-Soviet, 1928 novel *The
Twelve Chairs*, composed by two brilliant Odessa-born journalists,
Ilya Ilf and Yevgeny Petrov. Whimsical and unassuming, *Chairs* is
a masterpiece that, like Bulgakov's *Master and Margarita*, became
cult reading for Soviet citizens yearning for literary release as they
were inundated with a numbing onslaught of Social-Realist fare. The
plot concerns the hunt for a set of old chairs in which aristocrats hid
their diamonds after the 1917 Revolution. The narrative's hilarious
journey from Moscow through provincial towns to the Caucasus bris-
tles with funny yet shrewd, often unflattering, observations about
everyday life under the then-new communist regime.

In keeping with the *Twelve Chairs* theme, in the Vrubel Museum
Italian-made chairs and vases, flowery Dutch still-lifes, French tapestries, pink Limoges porcelain, and blue Wedgwood pottery

bear captions with witty quotes from the novel (sample: "*Spasenie utopayushchikh delo ruk samikh utopayushchikh*," or "The rescue of drowning people is the responsibility of the drowning people themselves"). The sum of effect is as humorous as it is telling and speaks to the predicament of so many in Omsk (and across Russia).

Outside the museum, Lenin Street presents pedestrians with wide faux-cobblestone sidewalks, equipped with park benches, well kept, and similar to those in Moscow and Tyumen laid down by Mayor Sobyanin. (Surely that is no coincidence. Even here what happens in the capital makes itself felt.) On our way from the museum to our next destination, the slick café New York Coffee, we noticed a book—Bulgakov's *Master and Margarita*—lying unattended on a bench. No surprise. After all, Bulgakov's satirical masterpiece was serving as an unofficial cicerone throughout our travels across Russia. In this case, this was particularly apt, for the café's interior resembled a scene from the novel.

New York Coffee's blackboard wall menu proudly announced "Trump coffee." The American president, it turned out, was just as consuming a topic of conversation in Russia as elsewhere. After all, he prevailed in an election Russians perceived would be, if not outright rigged, then at least arranged after one fashion or another to put their arch-enemy Hillary Clinton (disliked for a slew of reasons, but mostly for her fiercely anti-Russian, anti-Putin stance) in the White House. Trump, if nothing else, won over the hearts, if not the minds, of many Russians because he repeatedly voiced his desire to "be friends" with their country. Few Russians considered him an upstanding individual, yet no other American presidential candidate was talking that way.

But in Bulgakovian fashion, it was not politics—that is, whether the café's Trump coffee was meant to glorify or mock the president—that a gaggle of teenagers in front of the counter was arguing over.

With skateboards under their arms—they had been practicing their moves beneath the nearby Lenin statue—they were quarreling about what sort of orange syrup you need to top the garish caffeinated concoction to achieve the exact tinge of Trump's hair.

Out of curiosity, we ordered the Trump. The sweet caramel drink had about as much to do with coffee as Trump had to do with presidential dignity.

"Is Trump coffee meant to marvel at or mock him?" we asked the waitress, whose name, said the button on her shirt, was Lyubov.

"As you like!" she said with a wry laugh.

"Clever. Have you actually been to New York?" we asked her after the young group settled on their drinks and ordered. (None went for the Trump.) "We're from there. Or at least one of us is."

The teenagers joined in, eager to meet their town's foreign guests.

"So how does the café compare? How do you like Omsk?" they and Lyubov asked.

"How do *you* like Omsk?"

"Don't try to leave Omsk!" they joked. Intimations of the Omsk Bird of Doom!

We chatted: the feeling that life was somewhere else, beyond Omsk's dusty borders, was strong, and permeated their banter. They were pleased that we were enjoying our stay in their city. They pointed out that Lenin Street was the main drag, with few places as cosmopolitan elsewhere in town. Other big Russian cities—Yekaterinburg, for example—had more to offer, with Saint Petersburg interesting Lyubov in particular. She told us that she planned to work at the Hermitage next year; she wanted to live in a beautiful city, one without "the pervasive feeling of depression and neglect behind the sense of doom emanating from the Omsk bird."

"Why do people want to leave?" we asked.

"Because of the local government."

"Are you going to vote for Putin in 2018?"

"Yes, for him and United Russia."

Yet it turned out that two of our impromptu young friends supported Alexey Navalny, the popular anticorruption activist. In fact, they were volunteering at his local office and believed him to be the future of Russia. The backing Navalny could count on from such young Russians made him a threat to Putin.

Later, we met Tatyana Bessonova, chair of the regional journalists union. Once a reporter for *Omsky Vestnik* (The Omsk Caller), Bessonova, in her early fifties, sported henna-purpled hair recalling the Soviet days and worked for the governor's office. Which no doubt accounted for her reluctance to answer our prickly questions, including those about the notoriously bad relations between the oblast administration and that of the city.

However, she sounded upbeat about the recent journalism project they had implemented, proclaiming Siberia the Territory of Hope.

She went on and on about this. Yet we had seen precious little evidence that the project had had any effect.

"We haven't seen much hope among the city's young," we responded. "Wouldn't the morale boosting go better if you had improved governance here?"

"Well, yes," she admitted, and straightaway opened up about the difficulties plaguing the journalists union. Located in an Art Nouveau building with a magnificent, if rundown, oaken staircase, the union found its property being eyed by the government. Bessonova told us that she was unsure how long they could fend off a state takeover of their premises. It hasn't happened yet, she said, because she was advising the authorities on public relations. As both a journalist and a government employee, she faced a constant conflict of interest. How could she report on the injustices committed by the functionaries and then promote their work? Doing both, she responded, was the only way to keep the union alive, to continue the work—conferences and symposia, mostly—that gives Omsk what little standing it has in Siberia.

Omsk did grow on us. Perm may have had more confectioneries, but those in Omsk did not disappoint. One wonderful bakery on Lenin Street bore the run-of-the-mill French name of Éclair, but the wares it sold were tasty. Before moving on, we stopped one last time by the Skuratov café, perhaps the most memorable such café from our wide-ranging travels around Russia. A tiny hole-in-the-wall joint next to the river port, the café offered the best espresso we had enjoyed in a long time, serving it in elegant stoneware cups. The Skuratov won us over with its sincere service, handmade multiflavored chocolates, and sophisticated clientele. In fact, Skuratov had recently expanded to Saint Petersburg, and opened its cafés in four central locations in Moscow—no mean feat in the highly competitive market of these two cities. A business moving from the provinces to major Russian cities—this was something rarely heard of.

We left Omsk—yes, you can leave Omsk, despite its notorious avian symbol!—feeling down. The city has so much potential and yet enjoys such terrible repute. Russian cities, and Russian people, are like snowdrop flowers—battered by tempestuous crises, swept away by changing regimes, and wilting under a warm miasma of mismanagement and neglect. Yet every spring when the winter ends, they reemerge. In Omsk we saw evidence of their hardiness, as they tirelessly strove to turn their city into the third capital with the European flare they imagine befits it.

On the way to our next Siberian destination, Novosibirsk, the Omsk train station appeared to be as conflicted as the rest of the city. Two doors lead to and from the platform—"exit" and "no exit." The "exit" door is shut, so everyone passes through another door—an entrance from the outside. We did so hesitatingly, but the security guard waved at us to proceed. It bothered no one but us that exit from Omsk happens through the "no exit" door.

7

NOVOSIBIRSK

....

A STORY OF SCIENCE
AND SERENDIPITY

TIME ZONE: MSK+4; UTC+7

"Can you fix a town in twenty-four hours?"

"Yes, we can."

"How?"

"Putin just has to say that he is going to visit not only Novosibirsk; he needs to say that he is going to visit the whole region, and decide on a town later along the way."

—A contemporary Russian joke

On the train to Novosibirsk, we shared a compartment with a young fellow best described as lupine: he was tall and wiry, with a pointy nose and close-set eyes; from his white tank top protruded arms covered in tattoos. If he resembled a wolf, he also looked like a hardened criminal itching to pull out a knife. With his lanky legs stretched across the floor, he controlled access to the door, thereby blocking the entrance of a grumpy porter in a dull gray uniform. Avoiding eye contact with him, we huddled next to the window, staring hard at the sea of white flowers blanketing the steppes outside—a healing sight for eyes often wearied by Russia's endlessly repetitive vistas of forest, steppe, and hardscrabble villages. Yet it turned out that this sea would have had something other than a healing effect on us had we dived into it, covered as it was, in places, with water hemlock.

The flat landscape of this, the West Siberian Plain, was a pleasing sight, though it eventually turned tedious, subjecting us to sky and earth, earth and sky, with nothing to catch the eye. Welcome variety came during our train's brief stops at tiny wayside stations, at which locals sold pies, pickles, jam, and even furs and whatever else they could come up with. But soon the fields disappeared, forest intruded, and the stations became larger and more orderly.

Our lupine compartment companion eventually pulled out not a knife but a laptop. He turned out to be a shy hardware engineer named Igor, who, warming up after hours of travel, told us he worked for a company that made air conditioners, with offices in Krasnoyarsk and Novosibirsk.

"I'm going all over the country," the "criminal"-cum-computer geek said. "Omsk is okay, they say. It has more sunny days than any other place in Russia. But Novosibirsk is the best. It's Russia's third largest city and perhaps, on the whole, its most sophisticated."

Four hundred miles deeper into Siberia than Omsk, prosperous Novosibirsk, with a population of 1.6 million and set amid taiga, fascinated us. Not that it was without its own contradictions. In places, cracked sidewalks cried out for Sobyanin-style cobblestones. On the banks of the Ob River, which cuts a magnificent azure loop through the city as it surges north, sits a dilapidated port befitting an outback Siberian town. Amid new structures gray concrete blocks crop up, recalling the Soviet past—and, of course, Lenin Square spreads a formidable expanse of cement; arising in its center, a mighty, if weathered, bronze statue of its namesake towers above lesser bronze figures depicting workers, peasants, and soldiers. As always, the Russian double-headed eagle makes its appearance on the adjacent Krasny (Red) Prospect, this time atop the Chapel of Saint Nicholas, erected in honor of Nicholas II. The city was founded under his reign at the turn of the twentieth century. Whence the city's name, translated as "new Siberian town."

In front of a shopping mall near the square also stands a billboard: "Don't know what to give as a gift? Buy a model tank from the Eastern Front" (a reference to World War II). Here as elsewhere in Russia, "European" enterprises abound, emblazoned with PARIS or ROME, including the garish business center called Rome, outfitted with its very own Roman columns. The usual Russian schizophrenia notwithstanding, the city and its inhabitants exude an unusual aura of self-respect. Novosibirsk is, after all, young, with little in its past to be ashamed of.

In 1891, the engineer and writer Nikolai Garin-Mikhailovsky, charged with drawing up plans for the Trans-Siberian railroad, originally wanted the line to pass through Tomsk, an old university town some 150 miles to the northeast. But he eventually decided against dragging the rails north to accommodate Tomsk, insisting that the latitude of the tiny Novonikolayevsk ("New Nicholas Village," as it was originally called) be exactly fifty-five degrees north of the equator.

Thus began the story of Novosibirsk—a story of scientific bravura and historical serendipity, and of clever administrators who managed to profit from their central location (about three thousand miles from both Kaliningrad and Kamchatka) and turn their city into the de facto capital of Siberia.

In 1912, just twenty years after lucking out with the Trans-Siberian Railroad—if it weren't for Garin-Mikhailovsky, Novosibirsk would have been just another forgettable stop on the way east where villagers hawked jam and pine nuts and whatnot—the shrewd municipal boss Vladimir Zhernakov lobbied in Saint Petersburg to add another rail line to the Trans-Siberian station of Novonikolayevsk. With his town strategically named after the czar Nicholas II, Zhernakov scored a rail line to Semipalatinsk (now just across the border in Kazakhstan), and thus turned the little town into a major transportation hub for the Altai region, serving the European and Asian parts of the empire.

Then historical happenstance aided the new town's fortunes. The Soviets retracted their communist blessing from Omsk, Tomsk lacked a rail line, and Krasnoyarsk, another regional rival, had too much czarist-era history. The 1917 Revolution cast a pall of doubt on all the monarchy's achievements. Novonikolayevsk, then boasting only twenty thousand inhabitants and precious little historical baggage, had only to change its name—to Novosibirsk—to showcase urban development in the new Soviet Siberia.

Novosibirsk, thus, became a symbol, if one of ambiguous meaning. Its local nickname is Ensk—the "city of N." Ensk has come to stand for a faceless, proverbial provincial town lost in the depths of Russia, a generic abode of misery. Nikolai Gogol's *Dead Souls*—a novel written two hundred years ago yet still, in many ways, valid as a portrait of Russia—begins in N. The provincial town from which Ilf and Petrov's Ostap Bender journeyed to acquire the twelve chairs was also called N.

But Novosibirsk has defied the misery to which its nickname would seem to destine it. It is no Ensk, but a stunning success.

All across the Soviet Union, Lenin Squares were built huge to reflect the grandeur of communist aspirations. Such is the case in Novosibirsk, but at least its Lenin Square stands for the achievements made during its century of history. In the 1920s the Soviet authorities began working on the city, erecting, in Constructivist style, faceless cement behemoths for the masses—buildings that could contain anything the government wanted. Running from Lenin Square, the 4.5-mile-long Krasny Prospect—the locals brag (possibly not accurately) that it is the longest straight city street in the world—is flanked by the imposing *Oblpotrebsoyuz* (Regional Consumers Union), which now rents out space to private enterprises, from KFC to polling research companies; the *Sibrevkom* (Siberian Revolutionary Committee), now a major state museum of art; and *Delovoi Dom* (Business Building), with its own metro entrance. (Novosibirsk is the only Siberian city with a subway, equipped with grand marble platforms and decorated with portraits of Lenin. The subway owes its existence to Leonid Brezhnev, who, after being pressured by local officials, ordered its construction following his visit in 1972.) In the 1930s these Constructivist edifices competed for prominence with buildings erected in Classical Stalinist style, including the elaborate *Stokvartirnyi Dom Rabotnikov Krayispolkoma* (the Hundred Apartment Building of Employees of the Regional Executive Committee) on Krasny Prospect. All these buildings were constructed to glorify the state, not to offer creature comforts to their inhabitants.

Even the opera and ballet theater, built in the 1930s on Lenin Square, just behind the Lenin statue, is both monumental and eclectic in grandiose Soviet style. Its giant metal dome shelters an equally giant stage, large enough to accommodate a thousand-member troupe. Even the most populous of Russian operas, Sergei Prokofiev's *War and Peace*, involves only five hundred performers. But there is another reason for its size. In the Soviet Union, art, as it were, belonged to the people. Hence the theater was designed to host not only ballets, but also circuses, a planetarium, and a cinema hall doubling as a tank for a circus water show. The largest theater in the world, its interior was also meant to permit the passage of huge Soviet parades.

The gigantic size of so many of Novosibirsk's buildings represents, most of all, the vastness of Siberia; nothing is for the individual, everything is planned for the masses. One can love the unimaginable geographic dimensions of Russia most readily when one abandons one's personal identity and joins that of the nation, a nation priding itself on the size of its territory.

Russia has always favored building huge, which often conflicts with building for style and comfort. Novosibirsk has managed this, though, better than many other Russian cities. Its relative youth may have well suited it to serve as the model communist city, yet its dimensions, miraculously, have not interfered with its inhabitants' humanity. It is a cheery, inspiring place.

Like other major Siberian cities during the Great Patriotic War, Novosibirsk became an impromptu industrial center. The Kremlin ordered factories moved here and, in some cases, had them expanded, even though, unusually for Siberia, the city has access to few natural resources.

But never mind that: Novosibirsk lucked out in the post-Stalin era, too. After Khrushchev's 1956 Secret Speech denouncing the dictator, the country began opening up to the world and to science that could serve more than just the military's need for modern technology and weapons. After the mass liberation from the Gulag's labor camps and the housing deficit of the Stalin decades, the state endeavored to construct reasonably comfortable living quarters for its citizens.

Enter the five-story buildings with studios and single-bedroom apartments, the *khrushchevki*, which kicked off what amounted to a housing revolution in the Soviet Union, allowing people to have their small private residences away from the watchful gaze of suspicious neighbors—and the state. And it was not just comfort the post-Stalin Soviet state was after.

Khrushchev, lacking higher education, was a great fan of the applied sciences and revered the learned academics—namely mathematicians Mikhail Lavrentyev and Sergei Sobolev and the physicist Sergei Khristianovich. They argued for creating an interdisciplinary scientific center in Siberia, far from the established institutions of Moscow and Leningrad. In Novosibirsk, they believed, young scientists would be offered their own *khrushchevki* and work in research facilities just a walk away.

The Siberian Branch of the Academy of Sciences of the USSR, Akademgorodok (Academic City), was established in 1958, eighteen miles south of Novosibirsk. The surrounding pine forest, a recently completed hydroelectric power station, and the nearby Ob River reservoir factored into the state's decision to dedicate to Akademgorodok almost 3,500 acres of land, of which one-fourth was wooded, which would come to host thirty-seven institutes of higher learning and research. The forest was to form part of an "ecological city" in which residential neighborhoods of modest and efficient housing and all the research institutes blended holistically.

The Institute for Advanced Study in Princeton, New Jersey, where Albert Einstein worked, served as the model for the new Soviet enterprise. Khrushchev believed mightily in borrowing from the West. After all, he is known as much for his denunciation of Stalin as for his mass planting of corn, an idea he borrowed from an Iowan farmer named Roswell Garst.

In the late 1950s, Novosibirsk was no more science oriented than any other outback city in the Soviet Union, and so would hardly have been anyone's first choice as a future hub of research and development. But it had successfully hosted at least two major Soviet enterprises, a secret uranium plant and *Sibselmash* (a Russian abbreviation of the "Siberian Agricultural Machinery"), a complex that focused

on the production of farm equipment. The existence of these factories buttressed arguments in favor of opening centers for the applied
sciences there.

The hallowed city of Tomsk lost out here again. Farsighted planners chose Novosibirsk to be a future scientific powerhouse because
it was situated at great remove from the halls of government and from
recognized educational institutions; this would afford young scientists a chance to work independently and creatively.

Though it might not seem so, the idea behind Novosibirsk's transformation was, in essence, communist: savvy planners would take a
tabula rasa city and turn it into a rival for the Soviet Union's established centers of science. This was, to be sure, a leap from the Princeton model. Princeton sits, after all, just an hour's drive from New
York City, whereas Novosibirsk is a two-day train ride or a four-hour
flight from Moscow. New Jersey has warm enough cold months, but
in Novosibirsk −25 Fahrenheit passes for mild winter weather. And
yet this Soviet attempt at building a scientific utopia succeeded well
enough, with, strangely, state planners fostering a civil society and
an intellectual climate propitious to free thought. In this Siberian enclave of freethinkers, the country's top physicists, mathematicians,
biologists, and chemists, be they old or young, have worked together
on everything from science to landscaping. Novosibirsk has seen the
number of its research institutes grow from fifteen to thirty-seven over
the course of sixty years.

One warm, overcast July day we walked along Akademgorodok's
broad avenues, interspersed with pine and birch groves, their names
meant to celebrate the town's strength and occupation—Builders, Engineers, Academia, and Institute. Some local traditions of collective
labor still hold—on the way to the famed Café Integral, we passed
by a few elderly academic types cutting grass. The Café Integral—
integral is a mathematics term—was long a legendary gathering

place for discussions and debates; habitués, while consuming the premises' renowned goulash or cheese sandwiches, and downing its weak coffee or strong tea, hashed out new ideas about freedom and scientific innovation. In 1968 the Café Integral held the first Soviet festival of bards, who were, then, mostly amateurs and included scientists and engineers writing and singing their own songs while playing their guitars. The smartest in the country no longer sang about the achievements of the communist masses, as they once did under Stalin. Instead, they heralded their own lives, often lamenting how the Kremlin bosses got in their way, even out here.

The preeminent dissident and bard Alexander Galich, known for his contemplative yet pointed criticism of the regime, made his only concert appearance there, in that year of protest. His performance frightened the authorities because he sang as he spoke and delivered a ballad in memory of Boris Pasternak in which he denounced both Stalin and Khrushchev as *palachi* (executioners), and Khrushchev for his opposition to *Doctor Zhivago*. The audience rose in silence, honoring his lyrics and his bravery in telling the truth. Brezhnev, then in power, was not mentioned, but he took the affront personally. And while the authorities allowed concerts by other bards to continue, Galich was firmly forbidden to officially sing in public ever again. Soon after he found himself forced into exile in Paris, where he died in 1977.

Today the old atmosphere of freedom on the rise has waned. The original 1960s minimalist furniture has given way to chairs and tables one could find in any modern restaurant. The cuisine is excellent, but few scientists hang out there nowadays; they are busy making money. The clientele consists of people like us, curious about the iconic place, wanting to experience it for themselves.

After the 1991 collapse of the Soviet Union, Akademgorodok's fortunes declined, as did those of most Soviet enterprises, research centers, and factories. The Yeltsin government, concentrating on the privatization of state assets, neglected the country's intellectual resources. Say what you will about the Soviets, they did promote science and education. During the Yeltsin decade, many scholars chose to immigrate to the West, where they could count on the high salaries and esteem due them.

With Putin's quest to increase Russia's global status and influence, science and scientists have become priorities for the Kremlin once again. The year 2010 saw the inauguration of the Skolkovo Innovation Center (which merges business and high technology) just west of Moscow. The project has been mired in scandal and has produced little of value, at least so far. But in Novosibirsk the government has been striving to harness and develop talents that contribute to the needs of the country's modern economy.

GlaxoSmithKline, along with other global pharmaceutical companies, have chosen Akademgorodok for HIV drug testing and research. This makes sense, given the scale of the epidemic sweeping Siberia and much of rural Russia.[1] With the Orthodox Church helping Putin to consolidate his rule, social conservatism has backfired on the population—the priests cracked down on sensible approaches to sexually transmitted diseases fueling the Russian crisis.

The oil field service company Schlumberger has a strong presence in Akademgorodok, as do Intel and its Russian software competitor Novosoft. To foster the birth of at least twenty successful tech companies a year and their growth, the municipal authorities oversaw the construction, in 2007, of Technopark, a fourteen-story glass-and-brick cubist structure shaped as the letter "n"—an eastern precursor to Skolkovo.

Innovation doesn't come without controversy, of course. Akademgorodok has now become a fashionable neighborhood, with its woods facing constant threats from luxury condo developers.

Apropos of this, we tracked down an activist named Natalia

Shamina, a professor of biology who, in 2013, found herself fired from Akademgorodok for her political views and who now heads the local environmentalist movement. Shamina had gained fame as a crusader against the destruction of the very forest that underpinned Akademgorodok's study of nature; in 2010 she went on a hunger strike for this cause. Most recently, in 2017, she was fined for disturbing the peace. We met Shamina, in her fifties, with her dark brown hair pulled back in a taut ponytail, during a protest: she was standing, alone, under Novosibirsk's Lenin Statue, holding a sign reading "Protect the forest of Akademgorodok."

"Why are you by yourself?" we asked. "No one else is interested?"

Major protests against plans for the forest took place in the spring, she explained, but by July most demonstrators had tired of their task and showed up to picket government buildings only a few times a week. The authorities also changed the law regarding demonstrations, making permits to conduct them more difficult to obtain. Individual protesters, however, don't have to file for permits, at least as long as they stand fifty meters apart. So Shamina was out there alone. For a month, she had been shifting, week by week, from Lenin Square in Novosibirsk to Builders Avenue in Akademgorodok.

"These forests are needed for research and cannot be destroyed," she explained wearily, but with conviction.

She has been waging her movement's battle for a decade and has had some success, saving the botanical garden from destruction and blocking the construction of an upscale medical center in the woods.

Shamina's chief concern is the preservation of Russia's academic glory. She shares this aspiration with other scholars trying to reconstitute Russia's scientific know-how after the disarray of the Yeltsin years. The problem, of course, is that in Russia, the government, distrustful of free thought, always wants to oversee innovation, to be able to meddle in it if it becomes threatening.

During our visit we heard much talk about Dmitry Trubitsyn's company Tion, which manufactures, to global standards, high-tech air-purification systems for hospitals. By upgrading the purifiers to greater energy efficiency without certification, he allegedly broke an obscure law that essentially prevents innovation deemed too fast and too free, and now he is facing five years in prison. Fellow scientists and entrepreneurs in Akademgorodok have collected over five thousand signatures in his favor, but to no avail. One newspaper headline about the matter read, "Cleaning the Air Turned Out to Be a Crime."

The Tion case highlights the tensions between the Kremlin's aspirations for dynamic private-sector research and its obsession with controlling the process. The result: the Russian government thwarts its own strategic goals for moving away from its dependence on oil and mineral revenues to a more diversified economy rooted in innovation.

At the time of Trubitsyn's indictment, in February 2017, Putin, who often travels to Siberia for power-vacations and to touch base with the empire's outback, visited Novosibirsk and voiced support for the initiative, "Akademgorodok 2.0," a huge endeavor launched by the regional governor Andrei Travnikov. Travnikov hoped to enact a plan "for the development of the Novosibirsk Science Center . . . and . . . its territory," encompassing its "scientific potential, engineering sector, and social infrastructure."[2] But Putin's visit and support for the large-scale project (rather than for smaller, more focused ventures with a good chance of succeeding)—shed light on what always hampers Russia, the desire for size.

The Russian state perennially works at cross purposes with itself. The government announces change and then fears relinquishing control of the change. Khrushchev denounced Stalin, yet the reforms he oversaw—the lessening of political repression—did not go far enough because he feared where they would lead. When Hungary, encouraged by Khrushchev's de-Stalinization, set out to forge its own path in 1956, the Kremlin sent tanks into Budapest to "protect socialism." Yeltsin declared democracy in 1991 and then, two years later, faced with opposition, opened fire on his own parliament, thereby putting the brakes on democracy; he further worsened matters with the adoption of a new, more presidentially oriented constitution—Russia's current one—later that year, which set the stage for Putin's centralized rule.

Kremlin control notwithstanding, Novosibirsk, almost miraculously, has managed to chart its own course. No matter what has gone on in Moscow, the city has flourished, just as snowdrops—a flower so common in Russian forests—bloom every spring, despite the punishing winter just past.

This has much to do with municipal and regional leadership that tends to listen to the people's demands. In the summer before our visit, the oblast governor—Novosibirsk is, naturally, the oblast's capital—canceled plans to increase fees for housing and communal services by 15 percent, because of public outrage. Earlier, Novosibirskans had held a March for the Federalization of Siberia and in Defense of the Constitution, calling on Moscow to abstain from pillaging the budgets of major Siberian cities. This led to accusations of separatism and the blocking of demonstrations. But other powerful cities, including Yekaterinburg, joined the movement and made their voices heard in Moscow, too. (Though, perhaps, not for long.) However, in contrast to what happened in Yekaterinburg, with its mayor Roizman, Novosibirsk's mayor Anatoly Lokot, a communist whose support for United Russia the Kremlin had questioned, was able to make a deal to stay on. He promised not to challenge the recent Putin-backed import to the oblast's governorship, Andrei Travnikov.

Back in town, we met with Yury Tregubovich, formerly a legal reporter for the regional office of the hard-hitting longtime opposition paper *Novaya Gazeta* (New Newspaper). In a gray T-shirt and jeans, looking like a balding, thirty-year-older version of Mark Zuckerberg, Tregubovich touted the intelligence and sophistication of the city's leaders. Local authorities, according to him, cannot get away with abuses common elsewhere. While visiting a relative in Kemerovo, another major Siberian city, he happened upon a local corruption trial but discovered that a judge banned journalists from the courtroom. "In Novosibirsk," he said, "the authorities would never dare do such a thing."

When Tregubovich once discovered that a district leader was having his school-age daughter chauffeured around town in a municipal automobile, he confronted the official and warned him that he would write about his improper use of the city's property.

"He never used the car again for that purpose," Tregubovich said, with a chuckle.

"Why did you give him advance notice of what you planned to write?" we asked.

"This is Russia, after all. He's a good guy. It's better that he's on our side than to have him as an enemy. Unlike in many other places, though, courts here do let people win cases brought against the authorities."

We met Tregubovich for lunch in a crowded café, Travelers, on Kalinin Square in the north part of town. Despite its out-of-the-way location, it was bustling with people stopping in for a quick bite to eat or a cup of coffee. Commenting on how busy the place was, Tregubovich explained that Novosibirsk is entrepreneurial, a city in which small businesses can excel.

For an oblast with a relatively limited number (by Siberian standards) of oil and gas businesses, smaller firms abounded, at least judging by the signs on the street. We asked him why.

"Research and entrepreneurship," he replied. "Every two meters there's a café or a gas station attached to it, or a slick car dealership.

"There is corruption," he continued, "don't get me wrong. We aren't without corruption and bribery, for sure. But opening, say, a coffee shop still allows for less graft than the construction of business centers. So it's good that people open places like this."

We found Novosibirsk to be a sophisticated city—no doubt the most sophisticated east of Moscow. Cafés and restaurants seem to occupy every corner and do brisk business. Residents dress modishly, but not outlandishly, sporting jeans, flat-soled shoes and sneakers, summery dresses, and T-shirts—just as they would in any major city in the West in July, the month we visited. In Ensk, the City of N, the "N," we came to see, stands for normalcy.

In some ways, Novosibirsk is better than normal. In two days of taking taxis around town, three of our five drivers were women—a higher male-to-female ratio than one would encounter in Manhattan. Two had raised children and were getting on in years, and declared that they could do anything they wanted but were driving cabs by choice. The third, a young woman named Tatyana, was studying law and philosophy at Novosibirsk University (located in Akademgorodok) and so drove to make extra money because it's "better than tending bar."

Tatyana took us to Lenin Square, to the Museum of Local Lore, which occupies a fin-de-siècle brick-and-granite two-story building once used as barracks for Bolshevik soldiers and later to house the city administration. Unusually for Russian museums these days, no portrait of Putin greeted us as we entered, though the Lenin Square subway station features a wall honoring soldiers killed in Chechnya and Ukraine overhung by Putin's words: "Every country has to support its heroes." On the day of our departure, on the way to the train station (which also serves as a spectacular museum for the West Siberian Railroad), we passed by a billboard proclaiming, "Europe is just a flight away." Never mind that there are only two direct flights to Europe—to Munich and Prague—the civilized atmosphere is unmistakable. The city feels central, connected: after all, it takes as much time (about four hours) to fly to Moscow as it does to Beijing.

The Chapel of Saint Nicholas standing on Krasny Prospect, just off Lenin Square, used to represent the geographical center of the Russian empire. The Bolsheviks destroyed this house of worship and replaced it with a monument to Stalin, which was removed after Khrushchev denounced him, so the center became a glaring empty spot. And though the chapel was rebuilt in the 1990s, the center has since moved elsewhere. Still, Novosibirsk remains central—the most coherent city we saw in Russia, where elements of the Soviet past peacefully coexist with the czarist-era legacy of the double-headed eagle. The city had well earned the right to its renown, which its citizens were too dignified, too self-assured, to flaunt.

8

ASIAN ABODES OF THE SPIRIT

TIME ZONE: MSK+5; UTC+8

God is the same everywhere.
Kings are the slaves of history.
—Leo Tolstoy, *War and Peace*

The Buddha, Shamans, and a
Throne for Putin

The redeye flight from Moscow some three and a half thousand miles east, to Ulan-Ude, the capital of the Republic of Buryatia, left us dazed, as much from the lack of sleep as from the stark change in scenery, almost equivalent to a change in planets. (If Russia was, as Obama famously declared, just a "regional power," its "region" now seemed to us, at least from the plane's windows, to encompass extraterrestrial realms.) Our Airbus descended through ragged skeins of mist paling with dawn light until, beneath us, we descried empty green hills stretching out in every direction, presaging the grassland steppes of Mongolia just a hundred and fifty miles or so to the south. Amid this expanse of green, Ulan-Ude, population 400,000, loomed into view, a jumble of concrete shacks and gray apartment buildings scattered about like trash on an abandoned lot, hugging the east bank of the Selenga River and bisected by the lesser currents of the Uda.

The Selenga! The Uda! The waterways' names bespeak, to Russian ears, impossible, forbidding remoteness and exotic non-Slavic peoples. The airport turned out to be nothing more than a tarmac and a terminal one might well mistake for a bus station. Awaiting us in the lounge we found a crowd of stocky Buryats, whose Asian features recalled their consanguinity with Mongols, as did their language, a dialect of Mongolian, agglutinative and thick voweled, totally unrelated to Russian. Russians here were relative newcomers, arriving in the seventeenth century, bent on mining for gold and trapping for furs. They could not have felt especially warmly toward the Buryats, who descended from Mongols, the leader of whom, Genghis Khan, exploded out of Mongolia in the thirteenth century with his armies of crossbow-bearing horsemen to lay waste to almost all Russia, massacring perhaps a third of the population, and even threatening western Europe. The Mongol empire Genghis Khan established had lasting effects, all baleful, on Russia's history, cutting the country off from Europe just as Europe was poised to undergo the Renaissance and, worse, introducing tyrannical rule to Eastern Slavs who had governed themselves democratically in the city-states of Kievan Rus. (Not that the Russian princes of the time should fully escape blame—they chose to pay their Mongol overlords to protect them from the Swedes and Lithuanians, instead of siding with Westerners against the Tatar-Mongolian yoke.)

Our taxi ride down potholed roads to Ulan-Ude's center revealed a roughshod town of few comforts, with locals negotiating battered sidewalks or gravel walkways, at times subject to assault from whirling dust kicked up by the hectic traffic and sporadic wind.

Our Buryat driver sat and steered on the right—his cab was an import from Japan, as were so many other cars on the road around us.

"The federal authorities keep forbidding us from buying these right-hand-drive cars," he said. "Putin wants us to buy Russian cars, not foreign ones. But it's no use. These Japanese cars are so much better, even with the steering wheels on the wrong side." The perennial dilemma of a country as large as Russia: what the central government in Moscow ordains does not always hold in the provinces, which may be nine time zones ahead of the capital.

Our hotel, the Geser, was a functional brick structure, but comfortable enough. To our surprise, it hosted tour groups of Westerners on their way to China and Mongolia. Yet outside the hotel the town appeared stark and hardscrabble, dominated by crumbling cement buildings painted, in places, gaudy colors and bearing gaudy signs, some in Chinese; and in fact Chinese businessmen were out and about. Ethnic Buryats, not Russians, made up the majority here; a good number of Buryat men had crew cuts, weathered faces, and jutting brows. Here and there scurried Mongols on shopping expeditions. All in all, Ulan-Ude resembled Moscow about as much as Portland, Maine, looks like Lima, Peru.

"What would we do out here without China?" our driver exclaimed. "They've built a lot here. Just look!"

He was right: ramshackle skyscrapers of blue-and-yellow glass and steel stood in colorful disarray against a leaden sky. Here and there were Chinese noodle shops, Chinese clothing shops, and Chinese bric-a-brac shops. Of course Chinese businessmen were out and about, too.

When local Russian friends met us as the hotel later that day and took us for a stroll, we could find no café open in which to sit down and talk. We espied the Venezia Restaurant, but it was closed. Even the sidewalk ice cream vendors had disappeared by nine in the evening. The city at such an hour, we thought, should have been bustling with people but instead stretched before us empty, its broad avenues sweeping away toward empty hills.

Our stroll took us to the Square of the Soviets. There we confronted, set against a row of larches, the gigantic weathered bronze Lenin head—the largest such statue on earth, standing twenty feet tall from nape to crown and resting atop a granite pedestal that raises it another twenty-five feet. If the streets were empty, Lenin, here, was always on duty, his brows furrowed in perpetual vigilance and subjecting passersby to his fierce gaze. Despite the monument's size, the few out and about barely seemed to notice him, save for a group of skateboarders honing their skills on its pedestal—a familiar sight in other Russian cities. Another one who noticed was the late North Korean leader Kim Jong-Il, who paid it a visit in 2011.

A few blocks away, on a promontory above the Uda River, we encountered a monument of a very different kind: one memorializing the city's victims of the Stalin-era political purges. Fresh wreaths of roses, laid by the children and grandchildren of the murdered, testify to the ongoing interest on the part of the relatives of the perished. We visited it the next evening, as the sun, already set, lit from below a scattering of clouds, giving them the appearance of molten boulders floating above the verdure of the surrounding hills. A black granite wall engraved with the names of the victims and the dates of their birth and death (the latter predominantly having occurred in 1938, at the height of the Great Terror) rose beneath a tangle of barbed wire, in front of which stood a faceless citizen carved in bronze.

A plaque on the pedestal reads:

In memory of those perished innocents!
In memory of those buried in labor camps!
It is a pity we cannot bury them!
Their remains cannot be found.

Another plaque says, simply, *"Za chto?"* (For what?)

Buryatia was the first place we visited with a large, distinct minority population professing a religion of purely Asian provenance. About one out of four people in Buryatia profess Orthodox Christianity and one out of five, Buddhism. (The number of believers may well be larger—older people who grew up in the USSR are often hesitant to formally disclose their religious beliefs.) Nonbelievers, the stats tell us, account for 14 percent of the population—another legacy of decades of atheist Soviet education. Nonetheless, near Ulan-Ude sits Ivolginsky Datsan, the most important Buddhist temple in Russia, one belonging to the Tibetan Vajrayana school and frequented by both Russians and Buryats.

"A Russian can go to church in the morning and light a candle for a dead relative, but then go in the evening to the temple and perform a Buddhist ritual or two for him there, just to be sure," a Russian resident of Ulan-Ude told us. "Buddhists are tolerant. They recite their mantras and don't give anyone any trouble, unlike the Muslims." Other ethnic Russians we spoke to, though, talked of tensions with the Buryats, with the latter calling the former "occupiers." Yet such hostile sentiments, we heard, usually emerged as a result of a surfeit of alcohol. The kind of tension characterizing relations between Russians and Muslims in the country's North Caucasus region does not exist in Buryatia.

One cloudy morning, a taxi ferried us fifteen miles west of Ulan-Ude through the surrounding hills on the plain where the Ivolginsky Datsan dominates the horizon. Twenty-five years ago, the temples,

with their Chinese-style flaring eaves, gilt spheres, and lama figurines, and their red, green, and blue decor, had once impressed visitors
amid an empty steppe; now, they stood surrounded by a multicolored
congeries of workaday shacks, log cabins, and souvenir shops and living quarters (housing visitors and monks, astrologers and healers
and masseurs), the space between them crisscrossed with telephone
cables droopily suspended between crooked poles. At the ticket office,
we hired a guide—a monk in sneakers, burgundy robes, and a matching fisherman's cap. He introduced himself as Torzho, a name, he
told us, that in Buryat is translated as White Pearls, or, alternatively,
Big Diamond, with the intended import of "peaceful."

We set out on our tour. Around us were mostly Buryats, who come
here to seek spiritual guidance from all over the area, some from hundreds of miles away. Many seemed poor local farmers, but others
were clearly prosperous, in colorful traditional silk Mongolian robes.

Navigating among other groups on narrow unpaved paths, our
guide mumbled his spiel in a barely audible staccato, as if bored and
in a rush. As we trod the dirt walkways, we discovered that the
temples each now charge a two-hundred-ruble (about $3) entrance fee
and were for the most part similar: green plank floors, red columns
around the walls, red tables covered with tapestries and holy books.
Chintzy-looking portraits of lamas seem to hang on every wall. Perhaps because of the fee, we were always the only ones inside.

Outside, around us Buryats and a few Russians enthusiastically
hurried to spin prayer wheels and affix prayer flags to their knobs,
with a few doing the ritual circumambulation of the entire premises.
Our guide recounted the details of samsara, the pursuit of nirvana; he
talked of the region's lamas and other holy men. He lamented the
repression the Bolsheviks visited on the monks, who, at the time of
the revolution, numbered some sixteen thousand.

Yet he praised Stalin for reopening the temple in 1946.

"He had a religious education, so he could see the value in it," he told us flatly, alluding to the bloody tyrant's years as a student at an Orthodox Christian seminary.

"Why did he see the value in these temples only in 1946?" we asked.

"There was a change in government."

There was not. Stalin revived the Russian Orthodox Church during the war, understanding that it would help rally Soviet citizens for the fight to save his regime. He doubtless thought little of faraway *Datsan*, but surely Buddhism's traditional pacifism weighed in the temple's favor. Moreover, rebuilding the country after the war, Stalin reasoned, people needed all the faith they could get.

Our guide reserved the greatest praise for Putin, to whom he referred always by his full name.

"There are two thrones in our country," Torzho announced. "One is occupied by our lama. The other by President Vladimir Vladimirovich Putin."

"What?" we asked. "Putin on a throne?"

"In the Kremlin president Vladimir Vladimirovich Putin sits on a throne. As does our lama. We're grateful to President Vladimir Vladimirovich Putin for restoring our temples here. And he's also restored our stadium."

Our guide went on to explain that President Vladimir Vladimirovich Putin shared a "holy background" with Prince Siddhartha, the Indian noble who, millennia ago, had become the Buddha.

"Putin?" we responded, amazed. "A holy background? He may act like a czar, but he has never claimed any such thing! Anyway, the Buddha renounced his throne. Putin is preparing to run for president yet again."

"We are grateful to President Vladimir Vladimirovich Putin, who sits on a throne in the Kremlin. We really are."

Putin sits on no throne, not physically at least, although his grand coronation-like inauguration for his fourth presidential term in May 2018 may suggest otherwise. The gratitude the monk voiced finds reflection in the president's ever-high popularity ratings—up to 80 percent, even after almost two decades in power, and the perception that he is, indeed, all powerful.

Soon after this, we parted and hired a taxi back to Ulan-Ude and the giant Lenin head.

One of our Buryat drivers in Ulan-Ude waxed enthusiastically about shamans.

"Shamans have a *lot* of power, it's really true. There are white shamans who do good. Best to stay away from the black shamans." White shamans intervened, he said, in the lives of many, and generally helped people. Even during the Soviet decades people consulted them, asked for their aid. Or, if need be, they entreated black shamans to harm their enemies. White or black, though, shamans formed a part of the region's age-old culture; Buddhism, in these parts, was an import.

Intent on visiting a shaman, one gloriously sunny, breezy morning we boarded a late-morning train for the eight-hour ride from Ulan-Ude west to Irkutsk, a city known as the Paris of Siberia and a jumping-off point for visits to Lake Baikal, the world's largest (and deepest) body of freshwater, water so pure that one can see clear through to the rocky bottom from almost anywhere on its surface. The trains run in such a way that windows face the lake, affording views for which one would certainly be disposed to pay extra. We would share our car with a great number of Chinese, who spent little time looking out the windows, engrossed as they were with watching television series on their tablets or slurping noodles from Styro-foam buckets.

Yet the vistas of Baikal did more than impress; they instilled a peace of sorts, curative, uplifting, and enthralling. The lake appeared suddenly, sixty miles out of Ulan-Ude and about an hour into the trip. The railroad tracks veered away from the grassy clearings and larch forests to parallel the pebbly bank, with the far (northern) shore so distant as to be almost invisible. Azure sky and azure-green waters, at times still, at others frothy with the wind, swept away from us, with the taiga-covered low mountains—*sopki* in Russian—on either bank receding and shrinking away into the north. The shores, with their cliffs of schist in places, taiga in others, sheltered secluded coves on which *nerpas* (Baikal seals) sun themselves and moose and bears roam. When mists roll in, as they often do when the seasons are changing, the tableaus Baikal presents rival the finest work of the impressionists. This lake and its surroundings, one finds oneself thinking, seemed to exude a spirituality befitting notions of shamans; of lost, ancient worlds where peace reined and mankind lived as one with nature.

Strolling in the Paris of Siberia

Such lofty Lake Baikal thoughts did not have much to do with Ir-kutsk, though. With its 600,000 inhabitants and chaotic, traffic-clogged roads, there is no hint of Baikal's beauty, though the city does sit on the majestic Angara River as it flows into the lake some fifty miles to the southwest. Nevertheless, on the evening of our ar-rival, we strolled down Lenin Street and entered what the locals call the 130 Quarter, the pedestrian Third of July Street, the southern side of which opens onto views of the Angara, where you feel the sort of café-life languor and *esprit de flâneur* one might sense in Paris's historic center. Except of course here the area in its current leisure incarnation is less than a decade old. On a typical evening bands played, terrace restaurants were crowded, and merchants hawked ice cream. Young women dressed in summer casual but with the highest of heels vied for the attention of equally hip young men with globally fashionable beards and man-buns; stately elderly women walked with canes holding the arms of men with handlebar moustaches, recalling grandees of old. Here and there renovated Soviet-era vending machines dispensed fizzy water in little cups, just as they would have decades ago.

That the Bolsheviks executed in Irkutsk the White Russian Admiral Kolchak, commemorated by a statue, seems fitting; after all, Czar Nicholas I exiled some of the Decembrist revolutionaries here, in order that they serve their sentences under the direct supervision of the Governor General of the Irkutsk *Guberniya*. Their houses, two-story, of wood yet of almost palatial grandeur, with gray or brown facades and ornate white trim, recalled their upper-class tastes and background. Being revolutionaries, the Decembrists had enjoyed the favor of the Bolsheviks, who left their dwellings intact. Otherwise, Irkutsk's best-known son is perhaps the Buryat-Russian playwright Alexander Vampilov of the Soviet period; Vampilov authored a play, *Last Summer in Chulimsk*, in which the protagonist is determined to keep order, whether it makes sense to or not: every morning he rebuilds a fence the locals have trampled down because it obstructs their access to a park. More recently, Irkutsk impressed the world with its native daughter Nazí Paikidze, a chess wizard who, refusing to don the obligatory Islamic headscarf, boycotted the 2017 World Chess Championship in Tehran.

Dusk lingered long, the sky a glowing ashen canopy, with the air chilling fast. This was Paris perhaps, but Paris of Siberia.

Mystic Lake Baikal

Yet not Irkutsk but Lake Baikal and its alleged mystic powers drew us to this time zone. One gray morning, we boarded a *marshrutka* (minivan bus) for the trip north to the mostly Buryat village of Khuzhir, population 1,500, on Olkhon Island, halfway up the lake's western shore, and accessible by ferry. Famous as a "pole of shamanistic energy," Olkhon attracts Russian aficionados of the spiritual arts and of shamanism in particular. The island's Cape Burkhan, with a cave within its bizarre marble boulder—called Shamanka—is regarded as the chosen abode of the deity Khan-Khute-Baabay, and draws worshippers from all over Russia. Nevertheless, the cramped, seven-hour ride through taiga and across drab, grassy plains hardly inspired. And neither did the island itself, a mostly barren rock outcropping dotted with scraggly conifers and gaunt grazing cows. Khuzhir stood on high ground, its weathered shacks and *izbas* (Russian log huts) lashed by winds that never let up and stirred dust storms on its sandy streets, causing people and the many stray dogs to wince. The island's western bank faces the mainland's majestic taiga, where bears prowl and moose roam. The eastern side flanks the open Baikal; on the high bluffs stand, here and there, firs, their branches covered in prayer ribbons—gifts, proffered by visitors, to the local gods.

In the age of tourism, shamanism, is, not surprisingly, a business in Khuzhir. As far as is understood, Asian shamanism originated with the region's Turkic and Mongol peoples. It involves, essentially, self-induced trances, chants, and a beating of drums that permit practitioners ingress into the spirit world and the power to heal and do harm among temporal earthlings. We found the most accessible shamans to be those with yurts—broad, quasiconical tents of animal hides, held up by poles—standing on the outskirts of the village. For a modest fee, you can listen to a lecture on the basics of shamanism.

This seemed like a good idea, so we dipped inside, paid, and took seats with a half-dozen Russians.

The shaman-instructor, a young Buryat man, explained that, long ago, the heavens sent ninety-nine *tengri* (deities) to earth to help us humans out. The *tengri* grant shamans their powers, which, in the case of the exalted Zarin shamans, include being able to fly. One who is called upon to be a shaman may die if he refuses. Becoming a shaman involves surviving a three-day ritual. The most prestigious and powerful shamans are the *shamany-kuznetsy* (blacksmith shamans). Blacksmiths are revered because they once forged items essential to life in the region. They also have a lot of sway in the two Other Worlds, being able to call for help from the seventy-seven blacksmith deities.

A man named Igor raised his hand. He had, he said, fought in various wars, but considered God his guardian angel. Nevertheless, he was critical of the Church.

"I don't like how the Orthodox Church charges seven thousand rubles [$112] for a baptism, when a lot of people make only about twelve thousand a month. What do you shamans charge?"

"We have no set fee. Each gives us according to the wishes of his soul."

We decided we needed more insight than the "shamanism 101" lecture we had just heard. So, we arranged to meet a prominent local shaman, Gennady Tugulov, who is a Buryat native of Khuzhir. Tugulov, in his late fifties, is a blacksmith shaman. He arrived at our inn one evening toting his tools—a tiny hammer, a tiny anvil, a tiny file, and a small silver bowl—along with his folded indigo blue felt shamanistic robes and matching cap, all emblazoned with silver suns, for a meeting out on the wooden porch.

"Mind if I smoke?" he asked, setting his load down on the table.

"Is it allowed?" we asked.

"It is for me! After all, I'm a shaman."

He promptly lit up. With his cigarette dangling from his lips, he put on his robes and cap and laid out his tools, puffing as he did so. No one really knows, he told us, who came first to this region—the Buryats, the Sakha (as the Yakuts call themselves), or the Mongols. He affixed a dagger to his leather belt, which sported a silver buckle and silver bangles; around his neck hung, on green-and-blue ribbons, disks of burnished silver and gold, one signifying the moon, the other the sun. "Their circularity symbolizes eternity," he explained. He then gave us a rundown of his qualifications: he was a thirteenth-generation shaman; of the nine levels of shamanism, he has one left to attain. One does not decide to become a shaman but is selected for the honor by one's clan.

"What are these tools for, exactly?" we asked.

"Well, I put this file in the fire to heat it up. When it's hot, I sprinkle it with vodka from this silver bowl and sprinkle the drink on people to help them. This little hammer I use to pound the anvil and call spirits. The bear claw I have here protects me. The silver plate hanging from my neck means I'm a white shaman. The copper one wards off people's bad energy. There's a lot of that around these days, so it's necessary for people in my profession. A shaman must never fear, even when meeting bad people."

He took a drag on his cigarette.

"Shamans help people, help the sick; we were once the healers and judges here. We speak to our ancestors and consult them for advice. You have to be a shaman or you can't hear them. We also divine things through reflection and can see things through dreams. We do a lot of good, as you see, that simple folk cannot do on their own. The Soviets repressed us, yet still they came to us when they needed us;

in fact, the very ones doing the killing came to us and sought our aid in purifying themselves after their bad deeds. In the 1990s we revived our profession and now practice it freely."

"So things are returning to normal here?"

"Normal? No. You have seen Shamanka?"

"The rocky outcropping on Cape Burkhan?"

"Yes. Well, it has a cave running right through it. Since Soviet times mankind has desecrated nature around the lake. People have built resorts on the shores. These have to close or they risk really angering Baikal. People even bathe and do their laundry in the lake, which they should never, ever do. They take from the lake but they don't give back. They need to ask permission from the goddess of water, and she must be asked politely, as you would ask a woman. When the lake gets angry, its waters will rise in terrible revolt. Terrible."

Shamans, he told us, commune in solitude with nature, learning the language of the birds, the bears.

"You talk to bears?" we asked.

"We listen to them. Bears are very perceptive. If you talk to them, they won't bother you. But they can tell you a lot."

He fiddled with the bear claw he wore on a black cord around his neck.

"All our world's problems come from people going against nature. Yet we must observe nature and obey it. We cannot go against nature. Nature will take its own."

Orthodox Christian Russians come to him for aid.

"They try to contact their ancestors, but they cannot. They say there's too much lying and corruption in their church."

That was a familiar complaint in Russia. We asked if shamanism allowed for an afterlife.

"Yes. When shamans die, we're cremated so that our spirits can rise to heaven in the smoke. I don't fear death. There is no hell. After death, I know future generations will be asking me for help." He tamped out his cigarette. "What we shamans want most of all is peace, the peace we find in the beauty of nature. We want that peace to last forever, for man and nature."

Later that windy, clear evening we attended a Russian Orthodox church service in a small chapel—the Church of the Ruling Icon—at Khuzhir's edge, overlooking the lake. Its blue onion domes, topped by gilt crosses, harmonized with the sky and shimmering waters far below. The priest entered, draped in his gold chasuble and black frock, and initiated the liturgy, aided by two parishioners, chanting a melodic, haunting hymn that blended with the whoosh of winds above and the crash of waves far below.

Orthodox Christianity is relatively new out here, on the shores of Baikal, but nevertheless, its rituals, with their timeless melodies, blended in well with the lake's otherworldly aura. If, thousands of miles to the west, the Decembrists had tried to overthrow the czar and found themselves exiled here, at the very least they could take solace in their homeland's soothing, sparsely inhabited, and almost limitless expanses of forest and steppe, lake and river.

We were headed even farther east, into environs more alien and daunting to Russians who came later and lived under a different sort of czar—one who would turn such pristine expanses into abodes of misery and terror. But what would these environs evoke today?

9

BLAGOVESHCHENSK, HEIHE, AND YAKUTSK

ROUGHING IT

TIME ZONE: MSK+6, UTC+9

I am fated to journey hand in hand with my strange heroes and to survey the surging immensity of life, to survey it through the laughter that all can see and through the tears unseen and unknown by anyone.

—Nikolai Gogol, *Dead Souls*

From Blagoveshchensk to Heihe: The Edge of Empires

I lack the skill to describe anything as beautiful as the banks of the Amur. . . . The Russian bank is on the left, the Chinese on the right. If I feel like it, I can look at Russia, and if I feel like it, I can look at China. China is just as barren and savage as Russia: villages and sentinel huts are few and far between. . . . The Chinese will take the Amur away from us, of that there is no doubt," wrote Anton Chekhov in his letter to a friend in 1890.[1] The perceptive Russian writer may be right—today the Chinese empire seems to operate differently from the Russian one, its identity not in question, so unlike Russia, which rushes from imitation to negation of all things Western while China borrows from the world to strengthen its own power.

For a city whose name decodes as "the Place of the Annunciation" (by the Angel Gabriel, to the Virgin Mary, that she was to bear the Son of God), Blagoveshchensk, in the Russian Far East, arouses less than holy associations among those Russians who have heard of it. Chekhov stopped there on his way east across Siberia, a journey he describes in harrowing detail in *Sakhalin Island*. He had one thing in mind: sampling Japanese prostitutes—the *Karayuki-san*, or Ms. Gone Abroad, women who at the time offered their geisha services all over the world, including Siberia—working in *doma terpimosti* (houses of tolerance). They giggled *ts-ts* during sex and yet showed amazing skill, he wrote. They gave customers the impression they were "riding a highly trained horse," and, afterward, ever so gingerly used tweezers to extract a cotton cloth from their shirtsleeve to wipe them dry, "tickling their belly" in the process.

Once dressed, Chekhov would have emerged from his "house of tolerance" in Blagoveshchensk to gaze upon rows of brightly painted, well-kept single-story wooden houses along the Amur river embankment, and, in their midst, men erecting an architectural curio no one would expect six thousand miles east of Europe: a small-scale, neo-Russian ornate replica of Paris's chief landmark, the Arc de Triomphe. Erected in 1891 to honor Prince Nicholas, the future Nicholas II, the Russian version supports two towers crowned with the Russian state insignia, the double-headed eagle, their eyes perpetually looking up and down the great Siberian waterway on which the town stands. The arc itself faces China, on the Amur's western bank—specifically, the town of Heihe.

Blagoveshchensk was tough to reach in Chekhov's day, before the

Trans-Siberian Railroad connected Moscow and Saint Petersburg with territories to the east (and Blagoveshchensk is not even on that line). Then, travelers made their way in carriages down bone-rattling dirt roads, muddy in warm months, iced-over in winter. We had an infinitely less arduous time in getting there. Yet still troubles beset us, even before we arrived one early August morn: fog closed Blagoveshchensk's small airport, forcing our flight to land in Chita, some six hundred miles to the west. Grumpy flight attendants deplaned us into the lounge in Chita's single-runway airport. Hours passed as we waited, wondering if we might end up spending all day there. Around us the other passengers sat glumly, patiently.

We asked airport staff for an update, but they responded only with miffed silence. A young woman holding a large bag with a map of Crimea and a "Crimea is Ours" logo gave us a dirty look, telling her little daughter, "Never mind them. Everybody is silent, but they *vystupayut* [speak out]." Truly, we decided, Russians are treated this way because they let themselves be treated this way.

Yet soon enough the fog relented and we found ourselves, for good or ill, aboard our plane and soaring east. We touched down just outside Blagoveshchensk, a city these days of 225,000 that embodies (and not because of the Amur River) the Russian noun *glubinka*—backwater.

It was a tense place. People seemed on edge. Don't ask extra questions, don't request extra service. In a restaurant the menu included a detailed "broken dishes" price list—from a teapot and a salad bowl to a place mat—in the event that customers were to become too unruly and start damaging equipment and dinnerware.

Just as we were settling into our hotel, a power blackout promptly killed the lights and, worse, the air-conditioning. It turned out that Putin was touring the Russian Far East to fish, hunt, and show off his aging but still taut strongman's chest. Which meant he was set to visit Blagoveshchensk and discuss investment projects and so, along the way, had decided to stop by the Nizhne-Bureisk hydroelectric power plant under construction a hundred miles to the southeast of the city. To please Putin, the plant's managers rushed to open one of its reactors ahead of schedule with, sadly, predictable results. The whole Far East went completely dark for hours. A million people suffered. That evening, bars and restaurants along the Amur embankment closed their doors; we couldn't even find a place for a drink to toast Nina's birthday. We had begun our Russia travels in Putin's footsteps; now he was in ours, making our trip a challenge.

So, we kept strolling down the darkened embankment, our gaze fixed on the bright Heihe just across the Amur. We learned later that a few Chinese locations were affected by the blackout, too, those connected by an international power line to Amur-Heihe.[2] But from where we stood—not much wider than the Thames in London or the Seine in Paris—the Chinese bank was sending its shining lights, their shimmering reflections set on the river's blue-gray surface, lending an impressionistic luminosity to our embankment. Here, women promenaded, bedecked in princesslike long mesh skirts—pink, turquoise, pale green. Couples, many with children, and mesh-skirted girls, despite the late hour, were ambling along, discussing the blackout. (We gathered it was not a rare occurrence.) A few bicycle riders zipped by us, jostling their lamps and ringing their handlebar bells to alert those walking.

Despite the darkness, there were a few stands selling *kukly oberegi*, little straw guardian dolls that are meant to be all-purpose protectors against all ills, from Satan to insomnia, bad luck, and of course the terrors of the night, the saleswomen assured us. Such pagan traditions have mostly disappeared elsewhere in Russia but, perhaps as embodiments of the Slavic spirit, have persisted here on the edge of the Chinese border, at the cusp of the non-Russian world.

We gravitated toward a bronze statue, glinting with light reflected off the waters from Heihe, of a vigilant border patrol soldier standing guard, a fierce-fanged German shepherd by his side. Erected in 2007, the statue conveyed the renewed patriotic spirit of Putin's Russia—the very idea, "We are all border guards here!" we heard expressed by the "drill sergeant" cleaning woman in the Kaliningrad Cathedral.

Kaliningrad resembled a third-rate European city—imitative of a hardscrabble town in East Germany—that was nonetheless militant, hiding its sense of inferiority behind a screen of belligerence. One would expect that Blagoveshchensk, seven time zones to the east, would show Chinese influence. After all, it occupies territory that a mere century and a half ago belonged to China. And yet, the town feels like just another corner of outback Russia.

Never mind the dust and power outages, Blagoveshchensk asserts its European identity. The town's Lenin Street features—with signs in Latin letters—a Charlotte Café, the tobacco shop Sherlock, the men's club "*Fishka* (Chip) Strip and Smoke," the *LaLique* beauty salon, the Austrian coffeehouse Julius Meinl. The best, by far, is a French restaurant Bel-Étage, which displays in English a quote from the German writer Goethe: "Beauty everywhere is a welcome guest."

Many of these establishments occupy space in buildings displaying nineteenth-century neo-Russian style, which, incidentally, originated in Germany and was encouraged by the czar's court architect Konstantin Thon, himself of German origins. A number of the structures look out onto the gilt Byzantine spires and domes of the town's main Orthodox cathedral.

Chinese restaurants, too, abound in Blagoveshchensk, yet in contrast to signs advertising European-style businesses, they announce themselves solely in Cyrillic. The only Chinese-Russian signs we observed graced the Heihe-sponsored racks for rental bikes and the Confucius Institute of the Blagoveshchensk State Pedagogical University. The latter, perhaps, not for long. With rumors of its closure surfacing, the institute's future is now in doubt thanks to rising, Putin-inspired Russian cultural jingoism. In the 1990s the Chinese government backed the foundation of the Confucius Institute ostensibly to provide lessons in Chinese language and culture. Critics, however, worried that it aimed to support the "One Belt, One Road" strategy of augmenting China's influence in neighboring countries. Eventually, the institute came under suspicion of being a "soft power" initiative to help China manipulate local affairs. The Russians have been pushing back against this effort. In recent years the Blagoveshchensk authorities have been investigating its records, which in Russia almost always signals the government's displeasure.

There is a Chinese market—a shopping mall with a Russian name *Avoska* (String Bag) on the outskirts of town, where stores cater to Chinese traders and sell cheap Chinese goods. Although it sheltered Chinese staff, who gossiped in Mandarin as they slurped their instant noodles, all in all *Avoska* resembled so many other markets found in many Russian towns big and small.

On Lenin Street, few businesses orient themselves toward Russia's Asian neighbor and Chinese visitors are rare. Except, perhaps, on Lenin Square, where Chinese tourists stand taking pictures of the granite reproduction of the onetime leader of the world's working class. Yet, you see this all over Russia. Strangely, the central square and its statue evince neglect. Next to the weathered Lenin, though, stands a shiny, incongruous accretion from Putin's era: a new monument to Saint Innokenty the Innocent, the famed nineteenth-century Orthodox missionary to Siberia and the Far East.

If Russians go to Heihe to shop, have meetings with Chinese clients, and visit the Chinese market, Blagoveshchensk remains, on the whole, oriented toward Europe, Moscow, or possibly Japan. In Ulan-Ude, by contrast, the Chinese language was everywhere: Buryats welcomed the Chinese building and owning business centers, hotels, and shops. However, we were told that Russian women in Blagoveshchensk have been increasingly marrying Chinese men, who are known to work hard, drink little, and rarely turn violent.

Nevertheless, in talking to locals, we discovered an interesting dichotomy—Russians don't mind China as a neighboring country, but they are wary of the Chinese themselves.

"Do you fear that China may take over the Russian economy? Or even take over the region by moving in?" we asked one taxi driver.

"No," he responded.

Ours, though, was a reasonable concern. China's economy is the second-largest in the world, Russia's is only twelfth. China's military budget is three times Russia's—$69 billion to $215 billion,[3] and Heihe counts the same number of inhabitants as does Blagoveshchensk, but by Chinese standards, Heihe is tiny. In fact, the whole Russian Far East contains about six million people, which is slightly more than the population of Saint Petersburg. China's Heilongjiang province has twenty times that number and, theoretically at least, could disgorge quite a few of them into Russia east of the Amur. No current stats exist on just how many Chinese live in Russia, but estimates range anywhere from a few hundred thousand to a few million. If the Chinese, hankering after space and natural resources, further increase their migration to Russia, they may test the Russian infrastructure dramatically—and possibly transform it. After all, with China prospering, they are no longer just transient workers and tourists; they increasingly control banks and businesses, from shopping malls to medical centers and construction firms. Moreover, in recent years the Chinese government, using the investment policy of a richer nation, has made a concerted effort to augment the number of Chinese citizens in Russia: we are not giving you our money unless you take our people, too.

Much of Russia's Far East, from the Amur to the Pacific Ocean, once belonged to China, with towns having their own historical Chinese names—Blagoveshchensk was Hailanpao, Vladivostok was Haishenwai, Sakhalin was Kuye. Should the border ever open completely, these territories may simply dissolve back into China. Visa restrictions currently impede mass Chinese entry into Russia.

"What if the Chinese do what the Russians did to them in the 1850s?" we wondered.

Then, a small contingent of Cossacks from the Baikal region wrested from the Chinese the left bank of the Amur around Blagoveshchensk (then Hailanpao). Since 1858 the Amur has been the mutually recognized border between Russia and China, and Blagoveshchensk began its official, czar-blessed existence that year. The Cossacks sought gold and found it. More Cossacks and gold prospectors soon followed, increasing the population of Blagoveshchensk to about eight thousand by 1877. The newcomer Russians eventually did brisk business, selling their precious metal to the Chinese across the water. In the early twentieth century peasants from central Russia moved in and began farming successfully, further securing the region for the czar.

When Chekhov visited Blagoveshchensk, he described it in letters to friends as a rich and liberal town. Yet the locals, he wrote—being mostly Cossacks, prospectors, and fugitives—were loud, aggressive, and fearless, just as one might expect in a frontier town. And they were predictably limited: "People here only talk about gold; those who buy, those who sell . . . and so on." Nevertheless, Blagoveshchensk was "as liberal as it gets, so far away from the center. . . . Forget Europe. . . . There is no one here to arrest; and there is no place farther away to exile."[4] (The twentieth century would prove him wrong.)

If Blagoveshchensk has, since Chekhov's day, lost its lauded "liberalism," it has retained much of its crude, even aggressive, frontier spirit. The city's Regional Museum, located in a turn-of-the-century ornate redbrick building that was once the Kunst and Albert German–owned shopping center, hints at this by showing the Russian takeover of Chinese Outer Manchuria as something similar to the French *mission civilisatrice* in Africa or the settling of North America's west.

The reality was simple: the Chinese could not resist the well-armed warrior Cossacks, whose raison d'être was the conquest and defense of land for the Russian monarch. The resulting 1858 Treaty of Aigun granted the expanding Russian Empire vast new territories in eastern Siberia at the expense of the declining China. The treaty legalized Russia's settlements east of the Amur but was seen as unjust by the Chinese—it set the stage for a Russo-Chinese war, and, more than a century later, the 1969 Sino-Soviet conflict over Damansky Island (Zhenbao or "Precious" in Chinese) further downriver.

The museum depicts other skirmishes as the massacres of Blagoveshchensk, highlighting the heroic Russian defense against barbaric Asiatic hordes. On display are fascinating old photographs showing the Cossacks, gold prospectors, fur trappers, shopkeepers, and tradespeople as missionaries of the good. The Chinese, on the other hand, are portrayed as strange and inferior, similar to how Hollywood movies once depicted them as subordinate "coolies."

On the other side, in the Heihe history museum, a guide in Blagoveshchensk told us disdainfully, the Chinese claimed their territory was stolen by the Russians in the nineteenth century. Before the Russian gold miners, there were Chinese gold miners, traders, and farmers during the Manchu Qing dynasty.

She went on, becoming quite worked up: "We allow the Chinese into our museum, but theirs is closed to Russians and other Europeans. They hide sensitive and inconvenient historical facts about Russo-Chinese conflicts over the Amur region, which we won. They depict Russians as murderous brutes. And who are they to call us *lao maozi*, hairy barbarians?"

"Why wouldn't they permit Russians to enter their museum?" we asked.

"They want to avoid questions or debates. Their perception of facts is at odds with the current friendly relations between our two countries. For the time being, their history is reserved for them alone."

What the Blagoveshchensk museum unequivocally displays is nothing less than a "white empire complex"—with people of the West (and Russians, for the Chinese, are, culturally, westerners) superior to those elsewhere. On and off throughout the Middle Ages Russia fought with Europe over influence and territory. Despite the two-century Mongol yoke, Russia retained its European identity, even as it rejected aspects of the West, including Catholicism, all the while admiring the West's technological progress.

In this, Russia is not the east, it is the edge of the West—the un-Western part of the West, perhaps—its relationship to Europe infected with a strain of envy, even of hostility. Kaliningrad wants to be German, even if Russians there might patriotically deny this. But few Russians want Russia to be China.

In his letters, Chekhov patronizingly described the Chinese as "good-natured and amusing, recalling kind pet animals." Blagoveshchensk's inhabitants do not speak of the Chinese this way now, but still their attitude reflects strong prejudice: the Chinese, for them, are more cunning than kind; they are pushy humans rather than pet animals.

For most of the twentieth century the Russo-Chinese border was closed, and Blagoveshchensk languished as a semi-industrial and remote city. The Soviets, with their planned economy and the collectivization of agriculture, wrought havoc on the local production of foodstuffs and consumer goods, but so did Yeltsin's economic shock therapy and his chaotic privatization program. The result: when Yeltsin visited Blagoveshchensk in 1994 he was taken aback by the poverty he encountered.

One "Potemkin" food shop in town had been stocked for his inspection, but he ordered his motorcade to halt by a store he noticed by chance along his route. Seeing nothing on the shelves, he grew angry.

"The Amur has more than three hundred kinds of fish in it, and here there are three cans of sardines!" he shouted.

As Ostap Bender of *The Twelve Chairs* once said, "The rescue of drowning people is the responsibility of the drowning people themselves." With little help from the newly democratic state, Russians, eager to become capitalists, were already, at the time of Yeltsin's visit, taking full advantage of the abundant wares available in the communist, yet capitalist, China. People from Blagoveshchensk and nearby areas began flocking aboard shuttle boats to Heihe. There they purchased inexpensive food, electronics, and clothes and brought them across the river to be resold in impromptu markets at home. (Yeltsin, had he visited these, might have had a different impression of Blagoveshchensk.)

Here and elsewhere in Russia, such traders became known as *chelnoki* ("suitcase" or "shuttle" traders). A bronze statue of a bespectacled (and thus presumably educated) man lugging suitcases of merchandise now stands in downtown Blagoveshchensk; its inscription reads: "For the hard work and optimism of the Amur's entrepreneurs." The *chelnoki* included almost anyone, from scientists to doctors of philosophy to librarians to factory workers and military analysts. Suffering from the collapse of Soviet-era economic structures and hit hard by Yeltsin's shock therapy, Russians from all walks of life found they needed to make a living any way they could. Shuttle trading offered them a chance to do so.

In recent years, Russia has touted its "pivot" toward China, and especially fraternal relations have prevailed between Putin and Chinese president Xi Jinping, masters of the world's largest formerly communist or communist giants. A special arrangement between Russia and China allows Russian citizens to travel visa-free between Blagoveshchensk and Heihe on the ferries making the trip several times a day. Not all the *chelnoki* are Russians going to China; many Chinese are crossing over to Russia to stock up on vodka, textiles, and foodstuffs. The Russians operate their ferries for Russians and everyone else with a proper visa—occasional foreign visitors, citizens of former Soviet republics; the Chinese boats take only Chinese nationals. Jeff, an American citizen, didn't have a visa to make the trip, so Nina had to travel alone.

This is her story.

The Russia "Made in China"

The next muggy morning, still unsettled by the blackout, I decided to venture across the river. Would this be a pleasant jaunt? After all, the distance was short, relations between Russia and China good, and the visa-free travel arrangement should have cut red tape to a minimum.

Blagoveshchensk's River Station, a brick-and-glass box of a building, was orderly and easy to navigate. There was not even a line to buy the 2,300-ruble ($40) ticket. With ticket in hand, I moved on to the passport control booths. The hour was early, but in front of the booths, tight-knit groups of grumpy *chelnoki*—Russians with empty bags and Chinese toting giant, blue-white-red checkered satchels—

crowded and shoved. I plunged in but repeatedly found myself pushed back, barred from advancing by the phalanx of traders. Alone, I was no match for them.

Twenty, thirty minutes passed. I was getting desperate. The boat's departure time was nearing, but I, shoved this way and that, was no closer to the booths than when I entered the fray. A young man in a parallel line took pity and encouraged me to cut ahead of an old Chinese man just in front of me dragging three huge suitcases.

"He's only Chinese," he said, gesturing to me. I couldn't do it.

Lyrics from a Soviet song from the 1950s came to mind: "All people are brothers, so I will hug a Chinese person." Putin and Xi Jingping might be hugging each other, I thought, but no such amity was to be found here on the border between their two countries. Nevertheless, I reached passport control, got the requisite stamp in my travel document, and soon found myself pressed by the rushing crowd out of the station, over the gangplank, and aboard the ferry.

More and more *chelnoki* piled on behind me. But finally, a deckhand tossed the gangplank aboard the dock and slammed shut the gunwale door. With a toot of the horn, a roar from the engines, and a lurch, we were on our way, pressed far too intimately into one another. The ferry took fifteen minutes to chug across the Amur. As we neared the other side, a young man with kind eyes and a rare, old-fashioned sounding name, Innokenty (just like the Siberian missionary), offered me a blank Chinese entry form.

"Just hang on to me," he said, offering his arm.

Innokenty turned out to be the son of bioengineers who took to shuttle trading after losing their university jobs during the Yeltsin years. He was leading a group of ten other traders. I lucked out! I could join his flock.

The horn blared again when we neared the port. As the boat maneuvered itself to the dock, the deckhand threw open the gunwale door and tossed down the gangplank. Our crowd rushed ashore, across the asphalt pier toward the customs building and through the glass doors. It was larger, more modern, and airier than its Blagoveshchensk equivalent. Inside, green-uniformed Chinese officers stood guard, indifferent to the frenzied Russians surging past. In the melee I lost Innokenty but navigated to passport control on my own.

"*Nalog! Nado nalog!* [Need to pay customs tax]," the officer barked in Russian, perhaps the only words he knew of the language.

I fought my way against the elbows and knees of the Chinese, mostly men, cutting the line and the Russian *chelnoki* battling them to move ahead. I broke free and ran to the payment booth near the entrance. Even in this rigmarole of immigration control I marveled at the cultural contrasts. The Russians looked at the Chinese shoppers with disdain; the Chinese treated the Russians with utter indifference, as if they were just obstacles to be overcome to reach a certain goal. But no time to waste, receipt in hand, I plunged back into the crowd. Panting, I made it to the passport line again and presented the officer with the receipt.

He waved, "*Net, net* [No, no]." Apparently their computer system had just gone down, which he and his comrades interpreted as a sign from heaven that lunchtime had arrived. They all stood up, formed a line, and marched out. Other officers pushed the remaining hundred of us back to the glass doors. No explanation.

The wait didn't seem to be worth it. I gave up. After all, I just experienced the flesh-and-bone reality of "fraternal" Chinese-Russian relations; that was my purpose here, not shuttle trading. I had yet to officially cross into China, but the battle to enter was too much; I decided to return to the boat. I set off across the blissfully empty pier.

I didn't get far.

"Hey! Hey!" shouted Chinese border guards, waving their automatic rifles at me, delivering incomprehensible commands in Mandarin. I halted, saying I didn't understand. The sole female officer among at least five men stepped forward, speaking English somewhat and giving me a sympathetic smile.

"One minute, my boss," she said, gesturing to the man at her side. He snatched my passport, slowly flipped through its pages, and then shoved it back into the young woman's hands.

"So, can I go back to Russia?" I asked.

"Sorry," she replied.

"Sorry for what? I just want to go back to the boat!"

The other officers laughed and pointed at me. Who was I, a Russian, and a Russian woman at that—I imagined them to be thinking—to protest and demand answers to simple questions?

So, I was trapped between Russia and China, two militaristic states with little respect for the individual. I felt helpless, reduced to nothing. Here either the state or the mobs of citizens would crush you.

"Don't make such a scene!" said my fellow Russians berating me, fearful that the Chinese would take out their displeasure at my protest on them, too.

The guards pressed us back until we could go no further, cramming us together in a sweaty mass. One hour passed. Then two. Then three. . . .

I thought about what I was experiencing here on this far-flung border: the *chelnoki* hated me just because I was there, I was a competitor for space, for air to breathe, and for a turn at the passport booth. Why weren't they furious with the officials and their callous treatment? They were brought up in a country where not only the mighty state takes all, but citizens count as little more than an inconvenience, as pestering peons. The peons, scared of the state, vent their frustration on each other, quick to turn on those who buck the established order, on those nagging reminders that resistance is still possible—but such acts entail risk. Besides, the *chelnoki* have it hard enough: they are perpetually in search of a client or a deal, hauling heavy luggage, paying bribes to handlers, competing with their fellows, and at times fearing for their lives. To do what they do, one needs strength, cunning, and sharp survival skills.

Being a shuttle trader "kills the humanity in you," one woman in line said to me, sighing, as she nevertheless shoved her way into my space. "If I were without bags, like you, I'd just squeeze in." She gave me a sinister smile. "But then, we'd beat you up, of course."

Weary of all this conflict, I stepped back.

Finally, lunchtime ended. The guards marched back in and slowly started letting people pass.

I waited my turn patiently, dearly sick of Heihe, without having even officially entered it.

I almost made it to the passport booth. But one of the officers remembered me and my rebellion outside. He stepped in, blocked my entrance, and let a man in a camouflage T-shirt with a portrait of Putin in military fatigues pass before me.

The crowd cheered. The officer jabbed his finger at me, shouting, "*Plokhaya! Plokhaya!* [Bad! Bad!]."

This was too much for me to bear. After hours of such humiliation and scorn, I broke into tears.

The officer was stunned by this expression of humanity and, suddenly, let me through.

I stepped up to the booth and handed the official my passport and receipt, which he began examining. On the counter was a little digital monitor wishing you a good day in Chinese, Russian, and English and asking to rate your experience at the border by pressing either a smiley face or sad face.

I pressed sad. Does anyone ever press the smiley?

The official shoved my documents toward me and waved me on.

I walked on toward the terminal's doors, passing a pink stone plinth marking the border.

I still wanted to return to Russia. I glanced at the departure hall; more chaos reigned there. Crowds of Russians and Chinese were pouring in, dragging their unwieldy bundles of merchandise and amassing by the passport booths.

I stood there, dejected. Possibly my sad countenance prompted a passing striking-looking young woman, tall and willowy, to ask if she could help me. I told her what I had been through. Introducing herself as Tatyana, she nodded sympathetically at my recounted travails and encouraged me to go into town.

"It is usually much quicker, but can also be worse! If you go back now, you'll be here for another two or three hours! So take a cab and see what's here. Just tell the driver 'Huaifu,' pay no more than ten yuan [$1.59]."

It turned out that Tatyana was a student at Tomsk University and had been visiting Heihe with her parents, who were standing next to her. They smiled at me. Her father was Russian, her mother Chinese; they seemed like a loving couple. I thanked Tatyana and took her advice. I stepped out of the terminal and hailed a taxi, my faith in humanity restored.

My driver was a woman. (I learned there are quite a few female drivers in Heihe.) She drove me to that mysterious Huaifu along the embankment, where people were fishing, strolling, and posing for photographs with Blagoveshchensk as a backdrop, where Lenin and Europe seemed so close. Heihe itself looked well kept and cleaner than other Chinese cities, resembling a small Taiwan suburb rather than Shanghai. It was also green. High-rises along the Amur loomed above landscaped parks and squares.

But for a shopping paradise it seemed rather empty on a weekday afternoon. My cab rolled along almost alone on the road, except for a few cyclists pedaling the bright green bikes available for hire from curbside racks. In Blagoveshchensk such racks stand empty; the streets are too dug up and potholed to make biking much fun.

Just a village a few decades ago, Heihe, following the Soviet collapse, oriented itself toward trade with Russia and became a booming frontier town. It makes Blagoveshchensk seem poor indeed, though the Russian city looks more settled, with old trees lining the roads and a less mercantile atmosphere.

Ten minutes later we pulled up in front of Huaifu, which turned out to be Heihe's main shopping mall. The cab deposited me on the Central Trade Pedestrian Street, which announced itself in Russian and Chinese on a pink stone plinth, similar to the one at the border. In front of me was a sight that Russians in the Putin era know all too well—a row of police cars, overseen by an expressionless border guard. Beyond them, out on the river, were anchored patrol boats—both Russian and Chinese. Their crews' green uniforms show drill preparedness for a confrontation that, despite the claims of friendship made by the two countries' governments, may occur at any moment.

Heihe's Russia orientation was mostly nonmilitary and manifested all over the place. The Chinese had catered to Russians' pride in their culture by erecting a statue of their favorite poet, Alexander Pushkin—with the words "Sun of Russian Poetry" engraved in gilt letters on the ocher-colored pedestal, in both Russian and Chinese—on a central square. After all, Heihe was trying to make money from its neighbor. Fur stores abound: Fur City of Paris stood on one side of Central Street, Catherine II [the Great] Fur on another, the presumption being that the notions of Old Europe and the Russian Empress would whet the Russian appetite for luxury.

They had done less well sating their appetite for Russian cuisine: the Café Arbat (named after Moscow's main pedestrian street), *Pita-*

nie Strit (Feeding Street), and *Russkyi Khleb* (Russian Bread) had all been shuttered. As was Restaurant Putin. Much use, apparently, had been made of Google Translate, with results comical enough to evoke howls of laughter or inspire a Bulkgakovian short story, perhaps.

Why was Heihe so empty of Russians? The crush of bodies on the ferry had led me to expect otherwise. The crash in oil prices beginning a decade ago had something to do with it. But the post-Crimea economic sanctions had almost halved the Russian ruble's purchasing power against the yuan, which left the shuttle traders with slimmer profits and thus less reason to travel here.

The Russian *chelnoki* who arrived with me must have dispersed among less central and touristy shops and malls, but a tribute to them stood right in the center of town: mimicking Blagoveshchensk, Heihe had raised a bronze statue to the Russian shuttle trader. It shows a young man sitting on a suitcase, mobile phone in hand, surrounded by bags of merchandise, looking tired and distracted.

If Blagoveshchensk's service culture leaves much to be desired, the streets of Heihe churn with the tireless Chinese entrepreneurs and zealous hucksters. Vendors stand outside their shops clapping to attract attention; sidewalk traders beckon; arrays of multicolored, illuminated signs flash their Chinese characters, as if beaming inscrutable prophetic messages. At one point, I sat down on a bench to take in this Brave New World and was immediately surrounded by men and women trying to sell me everything from socks to toys, cigarette lighters and cell phone cases with Putin's portrait. One especially forward young entrepreneur turned on his hand massager and was about to apply it to my neck until I fled to another bench.

Even though suitcase trading has suffered a downturn recently, in Heihe people seemed to be particularly excited about the possibility of building a bridge between their town and Blagoveshchensk. In fact, for years China has been offering to fund the project.

"The Chinese always take the initiative. They need us more than we need them," Innokenty had explained to me on the ferry that morning. "Especially now, Heihe is eager to restructure." To overcome problems stemming from the dwindling border economy, the city, he said, plans to focus not on *chelnoki*, "but on turning itself into the new Harbin"—the capital of Heilongjiang province, the famed home for Russians displaced by the 1917 Revolution, and now a major manufacturing and tourist center.

"From the fake Russified China of Heihe, the bridge will lead to the real Russia, so the Chinese can come and enjoy our many Lenins on their Red Tour," Innokenty added with a chuckle.

In Blagoveshchensk there is less enthusiasm for such a bridge. First suggested by Yeltsin but shot down by his economic advisors as unviable, the project has, at least until recently, lost what allure it had. Russians have become accustomed to the ferry and don't see much need for another means of crossing the Amur. Recently Putin's government has been displaying renewed interest in the idea. With the Crimea Bridge completed, he can now start another bold enterprise. The bridge, after all, would create more formalized and better functioning trade zones and areas of cooperation—matters Putin and Xi Jinping have discussed—and thus help better control Chinese emigration to Russia.

One of the reasons the Russians have been slow to respond to the Chinese advances is their fear of a further increase in economic and demographic inequality.

Trying to stave off a possible Chinese takeover of parts of Siberia, the Kremlin, in February 2017, announced the Far-Eastern Hectare project, which involves offering free, single-hectare plots to Russians who move there and exploit the land in the first five years. One would think that giving away land to encourage frontier settlement would excite a lot of interest. After all, the United States passed the

Homestead Acts to settle parts of the country west of the Mississippi with offers of 160-acre plots to homesteaders. But Russia's meager one-hectare plots, located in frigid Siberia, no less, are not attracting many takers.

For now, the Kremlin has been intensively funding just one project in Blagoveshchensk: its newly expanded embankment. The Chinese have made Heihe's waterfront along the Amur shine, so Putin decided to follow suit. Blagoveshchensk's new redbrick high-rises (resembling, incidentally, those we saw in Kaliningrad), the bronze border guard with the dog, the Soviet-era yet recently renovated stark gray monument to the Great Patriotic War (a none-too-subtle reminder that Russians know how to fight those), and even the Arc de Triomphe (spiffed up not long ago)—all these are symbols of Putin's Russia.

After my taxi ride around town, I decided to get something to eat. This took some work, as waiters in the pizzeria-like cafeteria I stopped in spoke neither Russian nor English. Nevertheless, I managed to procure a small pizza, served with a plastic glove, instead of a napkin and a fork. While eating I stared at the wall adorned with an intriguing world map: on it, the Eurasian continent was titled Asia, and Russia wasn't identified; Europe was small; and only the Americas and Africa were depicted in scale.

Once finished with my pizza, and having stripped off my glove, I set about searching for a cup of coffee. This, it turned out, posed a challenge here. Even in parts of Russia, it is sometimes tough to find anything but instant coffee. But in China a sign saying café rarely means coffee at all; there they mean food. In Heihe one café, Parizh (Russian for Paris), promisingly had fancy pastries in the window, an Eiffel Tower on its wallpaper, and a bistro table with two chairs in front of it. What was lacking was coffee. "Coca Cola?" the shopkeeper asked.

I then ventured down "The Street of Russian Goods" (as the sign in Russian translates). It called to mind Canal Street in New York's Chinatown—behind every door they sell something—although here I was the only customer. Cheap, colored furs—red, yellow, orange, even green—hung from the awnings, marked RUSSIAN FURS, yet they were made in China. Huge shop windows displayed, in bulk, Russian canned goods, flour, sugar, and candy. Posters with writing in Chinese advertised Russian ice cream with a picture of Putin licking a cone—a clever mixture of hard and soft power.

Heihe, I came to think, seemed unreal, chintzy, slapped-together—a reified, steel-glass-concrete "made in China" slogan. Yet there were authentic moments—a group of older women sat on a bench, laughingly shielding a friend while she was changing into a new pair of trousers freshly purchased in the shop *Mir-Bryuki Nizkoi Tseny* (World-Pants at Low Cost). In the restaurant where I ate my pizza, teenage girls chatted away. On a side street, four men played mahjong, an ancient board game, with scores of spectators huddling around their table. I also uncovered a mystery of the Blagoveshchensk fashion of wearing princesslike mesh skirts in a variety of jewel tones—seemingly a dress code of every little girl in Heihe.

Evening was coming on. Still reeling from crossing the border, I considered spending the night in Heihe. I espied a new, palatial hotel, called the Saint Petersburg. At least from the outside, it seemed like a good option, so I dropped in to check it out. But in the fancy lobby, plastic glitz was already peeling off the walls, and I spotted a cockroach in the restroom.

Never did I want to return to Mother Russia as strongly as I did then and there, in the Saint Petersburg Hotel, Heihe-style.

So, I walked back to the port. This time, I would not go it alone. In the terminal, a young woman approached me.

"You don't look like you're from here," she said. I replied that she didn't look local, either.

Her name was Anastasia. We started chatting. It turned out Anastasia was originally from Blagoveshchensk but now lives in Beijing. It would be easier to battle stonewalling Chinese officials and angry fellow Russian travelers together, so we teamed up and got in line with a large group of men and women who oversaw a mountain of bulky bags and cardboard boxes and eyed us with outright disdain. And they were even angrier that the guards let any Chinese who showed up board, while leaving the Russians to wait—for hours.

Anastasia spoke fluent Mandarin. The impressed Chinese guards explained to her what was going on.

"Damaged by the blackout, the computer system doesn't allow us to switch between Chinese and Russian travelers without a glitch," Anastasia said, translating the guards' explanation. The group was unconvinced.

"A payback to Putin! They hate the Russians. That Xi and Putin friendship is bullshit," they grumbled.

I have never seen such angry people in my life, never felt as unsafe as then, while I languished between two gigantic, belligerent states and among those who have dedicated their lives to making small profits at any cost. Yet Anastasia and I boarded without incident, trying to find a spot to stand—the deck was jammed with merchandise, including even small tractors that enterprising Buryats were bringing back to Ulan-Ude.

Across the river on the Russian side, the rancor between the Chinese and Russians rekindled, with each group treating the other as inferiors. But now the might was on the Russian side: a stone-faced border guard pushed aside scores of Chinese and their bags to allow all the Russians to cross through customs first.

With last night's blackout now a distant memory, Jeff and Nina settled in for a drink at the Europeanish Café Sharlot, where service was slow but not uncaring.

Over wine and coffee, we spoke about Nina's day in Heihe. If they ever build the bridge, spending time on the other side of the water may prove less traumatic. But for now, a lone traveler feels like a non-person when confronting the reality of the Russia–China alliance, an alliance between two countries vying for superiority and whose leaders value state might above the well-being of the citizens over whom they rule. What's more, we thought, the Kremlin has turned a cold shoulder toward Europe in Kaliningrad, but when it turns east—the Chinese are overwhelming, making this edge of the frontier just as tense and testy, and more threatening perhaps, as the border to the West.

Yakutsk: Prisoners of Empire?

It was a brilliant azure evening of the sort that lingers endlessly during the summer in these northern latitudes. Sinking into damp eluvium—a sediment composed of white pebbles and rocks, sand and silt—we descended the steep bank tentatively, backtracking at times when our feet would not take hold. We slow-walked toward the docks at the Yakutsk port, from where a captain named Georgy was supposed to take us on a boat tour up the Lena River. As we treaded, we gazed down at the numerous makeshift piers jutting out into the green-blue water. Which one was ours? We had arranged the tour by phone but had no idea what sort of craft awaited us. A taxi speedboat that takes people to the other side of Lena, and to its many islands, some large enough to be habitable? A sleek modern cutter? Once at the waterside, we traipsed among disorderly clusters of skiffs, dinghies, and schooners, asking for Georgy, but found our queries met with shrugs and blank stares. We finally located him standing by a serviceable wooden craft that could seat fifteen passengers but, this time, would take us alone.

We climbed aboard. Brawny, sun-bronzed, and about forty, Georgy untied the mooring ropes and switched on the engine. We lurched away from the dock and out onto the Lena.

The previous day we had arrived in the capital of the sprawling Sakha (Yakutia) Republic, whose 1.2 million square miles of taiga and tundra are home to fewer than a million people, about half of whom are Sakha, descendants from Turkic tribes from Central Asia. (Yakutsk itself has about 270,000 people.) This part of eastern Siberia was long called Yakutia, but after the Soviet Union ended, as nationalism rose, it renamed itself Sakha Republic. The Sakha now claim that the names Yakutia and Yakut were given to them by Russian colonizers, but Sakha is what they call themselves, their land, and their language. Most of the republic's non-Sakha are ethnic Russians, in addition to small numbers of Evenks and Evens, people of Tungusic stock. During the Soviet decades, Russians involved in resource extraction made up a majority of the republic's inhabitants and accounted for about 500,000 people, with the Sakha and other local peoples accounting for 300,000. Today indigenous folk far outnumber the Russians. And although the Kremlin has called for settlers to head out to Siberia and the Russian Far East, there is little evidence of new arrivals.

In mineral resources, Sakha is the richest administrative territory in Russia and ranks fourth globally in diamond production. Nevertheless, Yakutsk and its port were chaotic and shabby. The actual port building resembled an oversized, blue-and-white cement shoebox sitting atop matchbox pillars. A dock on the river served larger boats, but most craft had to make do with rickety piers and even gangplanks. This, in the wealthiest region of Russia. Where was all the money going?

The Lena, at 2,779 miles in length, is the third longest river in Russia and the eleventh in the world. It is the only major river flowing entirely through zones of permafrost; almost half of Sakha lies within the Arctic Circle. Unique among bodies of water, the Lena freezes from the bottom up. It originates as a narrow rocky stream in the mountains just west of Lake Baikal and courses northward to emerge into the Arctic Ocean's Laptev Sea. At Yakutsk's latitude, the Lena's bed is some seven miles wide but strewn with a multitude of sandy islands overgrown with saw grass, so called for its serrated blades that can reach six or seven feet in height. Tributaries flow into the Lena from numerous tiny lakes—Yakuts say they are as many as stars in the sky—nestled away in the surrounding taiga.

Cossack explorers first reached this part of Siberia in the early 1600s. They took the name Lena from local appellations—Elyuene or Lenna, meaning "big river," in the Manchu Tungus language. The Lena's majestic expanses so impressed Vladimir Ulyanov, who did a stint of exile near its banks, that he adopted a version of it for his pseudonym, Lenin.

Georgy piloted his craft out onto the magnificent Lena, which resembles the region through which it flows—undeveloped and little exploited, despite its riches. We inhaled fresh air—there are no factories anywhere near. We watched the reedy islands slide by as we sailed south, against the current, our bow splitting the glassy turquoise panes of water spreading from shore to sandy shore.

Georgy, sounding bitter, commented on how strange Sakha and its chief river were.

"There are so many minerals out here. The Yakuts have a folk tale: when God was distributing riches around the world, he got so cold in Yakutia that he dropped all the minerals—a whole periodic table of elements of them. But they aren't exploited as they should be." He then pointed toward the banks and changed subjects. "Look at the grass on the islands. It only grows here and is so invasive that if you come back in five years, these islands will have been overtaken by the grass. Of course, in other places this growth would be managed. Here people leave the river alone."

The Lena's most famous natural wonder is the *Lenskie Stolby* (Lena Pillars), some 160 miles south of Yakutsk. There the river cuts through uplands, forming a channel of steep yellow-and-brown limestone and slate walls that, in places, reach more than a thousand feet in altitude. The pillars rival the Grand Canyon, although few outside Russia have heard of this Sakha marvel.

We would not make it that far, but Georgy often did.

"I make a lot of money taking people to the pillars," he said. "For a group of eight I charge as much as a hundred thousand rubles a day [about $1,700]. All the Russian officials and diamond businessmen who come to Yakutsk want to visit them. The pillars, the beauty of the scenery, the vodka, the *shashlyk* (kebab)—they have a good time out here with me."

We peacefully glided up the Lena, which now was growing astoundingly asymmetric: the eastern shore was flat, the western steep, high, and rocky. And the farther we got from Yakutsk the more stunning it was, erasing our memories of the messy port and docks.

Over the course of the next few hours, Georgy regaled us with his story, which was typical for this part of Russia—the difficulty of keeping a small business going and a desire to move out west, to the better lands with more opportunity. He had grown tired of Yakutsk and its ethnic tensions; he was thinking of moving to Novosibirsk or Krasnoyarsk and starting up a similar boat service on one of the rivers passing through them, the Ob or the Yenisei.

Part of the reason Georgy was thinking of leaving had to do with what happened to the port following the Soviet collapse of 1991. Here, as along so many river towns across Russia, in the Yeltsin era the government privatized the port, dividing it up between a number of owners. Owners tried to squeeze out as much profit as they could from their sections, bribing local authorities as necessary and creating, as a result, a generalized chaos that suited no one. In the 1990s and early 2000s, Russian railroads languished in similar disarray, owned by multiple proprietors. When Putin became president, he made it his priority to put crucial pieces of Russia's infrastructure under full Kremlin control. And although he managed to reorganize the railroads, the exploitation of natural resources, and even the postal service, which he restructured, the waterways are still waiting their turn.

"Imagine," Georgy complained, "despite its size, the Lena has no bridge across it. A bridge was in the works, but with the Crimea annexation the state shifted funding to Crimea, to the bridge that is being constructed there" across the Kerch Strait.

We nodded sympathetically—this Crimea diversion, we had seen, had happened in many other places across Russia. Reporting on the news of its opening in May 2018, one Italian newspaper quipped that Putin "built his career on bridges"[5]—in Ulyanovsk, Vladivostok, and elsewhere. It is also worth noting that the Crimea bridge construction dream dates back to the last czar. Stalin also made an attempt to build it in 1945, but it was quickly destroyed by ice. Putin then succeeded where the previous greats had failed, which must be a tremendous point of pride for the current Kremlin leader.

Answering our question about his own future, Georgy insisted that all ethnic Russians, like he is, would leave Yakutsk soon enough—a lack of opportunity and rising ethnic chauvinism were to blame. His sister had already moved to Krasnoyarsk—"a nice town, less to compete with than in Novosibirsk. They need entrepreneurs more there, so I am getting ready."

Judging by his almond-shaped eyes, Georgy probably had Yakut blood, even though he spoke passionately of his Russianness, with a whiff of disdain toward the indigenes.

"The Yakuts don't even know how old they are," Georgy said. A giant banner on top of the port building announced Yakutsk's 380th anniversary. Yet on Lenin Square it is listed as 385, and 384 elsewhere.

Nevertheless, Yakutsk is indeed old. Once a settlement in the taiga, it existed long before the Cossacks, led by the Ataman (chieftain) Pyotr Beketov, who reached it in 1632. The Sakha had fled north from the rampaging armies of Genghis Khan and finally settled here, where the freezing winters and summer swarms of mosquitos and midges would dissuade intruders. The Sakha herded reindeer and cattle, hunted, fished, and even bred horses—diminutive, robust ungulates capable of surviving on limited fodder during fierce winters. The coldest winters on earth—temperatures at times hit −94 Fahrenheit—preclude much in the way of agriculture. Not surprisingly, in recent decades scientists have found more remains of woolly mammoths—three entire specimens—in the republic than anywhere else. Proud of these discoveries, Yakutsk hosts a mammoth museum—the only one in the world—though its unique exhibits, as we would see, could use better upkeep.

The indigenous peoples lived in harmony with nature, unforgiving as it was, whereas colonizers brought their own habits and rules. In the seventeenth century, the newly arrived Russians were brutal in establishing themselves here, killing Sakha by the thousands, according to numerous sources, when the natives rebelled against taxation or relocation.[6] The Russians trapped for furs but also prospected for gold and diamonds, resources not previously exploited in the region. Unfortunately, they also introduced alcohol. As is the case with Native Americans, the indigenes lacked the enzyme that metabolizes alcohol efficiently, which left them prey to alcoholism. Alcoholism is a plague now as it was then, with a frightening death toll, more than three times higher than in the rest of the country.[7] During the week, we noticed an unusually high number of intoxicated young Sakha begging for money on the streets but saw few Russians out and about. Russians joked to us that they work while the Sakha drink. On weekends, though, the ethnicities mix and tipple together. The climate here, at least in winter, surely drives many to drink.

Walking around Yakutsk, we couldn't shake the feeling that even after almost four hundred years since the Cossack arrival, the Russian world is still colliding with the indigenous one. It was hard to call Yakutsk Russian at all. Russian towns, as a rule, have a certain logic—there is a Lenin Square, a Lenin Street, and central avenues and streets, usually well maintained, radiate from there before falling into disarray further afield. Here, from Lenin Square—the only one in good shape—radiate streets as dusty and rough as gravel roads.

Just stepping off Lenin Avenue to a side street, we encountered a huge pile of dung—from the times of the woolly mammoth, perhaps. It was a few yards before we got to the Treasury of Sakha, an ultra-modern structure of slate-gray glass and steel. Inside we would gaze upon the pride of the republic, the national treasures of Sakha: gold, precious stones, diamonds, and figurines carved from bone depicting hunters, animals, and scenes from traditional family life. Wouldn't someone think to clean the street in front of the building housing such a stunning collection? To be fair, though, even if Yakutsk were to spend a fortune paving and maintaining its roadways, it might not do much to make the city more livable. During the all-too-brief summer, temperatures reach 104 Fahrenheit, and, we discovered, midges and gnats swirled around our faces all day long and even after sunset. No surprise, really, given that the terrain surrounding Yakutsk is bog. Locals say, "Repellant doesn't help, but a paste of reindeer fat and gasoline does." But who wants to walk around town smelling like a car!

The Siberian chain of cafés, Traveler's Coffee, often provided us with some consolation, though we spent thirty minutes waiting for a cappuccino. We took greater pleasure in the flower market covering the giant Ordzhonikidze Square. Even stands selling simple petunias drew scores of buyers—Russians, Yakuts, Evens, and others—from all walks of life. In Sakha, where it is cold nine months a year, petunias must seem as fancy as orchids. One Sakha woman confirmed that any flowers are better than none: "With this climate we have here—the pole of cold—we do like flowers."

Yet just a couple of blocks from Lenin Square, in the wooden quarter of town called the Old City, we came upon tall, yellow-orange-scarlet-pink Siberian lilies (the *Lilium dauricum*, scientifically speaking) peeping through patches of overgrown grass. Elsewhere such flowers would be considered precious and rare, but here they grow unattended, unnoticed. The Old City itself seemed more rundown than antique—a few dilapidated Russian huts, a handful of "traditional" restaurants, and incongruously standing amid them, the boutique Mascotte; a beauty salon called, puzzlingly, Lime.Fink; and the log-cabin Museum House of Maksim Ammosov, one of the founders of the Yakut Soviet Autonomous Republic and one of its first leaders. Nearby stood the nineteenth-century Cathedral of the Transfiguration. In front of it lay another pile of dung. No one was rushing to clean it up.

We did find a stately and well-kept street in Yakutsk—Dzerzhinsky Street, named in honor of Felix Dzerzhinsky. Iron Felix, as he was known for short, was the founder and first leader of the dreaded

Soviet Cheka, or secret police, a precursor to the KGB and other Soviet security organs. Putin's own KGB past may have contributed to
Dzerzhinsky's standing in Yakutsk. Still, if the notorious Dzerzhinsky is no longer considered the villain he was before Putin, few cities
rush to memorialize him with statues and street names. In Yakutsk,
Dzerzhinsky's bust rests in a little birch park on Dzerzhinsky Street
next to the imposing, sleek, cream-and-chocolate Ministry of Internal Affairs of the Sakha Republic, which looks more like a five-star
hotel than a Sakha version of the FBI. Next to it stands the less
pompous but still impressively sleek police headquarters. Such is the
current Russian trend—public infrastructure for simple citizens
might be deteriorating, yet the *karatelnye organy* (punitive organs)
are doing just fine.

This is no accident: the city has even tried to rehabilitate Stalin,
in a way. Plans were made to install a Stalin bust in the Veterans Park
further down the street, but Yury Zabolev, then mayor of Yakutsk,
supported by the journalist and media entrepreneur Leonid Levin,
pushed to sway public opinion against the idea. Surprisingly, they
won out. Off the dusty Chernyshevsky Street, though, in a private
yard belonging to the Diamonds of Anabara company, a Stalin bust
was nevertheless erected. Beneath his stern gaze, veterans, pension-
ers, and communists now gather to remember the Soviet's grandeur
during his decades in power.

We wondered, why would the Sakha still esteem Dzerzhinsky
and Stalin? After all, their republic for centuries suffered under the
Russian yoke. Only since 1991, with the emergence of a movement
for self-determination, have they begun to reevaluate their history.
In fact, Sakha was originally determined to achieve independence.
Its first post-Soviet leader, Mikhail Nikolaev, negotiated with Yeltsin
and won the right to be called president and quasiindependence
from Moscow. Not that Yeltsin meant it, really—two Chechen sepa-

ratist wars followed his declaration. The Sakha would not revolt against Moscow, though. Eventually, the independence movement waned. The Kremlin no doubt rejoiced, since the republic paid so much in taxes to the federal government. Yet the movement had a salutary effect on Sakha's finances: revenues from at least some of its resources—fur, gold, diamonds, copper, and other precious and semiprecious metals—would go to the development of the republic. In previous years, only limited funds went to local projects, leaving the Sakha to mostly drink and waste away in poverty.

Enjoying, for the first time, revenues from their minerals, the Sakha have turned away from the phony internationalism that was such a strong part of Soviet communism and begun to reevaluate their own heritage. Glorifying Dzerzhinsky and Stalin, we thought, should have had nothing to do with that. So what was going on?

To seek answers, we arranged to meet Leonid Levin, one of the opponents of the Stalin bust, and editor and publisher of the *Vecherny Yakutsk* (Evening Yakutsk) newspaper, in his office, a wooden two-story bungalow on the outskirts of town. (It happened to stand adjacent to the London Hotel, another bungalow whose only connection to the British capital was a painting of Big Ben on the front wall.) Upbeat and charismatic, Levin, to our surprise, blamed the local government for the glorification of Stalin, but he absolved Putin.

"Putin is not a Stalinist," said Levin. "He just uses elements of Stalinism as tools to unify the country."

Isn't it the same thing, we wondered? In Russia, there is almost always a desire to justify the central state even among those who suffer from it. We were surprised to hear such words from one who militated against glorifying Stalin.

Our talk turned to other topics. After 1991, Levin told us, when the Republic began receiving revenues from its diamond mines, the leadership chose to spend them on transforming the city into a megalopolis, at least as the Sakha understood it, rather than on health care and education. Yet they did designate some funds for the cultural sphere. The resulting ethnic revival helped quell separatist aspirations, with the Sakha finding themselves free to be Sakha in their own land. A more practical question did arise: namely, just what purpose independence would serve. Yes, Sakha's resources would make it the richest country, at least per capita, on earth, but most businesses, particularly those in the diamond sector, are run and owned by Russians. Ethnic divisions do remain: the Sakha tend to hire Sakha; Russians prefer to deal with Russians.

"A balance between ethnicities has not been found on the republic's level," Levin said.

He was right. Time and again, we heard from Yakutsk Russians, who had little positive to say about their city, "We'll all leave, and those Yakuts can stay and do what they want." On the flight from Blagoveshchensk, a young Russian woman sitting next to us kept repeating, "I can't wait to move to Blagoveshchensk, from this godforsaken Yakutsk—hot, cold, dirty, with mosquitos and nothing to do."

Yet these Russians vastly underrated their Sakha conationals. We saw evidence of this in *Vecherny Yakutsk*, where Russian and Sakha journalists worked side by side, and a young Sakha photographer whose name, Saidam ("talented, savvy" in translation), described him well: he really impressed us with his knowledge of cities via 2GIS, a Russian search engine company (developed in Novosibirsk). He was also an expert on New York jazz clubs, though he had never traveled abroad. So removed from the world, the Sakha were as ambitious as anyone. Perhaps, in fact, their remoteness gave them special incentive to nurture their ambitions.

Levin told us that although couples were, in Yakutsk, having fewer children than ever, the drop in population was compensated for by an influx of out-of-work youths moving in, as reindeer farms in the outback are running into hard times. The republic's cultural rejuvenation, has, moreover, had one negative consequence no one expected: imbued with Yakut nationalism, many schools now offer education only in Yakut, which means students are not learning proper Russian.

"These kids," he said, "will have no college in their future, since nobody teaches classes in the local language. Education levels and expertise in various fields will be falling."

That being the case, how could the Sakha, if independent, run the diamond and gold businesses, revenues from which sustain the local budget? To take advantage of the recently emerged hesitation in Sakha about independent statehood, and also following his own growing autocratic tendencies, Putin did away with the title of "president" and replaced it with "Leader of the Sakha Republic." It is unconstitutional to have two presidents in one country, Sakha was informed. Given all the potential complications from splitting away, perhaps it was for the best that Sakha remained part of Russia.

The day was ending, and we walked outside with Levin, where his son awaited him in a spotless black SUV. The languid blue-gold light of evening was coming on, the mosquitos and midges were whirling in dark columns against the sky. He had given us a frank assessment of how things were in his republic, free of the ethnic chauvinism so many Russians evince toward Yakuts. We thanked him for his time and parted ways.

In the Oyunsky State Museum of Yakut Literature (dedicated, as the name indicates, to the native-born poet and writer Platon Oyunsky, who lived from 1893 to 1939) our poet-guide Nikolai Vinokurov told us, in accented Russian, the heroic story of how the Yakuts both resented and embraced Russian culture. This Sakha man, like many here going by his Russian name, spoke of the "civilization" the Slavic outsiders brought with them. One panoramic painting illustrated the gist of his message. It showed a landscape of tundra, low hills, and yurts with hearth fires that kept burning in summer to ward off mosquitos and midges; Sakha herding cattle and riding horses; and old men reciting the tales of the *Olonkho*, their traditional oral epic. (The United Nations has recognized the *Olonkho* as part of humanity's "intangible cultural heritage.")

The Yakuts, as the painting had it, dwelled in a sort of prelapsarian, boreal idyll before the Russians arrived.

However, the story isn't so simple. Sakha owes at least its written literary traditions to Russian missionaries who arrived in the nineteenth century. Under the direction of Bishop Innokenty—later canonized as the Siberian missionary—Saint Petersburg's scholars and writers adapted the Cyrillic alphabet for the Sakha language, and priests began translating the Bible into it, thereby laying the foundation for the emergence of Sakha literature. As had Ammosov, Oyunsky stood at the beginning of Sakha's transformation into a Soviet socialist republic; he composed his poems to resemble the *Olonkho* but imbued them with Soviet themes. Like many in the 1930s, he was arrested for his "counterrevolutionary" ideas and died in prison.

"It was strange that he was arrested," said our guide, Nikolai. "He was a good Soviet citizen." As if being a good Soviet ever protected anyone from Stalin and his security apparatus.

The city's Museum of Local Lore exhibits document more than a hundred labor camps for political exiles on the Republic's territory and also show the plight of the Sakha during the Stalin decades. By and large, the Sakha themselves were not victims of the Gulag. Most of the prisoners came from elsewhere in the Soviet Union. Nevertheless, the state did prosecute untold numbers of Sakha for the alleged crime of ethnic nationalism.

After Khrushchev's Thaw began, Soviet authorities maintained that no purges had taken place in Sakha. The Sakha saw things differently. Many farmers, accused of resisting collectivization (of reindeer herds, for the most part), were forcibly relocated to other areas but given little time to pack and prepare. Thousands died from cold on the road.

Yet contradictions abound. The 2003 monument to Oyunsky, a victim of such Soviet repression, stands on a square with Dzerzhinsky's bust, on Dzerzhinsky Street, just behind him. Stalin's own bust lurks a few blocks away—two monuments to murderers and one to a victim of Soviet repression.

As we walked out to look for a place to dine one evening, black clouds massed over the flat bogs and taiga sweeping away from the Old City at the edge of town. We came across the *Dikaya Utka* (Wild Duck) pub, one of Yakutsk's restaurants offering "traditional" cuisine, and chose it for our meal.

We walked inside to confront a bizarre scene: diners, all Sakha, were playing Hollywood Bingo. Images of Mel Gibson, Bruce Willis, Julia Roberts, and other American actors flashed on a giant plasma screen as the players marked their cards accordingly. In this remote city on the shore of the Lena River, where the wilderness is vast enough that it has served as a realm of exile, and where woolly mammoths are the objects of local pride, American movies serve to connect the inhabitants to people in the outside world.

The juxtaposition of Mel Gibson's image above Sakha gamesters, of bingo inside and bog outside, combined with the palpable sensation of being far from anywhere we knew induced a disorienting feeling of alienation. Yakutsk, even though ever more "Sakha" and less Russian, did not seem to belong to Asia, but, like Russia as a whole, to a middle area, a gray zone. Often presenting themselves as "prisoners of the empire"—their 64 percent vote for Putin's fourth term was one of the lowest in the country—the Sakha still seem to embrace their in-between status more than ever before.[8] They now freely foster their ethnicity but can leave big decisions on statehood to the man in the Kremlin.

10

VLADIVOSTOK

Rule the East!

Time Zone: MSK+7; UTC+10

Beyond Paris, Vladivostok is probably the most fascinating city on
Earth at the moment. . . . We are so very lucky to witness so many
interesting things happening around us here and now in Vladivostok!

—Eleanor Lord Pray, *Letters from Vladivostok*

From the grim concrete ramparts of Vladivostok's Fort Number
Seven, the Gulf of Amur spreads to the west, its leaden waters
barely rippling one August afternoon under an equally leaden sky.
Turn north or south and your gaze falls on high-rises and apartment
blocks scattered over hills that, with their two suspension bridges,
give the city of some 600,000 the floating, elevated feel of a Russian
San Francisco.

The fort's hulking heptagonal walls enclose an array of cannons
and heavy artillery guns and ammunition storage bunkers capable
of withstanding sustained incoming fire. (Stalin's executioners did
their work within these dungeonlike structures.) Just beyond the
walls, on the square in front, decommissioned Soviet-era missiles lie

on mobile platforms, belying the age of the fort, built at the end of the nineteenth century.

The city itself, founded in 1860, is now the terminus of the Trans-Siberian Railroad—a column on one of the platforms reads "9,288 km" (5,771 miles), thus marking the distance to Moscow. It owes its origins to Russia's successful attempt to secure the terrain from the Amur River east to its coast, on the Sea of Japan, which it legalized by signing the 1860 Treaty of Beijing with China, when that country was too weak to resist. (Japan lies only some five hundred miles away.) Head southwest for fifty miles, and you run into the border with the People's Republic of North Korea. Just to the north is China's Heilongjiang province. In strategic importance, Vladivostok rivals another port town we had visited, Kaliningrad, almost six thousand miles to the west, and well deserves its name, which translates as Ruler of the East.

As we rode in from the airport through leafy green hills, a sign caught our eye, proclaiming *"Ostrov Russkiy, Krym Rossiyskiy"* (The Island Is Russian—the island being the Crimean Peninsula—Crimea belongs to Russia). In Vladivostok, as in Kaliningrad, on the other end of the current empire, Crimea, though distant from both, haunts the Russian consciousness. Russia's chief far-eastern port city celebrates the return to the motherland of another territory, a long way to the west and strategically vital for its own port, this one on the Black Sea.

"Ever since the 2012 summit"—the summit for Asia-Pacific Economic Cooperation (APEC)—"things have been looking up here," our taxi driver, a middle-age fellow named Nikolai, told us as we sped up and down the undulant highway toward town. "We got new roads, better services, and more investment. Before that Vladivostok was reeling from neglect, all the way back to the Yeltsin days." But with

Putin in charge, the city has built "three new bridges in less than ten years."

For more than a century the town dreamed of a bridge to Russky Island. It was painted on postcards and drawn on city plans but never materialized on account of war and bad management—the usual reasons. But then, in 2009, the Kremlin announced that it was going to erect not one, not two, but three bridges, two to the nearby Russky Island alone. "Across Golden Horn Bay, the Golden Bridge—like the Golden Gate in San Francisco—the Russian Bridge over East Bosporus Bay, and another one across Amur Bay."

Though China and Japan had, Russia had never endeavored to construct bridges over sea straits, as it did here. And yet, looking west as ever, or maybe following the Kremlin's orders, the Russian east sought help not from Asia, but from the engineers in Saint Petersburg and France. Nobody believed construction could be completed in three years (in time for the APEC summit), and yet it was. "Another thing that ties us to San Francisco"—the construction of the Golden Bridge—"was also deemed impossible. The bridges are a Vladivostok miracle, a testimony to our spirit," said Nikolai.

Taking advantage of a pause in his impromptu introduction to the city, we squeezed in a personal question.

"Are you from here?"

He was not; he had moved east from Krasnodar some thirty years ago. He wasn't the only one. "People come from western Russia for a visit, see the fish swimming in the bluest of oceans, try Pacific smelt, and find it much tastier than smelt in the Baltic Sea, and stay." (Apparently here in Vladivostok the east–west Russia rivalry boils down to fish.) "The population keeps renewing itself. The port is doing well, new international businesses are opening up, and our Far Eastern University is an international hub."

We had heard his latter claim supported by others in Russia, though the year previous to our visit, at the Eastern Economic Forum, the Kremlin did announce ambitious plans to turn Vladivostok into Russia's San Francisco, with investments of as much as $46 billion coming from the state alone, with outsiders invited to take part. In any case, this windy Russian city of many hills, with its offshore waters and sky at times melding in blue mist, with fog often blanketing inland vistas, and with its soaring bridges, already feels like the white and windy city of northern California. And as in San Francisco, the Paris of the West, so in Vladivostok, the Paris of the East (although, as regards the latter, it competes for this title with many other cities, from Irkutsk in Siberia to Harbin in China), foreigners abound.

Even Vladivostok's railway station, so reminiscent of Moscow's busy Yaroslavsky Station, has a cosmopolitan flare and bespeaks a connection to the center. It was built in the early twentieth century in neo-Russian style, with pink-and-white towers, arches, and columns decorated with the image of Saint George the Victorious on a white horse.

Soon we reached our hotel—a modern, toffee-colored double-towered skyscraper with a view of the Gulf of Amur from one side and the Zolotoy Rog (Golden Horn) Bay from the other. Once inside we confronted an atmosphere we had never seen before. In the Soviet era Vladivostok was one of those "closed" military port cities, but now Chinese and Korean tourists and businessmen filled in the broad, high-ceilinged lobby, emitting an earsplitting roar of enthusiastic chatter that compelled us to shout so that the clerk could hear us and cup our ears so we could understand her response. There were Japanese guests, too, but they sat in small groups, quiet and reserved. Despite our having traversed Russia from east to west, we immediately sensed we had arrived in a place resembling no other in the country.

Later, as we walked Vladivostok's paved, well-kept Sportivnaya Embankment along the Gulf of Amur, we encountered sailors—many of them—out and about in their blue-and-whites, strolling on leave under elegant lampposts, passing a gushing fountain, street acrobats plying their trade, and a pair of Amur tiger cubs (made of bronze, that is)—placed there in honor of the Amur tiger, a symbol of the Russian Far East.

A Ferris wheel rotated slowly, the children in its tilting cars laughing; sidewalk merchants sold candied corn and saucer-size pizzas from wheeled, multicolored carts; kebabs roasted on grills scented the air, recalling the North Caucasus homeland of their cooks. Here and there we heard American English and caught snippets of conversation, apparently American men courting young Russian women. The men wore sneakers and baseball caps; the women, dresses and sneakers, the global fashion of the young. On Svetlanskaya Street, an Orthodox church and a Lutheran cathedral coexisted—a rarity in Russia, which during the Putin years has become increasingly traditional. A Hare Krishna group walked by us, dancing and chanting, with many passersby looking on with amusement.

On the other embankment, Korabelnaya, facing Golden Horn Bay, we came across a well-executed bronze statue of the famed dissident writer Aleksandr Solzhenitsyn. Solzhenitsyn, after decades of exile in the West, did arrive here in 1994—his first stop on Russian soil—to begin a journey on the Trans-Siberian that would end with him taking up residence just outside Moscow, where he remained until his death in 2008.

Further on, the Golden Bridge, with its twin suspension towers, linked one side of the bay to the other. It is no wonder that our driver Nikolai was so taken by the bridge. Before it appeared, the trip around the Golden Horn Bay often took almost two hours; but now, it took just five minutes. Above the bridge a funicular line climbed a hill to a lookout from which a statue of Cyril and Methodius (the Bulgarian monks who created the Russian alphabet) looked down on the city, holding a large Christian cross and an open book showing their creation. The statue, though smaller, resembles the cast-iron monument to Prince Vladimir in Kiev. Perhaps the officials who erected it meant to emphasize the city's Russianness, but it also highlighted the diverse sources of the country's civilization. The Cyrillic alphabet was itself created from the Greek.

Walking from the embankment up Vladivostok's often steep, zigzagging streets we thought of a line from a poem by the Soviet poet Robert Rozhdestvensky, "Vladivostok is like a swing: up and down, up and down." The landscape turned our trips by taxi into something like free-range roller-coaster rides, made hairier by the right-hand-drive steering wheels and the imprecision they necessarily introduced when maneuvering in left-side traffic.

On the historic Svetlanskaya Street we encountered a range of tony shops and fancy restaurants and eateries serving everything from pizzas to Chinese food to Russian dumplings (and burbling hookahs) to Italian cafés to French cuisine and locally caught seafood. Here and there hung banners announcing "Open to the World for 130 Years"—highlighting Vladivostok's internationalist aspirations and ignoring its status as a "closed" city during most of the Soviet decades.

In fact, the buildings housing diverse private businesses betray Soviet-era origins, their owners having rented out premises in willy-nilly fashion, obligating customers to, for instance, pass through a drugstore to get to a dumpling eatery, or through a real estate firm's lobby to reach a café. Mementos, at times chilling, of the Soviet era did appear: on Aleutskaya Street, for instance, sat a hulking, four-story building with turretlike domes belonging to the city's branch of the Interior Ministry; it had once, naturally, sheltered Stalin's dreaded NKVD, the KGB's predecessor.

And on Ivanovskaya Street rises a memorial honoring border guards who perished in the line of duty: four guards (including a seaman), modeled in bronze and painted black, and dressed in uniforms from various eras of Russia's history, stand vigilant, a German shepherd at their side. The statue is recent, dating from the fiftieth anniversary of the end of the Great Patriotic War, and manifests Russia's concern for the future of this city and the Primorsky Krai (Maritime Region), of which it is the capital.

And yet, not far away, two other statues convey a different, independent and cordial message. In a nearby park, a monument to bard Vysotsky shows him sitting in a relaxed pose with his guitar, and in the very center next to the main post office, built at the turn of the last century in Neo-Russian style, stands another figure in bronze—of a woman in a Victorian dress who is hurrying to drop a letter into a mailbox. This is the American Eleanor Lord Pray, a native of South Berwick in Maine. Before the revolution, Pray spent more than three decades here with her American husband turned local businessman. Every day for years she composed letters to relatives in America and China; they now constitute a detailed, if unofficial, chronicle of life in Vladivostok. (Her *Letters from Vladivostok* were recently published by the University of Washington Press.) Here they call her their "first blogger."

Pray also sent her relatives pictures. Her texts and photographs show just how cosmopolitan this far-flung city was—more than anywhere in her native Maine, no doubt—with residents from Europe, China, Japan, and Korea living and working alongside Russians, Ukrainians, and indigenes. Vladivostok was, thus, a crossroads for a unique mixture of cultures from Europe, Asia, and even North America.

And that's not all. On the previously mentioned Aleutskaya Street lived the most important regional entrepreneur of the time,

Swiss-born Yuly (Jules) Briner, whose Far Eastern Shipping Company stood at the origins of Primorsky navigation. Yul Brynner, the future Oscar winner and star of *The King and I* and *The Ten Commandments*, was born here, in his grandfather's home. Near the family house now stands a stone monument to the actor; its caption reads, "Yul Brynner, the King of Theater." This seems fitting in such a city of inclusivity. Walking about, we encounter references, often uncanny, to other familiar places—Moscow in a train station, Kiev in a statue, San Francisco in a bridge, New York's Fleet Week in gunnery sergeants and naval officers ambling around town.

The takeaway: Vladivostok, like the rest of Russia, though less dramatically, suffers from a split-personality syndrome. It is both open to the world and fearful, as it lies so close to China, a country with a population more than ten times Russia's size.

One afternoon in our hotel's lobby, we met Andrei Ostrovsky, the regional editor of *Novaya Gazeta*. The thin, tall, energetic Ostrovsky had traveled much in the Russian Far East and in China. To escape the ever-present din from the Chinese and Korean guests, we retired to a secluded table near the elevators. We asked him about the Chinese presence in town.

"We have about 300,000 Chinese visitors a year here," he replied. "Most are tourists but some are investors, businessmen. Our Primorsky Krai has only six million people, but the province across the border has 100 million Chinese. We've had to make it illegal for them to enter Russia by car here, or our streets would be totally jammed."

"Do you feel threatened here by the Chinese?" we asked, as we had asked in Blagoveshchensk, another city on the doorsteps of Asia. He gave the same answer we heard there: "No, I do not feel the 'China threat' you hear so much about." He explained: "If the Chinese want something from us, they can just buy it. They hire Russians, which is good. The problem is they send their profits back to China, which doesn't help us. But there's no real xenophobia toward them. Our relations are all about doing business. The Chinese also come to study, too, at the Far Eastern University. We're trying to attract investment and have just begun issuing electronic visas to twenty countries, including China."

Tourism was also a major draw, he added, as "we have the most varied scenery in Russia. We have tigers, the Amur tigers! Plus killer whales off the coast." Moreover, young Russians in Vladivostok study Chinese and other Asian languages to improve their chances of finding work. "Most of us have been to Japan or Korea or China, and much less to Moscow. We're looking east; in fact, we're looking everywhere."

Surely the demographic trends of the region worried him, we insisted. But he denied this. "Look, the population in Primorsky Krai might be dropping, but Vladivostok's isn't. We have people arriving from all over the country. Historically, it was the risk-takers and entrepreneurial folk who came out here, and this is still true. They come to this special city of ours because they want to really *achieve* something. They are good for us and our economy."

One evening, as the sun fell, casting its orange light over Vladivostok's staggered cement warrens and the forested *sopki* beyond them, we took a taxi to the lookout point. (The funicular, for some reason, was not running.) The driver sped up and down the hills, but mostly up, until we reached the summit, with its view of the soaring, V-angled towers and taut cables of the Golden Bridge, teeming with traffic, over the Golden Horn Bay, busy with cutters and small chugging craft. In the time we had spent in town, no one had spoken to us about immigrating to Europe or the United States—a common topic of conversation elsewhere, including in Yakutsk, where we had just been.

Vysotsky's lyrics came to mind about "the open 'closed' port of

Vladivostok." As did words from the next line, meant to be ironic: "Paris is open, but I don't need to go there." (He was married to the French actress Marina Vlady, so Paris was not off limits to him, as it was to other Soviet citizens who were not allowed to travel abroad.) Presumably, though, if Russians here wanted to go anywhere, it was not just to Europe, but to Seoul, Beijing, or Tokyo.

The bard penned these words in Moscow decades ago. But they hold now, in this hospitable port city, on the other end of this vast country.

11

FROM THE GULAG CAPITAL TO THE VALLEY OF DEATH

TIME ZONE: MSK+8; UTC+11

People who think you can use terror are quite wrong. No, no, terror is useless, whatever its color—white, red or even brown! Terror completely paralyzes the nervous system.

—Mikhail Bulgakov, *Heart of a Dog*

Land of Bones and Ice

My friend has left for Magadan.
Take off your hat!
He left as a free man,
Not a convoyed prisoner.

Perhaps someone would say: Insane!
Why would he decide to leave behind everything, just like that?
There are only labor camps there,
With murderers and killers!

He would reply: Don't believe everything you hear.
There are no more of them than in Moscow.
And then he'd pack his suitcase,
And would go, to Magadan.[1]

Thus sang Vladimir Vysotsky, standing casually with his guitar on the shore of Nagayev Bay, on the frigid Sea of Okhotsk, which flows into the northernmost expanses of the Pacific Ocean. Actually, the bard died in 1980. His raspy recorded voice here came from a speaker hidden behind his weathered bronze statue erected in his honor in 2014. The recording plays twenty-four hours a day, seven days a week, all year, in memoriam both of Vysotsky, who visited here, and the millions of Gulag prisoners. For them this seascape was the last they would set eyes on before being marched to labor camps in the interior of the wild, bear-haunted province at our backs now called the Magadan Oblast, but historically, and so evocatively, known as Kolyma Krai. The Kolyma was the Stalin-era Soviet Union's terrestrial Hades, a deathly cold boreal realm populated by living shades, remnants of men and women being worked to death for political crimes more often imagined than real. Stalin's NKVD dispatched almost twenty million Soviet citizens to the Gulag, and the most unfortunate landed here, by boat, shipped around Russia's eastern coast from the railway line ending in Vladivostok, or from the White Sea through the Arctic Ocean to the Sea of Okhotsk.

We stood by the statue and turned to gaze back at the barren landscape of gray, rounded *sopki* dotted with dwarf pines and lichen-mottled stone overlooking freezing (even when not frozen) sea waters and a rocky shoreline. Vysotsky's posthumous electronic performance here was, we found, improbable and yet possible in today's Russia, striving, as it is, to bring together the divergent, often mutually contradictory elements of its past and present.

Vysotsky's song from the 1970s reflects Kolyma's Gulag history and that of Magadan, its capital, a city shot through with reminders of the inhumanity that long ruled these realms. A banner in the airport met us with what seemed a hideous, mocking greeting: "Welcome to Kolyma, the golden heart of Russia!"

Was this a joke? No, it referred to the gold mines abounding in the region. Yet strangely, just as Vysotsky sang—it is, indeed, the golden heart of Russia, the measure of man's endurance, kindness, and forgiveness, if that heart beats, as a Gulag-era song has it, in Kolyma, a "wondrous planet, with ten months of winter and all the rest of the year summer."

Riding back to our hotel, we passed a statue called *Vremya* (Time) depicting a woolly mammoth, brown with rust and covered with clocks. Once again, improbable and yet appropriate: here time absorbs all, from prehistoric animals, the relics of which are still found in the vicinity, to the remnants of labor camps that once dotted this vast northern *krai*.

Kolyma's history is tragic. Its main, and almost sole, thoroughfare was and remains the Kolyma *Trassa* (Route), running from Magadan north and then looping west to finish 1,300 miles later in Yakutsk. Historically synonymous with grief and unimaginable remoteness, it became something other than a dirt road only a decade ago, when parts of it were paved and others graveled over. (It is now officially known as the R504 Kolyma Highway.) Yet another Kolyma prison folk song—there are many—mourns the *krai*'s icebound isolation from the *materik* (mainland)—an isolation long so complete that one spoke of being *na Kolyme* (*on* Kolyma), as if on an island. Until recently, getting to Magadan by road from, say, Irkutsk, could take weeks. (Gulag prisoners, again, came by sea.) Ports at Nagayev and other local bays "welcomed" new arrivals during the brief summer months of navigation, when transport ships brought inmates in their hollow hulls, discharging them offshore at low tide. The exhausted, malnourished prisoners would stumble toward land in the chilly waters, with those who faltered washed out to sea by the hundreds.

The Soviet government established Magadan in 1929, in what may charitably, and without too much exaggeration, be described as the middle of nowhere. No permanent population dwelled along the seacoast here, and even indigenous reindeer herders were scarce. Yet Stalin's state was eager to exploit the precious metals and other natural resources his geographers had discovered inland. The dictator's crash industrialization program needed raw materials, and quickly. The gold and uranium mines of Kolyma provided many of them, and they passed through Magadan to be shipped west. The Soviet song *"Aviamarch"* once declared, "We were born to make our dream a reality," and it was Stalin's dream to turn the Soviet Union into a superpower. There were other cruel yet lucrative endeavors of this sort, from the White Sea–Baltic Canal to the Baikal–Amur Railroad (BAM); these were also projects carried out at great cost in human lives. Yet ultimately, they all had limited practical use. They only brought short-term dividends—they enhanced Stalin's industrialization program—but were not economically viable until redesigned decades later.

In the early 1930s, Stalin sent Gulag prisoners, many from SLON on Solovki, to build the White Sea–Baltic Canal. To impress the dictator, construction was hurried to finish ahead of schedule. (Recall the Nizhne-Bureysk hydroelectric plant that failed before Putin's visit, and ours, to Blagoveshchensk.) Builders dug the channel too shallow, thereby limiting its use. Though dating from the late 1920s, the Kolyma Route connecting Yakutsk and Magadan became a viable, year-round highway only during the Putin years. BAM began as a forced labor enterprise in the 1930s, but, under Brezhnev decades later, morphed into a volunteer "youth" construction project. It took decades more to make it actually work.

The Kolyma region subsists off gold mining—it is the third largest supplier of the precious metal in the world, in fact. On its 287,500 square miles dwell only 140,000 people. Still, 40 percent of its budget comes from Moscow—a bizarre arrangement for such a rich place. In Russia, regional prosperity often depends on the oblast governor, and Vladimir Pecheny, the man in charge until 2018, was not particularly entrepreneurial or honest, at least according to locals with whom we spoke. They envy Chukotka, the oblast to the north that once belonged to Magadan's zone of authority but is now autonomous. Chukotka was the domain of the oligarch Roman Abramovich, its former governor and the current owner of the British Chelsea soccer club. Abramovich, according to the envious locals, "brought it into the twenty-first century by finding gas, improving infrastructure, and making their salaries one of the highest in Russia."

Magadan, as yet another prison song goes, is simply "cursed" by the millions of convicts passing through its "inhumane heart." In 1929, before the Gulag mentality firmly took hold in the Soviet Union, the newly established settlement welcomed contractors. Most were demobilized soldiers from the Red Special Far Eastern Army, and they would dig for gold and build roads and other infrastructure for the state. But the rough conditions in these northern lands—Chukotka and Magadan, bordering Sakha to the east—ultimately proved too trying for these hardened military men. Even the high salaries they earned were not sufficient to motivate them to toil in the region's inhospitable climate. In fact, the aboriginal tribes of Chukchis and Evenks, along with the rare exile, barely survived the climate, in which winter temperatures drop to −80 Fahrenheit.

Then change came. In the early 1930s *Dalstroi*, a Soviet bureaucratic abbreviation for the Far-Eastern Construction Directorate, decided to employ *zeki* (inmates) to develop gold mines and build roads. But the brutal conditions killed most of those imported—both *zeki* and their guards—during the first years. The first thousand workers failed to turn *Dalstroi* into a workable enterprise. That would necessitate the mass import of prison labor. Thus were born *Berlag* (Coastal Labor Camp) and *Sevostlag* (Northeastern Labor Camp), as the networks of forced-labor facilities in the region were known. The Solovetsky camps on the White Sea provided for excellent models to replicate.

Benefiting mightily from the Great Purges, Magadan in 1939 officially acquired the status of a city. The locals grimly joke that the sham judicial proceedings leading to the detainment and imprisonment of millions were carried out to populate Magadan and man the resource-extraction industries it served. Of the almost two million arrested in 1937–1938,[2] according to the human rights organization Memorial, many would be shipped to Kolyma. Forced labor fully replaced the paid workers.

Yevgenia Ginzburg, author of the critically acclaimed and heartbreaking dissident memoir *Journey into the Whirlwind*, published abroad in 1967 and censored by the Soviets until the era of Gorbachev, described her years as a victim of the purges in Kolyma Krai. She survived her ordeal to write a book that became the manual for understanding the Gulag experience for decades to come.

Ginzburg described the detention camps as ghastly, cruel institutions and explained the labor camp system as a product of policy, politics, and the mentality of the ruling regime, which set about persecuting entire segments of the population; executing potential opponents; and, most of all, exploiting them as forced labor. (Nina as a child knew Ginzburg and considered her a woman of extraordinary spirit.) Despite all the horrors she had experienced, Ginzburg continued to believe in the bright communist future officially proclaimed as inevitable. More than anything, though, she believed in the fundamental goodness of humanity—an astonishing paradox, common to many former Gulag prisoners. The leaders may betray them, they thought, but not the ideal of the communist brotherhood on earth.

The message, indicative of Russia's split-personality syndrome: one-half of the population was imprisoned, the other half guarding it. One would imagine the rancor of those years between prisoner and the imprisoned would survive in some fashion here. Yet despite the Gulag heritage, or maybe because of it, we found people in Magadan to be helpful and disarmingly openhearted. Vysotsky sang that there were no fewer "murderers and killers" in Magadan than in Moscow. Walking around town, we began to understand what he meant.

A city mostly constructed during Soviet times, it fit the purposes it was built for. Edifices in the center, as if defying the wild, and desolate *sopki* to the west rose grandly in Classical Stalinist style; sweeping, broad avenues bore the names of Lenin and Karl Marx, and spires topped with red stars stood against a boundless azure sky. The Cathedral of the Holy Trinity, its white walls rising towerlike to finish in gilt onion domes, replaced the never-completed House of Soviets, which was torn down in 1985. The house of worship faces a hulking, Soviet-era structure that once housed the *Dalstroi* administration, with a statue of the Siberian missionary Saint Innokenty standing between the two. By a twist of post-Soviet irony, Magadan's statue of the fiercely atheistic Lenin used to occupy the spot, but authorities have moved it to Cosmonaut Square, which today is dull, dirty, and invaded by pigeons, occupied by a huge hexagonal apartment building reminiscent of, well, the Pentagon—with, of course, an additional side. Cafés are a rarity in Magadan, yet bakeries offer a variety of buns and pierogies to rival those on offer in hospitable Perm. After a few days in town, we concluded the people were the most genuine we have ever encountered. No matter what the past, in such wild Siberian realms, at the edge of a thrashing cold sea, human kindness thrived. Few Russians from outside the region visit to discover this.

An eight-hour flight east from Moscow (almost the same amount of time it takes to fly to New York from the Russian capital), Magadan sits at the edge of Russia, just as it long represented the limits of human suffering, of almost unimaginable misery and pain. We arrived aiming to travel by vehicle the way Ginzburg once was forced to tread on foot the Kolyma *Trassa*. She did her time at the Elgen and Ust-Tuskan camps 600 miles north of Magadan; we, however, wanted to visit Butugychag, a uranium mine once manned by Gulag inmates about 160 miles to the north of the city, one of the sources of the radioactive mineral used in the first Soviet atomic bomb.

In the late 1930s, Magadan functioned as the chief distribution center for the region's 250 labor camps,[3] dispatching prisoners into the interior to log and build roads and to dig for gold and other precious minerals, including uranium. The "lucky" ones—including Ginzburg's fellow inmates—did their "light" time cutting firewood for the Tuscan Food Processing Plant.

Almost wherever one looks, one's eyes fall on edifices that once sheltered the bureaucracy required to keep the camps staffed with their half-dead inmates. Yet, strangely, locals told us, "Nobody here is interested in the past." This was an astonishing statement, considering that the past in Magadan intrudes so starkly on the present. It stands embodied in, say, the half-ruined sorting facilities of *Dalstroi*, overgrown with high grass and fireweed plants. *Dalstroi*'s barracks are now nothing more than carcasses of stone and rotting wood. The barracks' windows, their panes of glass long since broken or looted, peer down like sightless eyes on the town through rusting skeins of barbwire running over the crumbled remnants of the surrounding fences. One part of the facility has been maintained; it is dilapidated but still used for a police headquarters. Why let what's left of the Gulag go to waste?

We set out into town on foot, listening to the mournful cries of seagulls, inhaling the briny maritime air. Despite the center's grand architecture, we found the sidewalks and pavestones chopped up, a legacy of the brutal winters and poor urban management. Rising above us, and visible from almost everywhere in town, was the imposing, fifty-foot-high Mask of Sorrow, a lead-gray concrete bust with one eye shedding tears that are themselves configured as faces shedding tears, the other eye nothing more than an empty socket, which, with a platform beneath it, serves as a lookout post for visitors. This magnum opus of grief is the progeny of the artist Ernst Neizvestny and was commissioned in 1996 when Yeltsin was eager to put to rest Stalin's murderous legacy. Each step on the way up to the monument's plinth bears the name of a labor camp, chiseled in stone. Atop the monument, a red lamp flickers in memory of those who perished here.

How could Magadan escape such a tragic past?

We spoke about this with Andrei Grishin, a twenty-eight-year-old local journalist. One of the few social activists in town and a supporter of Alexey Navalny, Russia's main opposition figure, Grishin found himself fired from his newspaper, *Vecherny Magadan* (Evening Magadan) for criticizing Russia's bellicose foreign policy. Pale, bespectacled, and wearing a ponytail, Grishin typifies the image of a Russian *intelligent*, a member of the intelligentsia.

Grishin spoke eloquently about what he called the "soft despotism of Putinism, when people are silent because they fear losing the little comfort they have—useful connections severed, a trip abroad blocked." Magadan, he said, lives in apathy, in a state of "arrested development." Most people here live "a postponed life," in expectation that another, more comfortable and rewarding existence awaits them elsewhere in Russia, which absolves them from concerning themselves with improving the here and now in Magadan.

What Grishin was describing was, in fact, an originally Soviet phenomenon. (He was clearly too young to have understood this.) When the state's victories—in the Great Patriotic War, in "building communism," in eliminating illiteracy or bringing electricity to the hinterland—no longer satisfied Soviet citizens, the desire for emigration to the West became overwhelming, especially in the late Brezhnev years. For most, daily life was a dull grind, even if the social safety net provided people with a material security that gave them the leisure to dream of something better. Russians, for most of their history, have wanted to move elsewhere and begin anew— Muscovites to Europe and America, the people in Omsk to Yekaterinburg or Saint Petersburg, those in the west of the country to the freer Siberian outback or cosmopolitan Vladivostok. Better economic opportunities draw them, of course, but there is more to it than that. In a country where the state's victories have taken precedence over individual prosperity and happiness, Russians have found themselves ill prepared to lead a life restricted to the pleasures of the present—say, enjoying a cappuccino. They have sought grandeur on the world stage, which has let the Kremlin use them for its own agendas.

"There is always a feeling that life would be better and have more meaning elsewhere," Grishin said. "This 'postponed life' comes from living in the shadow of the Gulag, from the constant state oppression. And yet the Gulag doesn't interest us anymore. The labor camps, the cemetery—they're all here, yes, but you can't dwell in the past all the time," he insisted. Everyone needs a present, a future.

One cannot, in other words, endlessly pity Ginzburg, who along with thousands of others, tread the Kolyma Route hundreds of miles toward her destination, he said.

Early in the clear morning of the day after we spoke with Grishin, we met Yevgeny Radchenko, our other local contact and a renowned Kolyma guide. According to him, *Ivan-chai*, or fireweeds (purple-petaled long-stemmed wildflowers that bloom during the region's brief summers) commemorate Stalin's victims, popping up in fields after fires have struck or bombs have fallen—in the wake of tragedy, in other words. From a Ukrainian family, fit and in his early thirties, with lively eyes and an auburn crew cut, Radchenko explained that fireweeds were both "flowers of misery and of resilience; a perfect metaphor for a country of death camps. Organic matter is what makes *Ivan-chai* grow; from all the people who died of hunger and hardship, marching on the road in convoys for weeks, for months, make fireweed grow into endless fields." He told us this as we were setting off along the Kolyma Route to visit Butugychag. Even now, the site is radioactive, so visits, if undertaken at all, must be brief.

As do most camps, Butugychag sits well off the road, on a dirt track long since largely returned to nature. To get there, we needed both a knowledgeable guide and an experienced driver. For the latter, we chose another Yevgeny, Yevgeny Viktorovich—Viktorovich was his patronymic, which we use here in lieu of his last name, which we never learned—a middle-age fellow with a tousle of white hair and a pair of translucent blue eyes. Yevgeny Viktorovich manned a sturdy yellow UAZ, a four-wheel drive vehicle originally produced in Soviet times for military use. Its independent suspension obligated Yevgeny to reach deep under the steering wheel to change gears. Yet the UAZ, we learned, could put Jeeps to shame and overcome almost any terrain.

When we reached for our seat belts, both Yevgenys looked at us with an air of contempt, as if to say, "Such wusses!"

And so we drove into the wilds of Kolyma, talking about the endless fields of *Ivan-chai* sweeping away from the road toward the *sopki* and labor camps, all the while listening to the life stories of our two Yevgenys.

Radchenko, in jeans and a khaki bush jacket—adept at playing up his Siberian he-man persona for foreigners—formerly worked as a distributor of technological gear. He has turned local historian. For somebody who takes visitors to Gulag camps, his lineage is surprisingly pro-Gulag and based in the military. Radchenko's grandmother came to Magadan to work as a naval code breaker during the war, earning a salary of seven hundred rubles—a fortune in the Soviet Union at the time, much more than the then-excellent salary of two hundred rubles in Moscow. His Ukrainian grandfather drifted north to work as a labor camp guard for even more money. After the camps closed, they stayed on. Raised in Magadan, Yevgeny decided to turn Kolyma into his profession.

Does he feel remorse for what his family did? we asked.

Not in the slightest.

"They just tried to get by in the country they lived in," he said, shrugging his shoulders. "If the leaders could be cruel, why couldn't others? They were just doing the job the state assigned to them. Do you feel remorseful?" he asked Nina.

Khrushchev was, after all, a Soviet leader. Even if he denounced Stalin, he did issue orders for mass repression in the earlier part of his career.

"I do," Nina admitted. "In fact, I'm in the habit of apologizing for the Soviet injustices, especially for those during my great-grandfather's rule."

Radchenko seemed rather keen on the Soviet state, though he lamented its "excesses." As he put it, "Well, people used to come here, workers, intelligentsia, as in Vysotsky's song, and they used to contribute to the country's might."

As did so many in Russia, he thought that Stalin had no other choice but to use forced labor to industrialize the Soviet Union, which Western powers hoped would fail. He did feel bad, though, for those who perished, for those who were made to work in inhumane conditions.

For one of Ukrainian heritage, Radchenko proved rather anti-Ukrainian. His family hailed from Ukraine's Russian-speaking, largely ethnic Russian east, and he complained that West Ukrainians took poorly to compatriots who felt more Russian than Ukrainian. Of course, Western Ukrainians accordingly disparage Russian domination in the east.

Some hours after leaving Magadan, we turned east off the Kolyma Route and picked up the Tenka *Trassa*—or Tenka in local speak—another highway that despite decades of road construction in the region remains a broad gravel road, with no markers or traffic lights. Occasionally, though, signs appear, reminding drivers to "follow the rules" and threatening them with fines. What rules? we thought. We were rolling along a dirt road in the middle of nowhere.

Radchenko explained: "Our government is great at making people guilty of its own shortcomings." He was once stopped for speeding by police hiding in the roadside bushes. When he argued that the *Trassa* has no signs and he would have followed the rules if the road were marked, he was fined double.

Mostly alone on the road, at times we caught up with giant orange oil tankers, construction rigs, and then a pair of trucks belonging to the Siberian wine company *Krasnoe i Beloe* (Red and White). Enveloped in a cloud of dust, we lumbered along behind it. It took all Yevgeny Viktorovich's skill at the wheel to pass them without provoking an accident. Truckers on such Siberian roads pay little heed to passenger vehicles.

After hours of ascending low mountains strangely reminiscent of the Italian Apennines—the Kolyma Upland, as the *sopki* around us were known—we stopped to stretch our legs. Before us spread a stunning green mountainscape pitted with the gray patches indicating uranium deposits. Yet at the bottom of an abyss opening up at the roadside lay the mangled steel of a yellow truck once used to transport gold from mines.

"Ukrainian," Radchenko said with a shrug.

"How do you know?"

"Only they drive on these difficult roads with no regard for others. They don't understand the locals' respect for each other. Those from the *materik* (mainland) can't comprehend that when you live in such harsh conditions, with such horrible roads, you have to be considerate of everyone. But they drive like maniacs, as if on an autobahn!"

Despite the Russian annexation of Crimea, he added, a lot of Ukrainians were still signing up for lucrative jobs in Kolyma's gold mines. They get along well with the Russians during the workday, but fights break out between the two groups in the evenings. The Russians, of course, are victorious in Radchenko's account, and he was annoyed that Ukrainians came and took Russian jobs. (In Russia, Ukrainians are known to be excellent workers, generally, while Russians, who could be, often are not.) As the "superior race," at least within the former Russian empire, the latter tend to be more careless than those born without such status.

Radchenko's political convictions were complex and confusing. He was for *Krym nash* ("Crimea is ours") and a strong Russia. But he had become disillusioned with Putin, and now supported Alexey Navalny, who built his reputation on exposing corruption. Some of his views coincided with those described by Grishin, as the belief in the passion of Kolyma residents for getting out of here to go on vacation.

"In our cold climate most people's major concern is to get out of Siberia, even for a short while. There's a lot of apathy about local problems. Here if they hold rallies against corruption, only a hundred people show up. Until your own roof collapses on you, people won't do anything." Collective concerns, in other words, hardly motivated people.

Perhaps such apathy leads Russian patriots to pardon the Gulag. After all, Stalin created it to "make the nation great"—*les rubyat, shchepki letyat* (chop down a forest and wood chips will fly). Navalny is a popular politician, however, Radchenko explained. Putin is the state leader—far away, unapproachable, with support in Kolyma running at 56 percent, the lowest score in the Far East.[4] Pecheny, as the governor, couldn't deliver acceptable polling numbers for his boss in Moscow and so retired early, in May 2018, to avoid being ousted by the Kremlin. (His replacement, Sergei Nosov, is a Siberian local.) People in Magadan expect little from the new governor, but Pecheny, they said, was the worst. He didn't have a reputation for caring about his electorate, which allowed Navalny to open his regional headquarters here ("a great coup," in Radchenko's words). People looked to Navalny to improve their quality of living, and to put Magadan on the map, and not just the Gulag map. "If Alexey," said Radchenko using the opposition leader's first name, "makes it further up the political ladder, many in Magadan will turn to him."

According to our guide, Navalny's appeal is that he appears to be as pro-state and Russian-nationalist as Putin—before his anticorruption crusade Navalny popularized the slogan "Russia for the Russians," insisting on the primacy of the Russian nationals—but he appears to be less vain.[5] Although some in Magadan appreciate Putin's affection for Siberia—he often spends his vacation in its wilderness—for most, he has discredited himself with, as they see it, "a fake show-off tough man persona," rarely venturing as far east as Kolyma. Putin last visited here in 2011.

Regardless of Navalny, Radchenko told us that he has thought about leaving "for Irkutsk, perhaps, to tour those gorgeous places around Baikal—with shamans, old churches, and Siberian beauty."

Though Butugychag lies only some 160 miles from Magadan, making it there in one day can be trying. It is better, Radchenko insisted, to drive to the settlement of Ust-Omchug (with a stop for provisions in Palatka) to spend the night, and travel to the labor camp in the morning. Palatka and Ust-Omchug would seem to have nothing in common. Both places, however, could serve as real-life metaphors for Putin's Russia. Their patriotic facades plaster over a deep despair.

Just forty miles out of long-suffering Magadan, Palatka is a town of some 4,200 souls founded in 1932 as an outpost to support prospectors operating in the area, and itself was once a home to three labor camps. The name Palatka would translate from Russian as "tent," as in enthusiastic communist youth camping, but in fact derives from an Evenk-Yugar toponym (*palya-atkan*) meaning "rocky," in reference to the adjacent river. Palatka, in any case, appeared to have sprung from the pages of Nikolai Nosov's didactic *Neznaika* (Dunno), a 1950s children's book about Soviet Smurfs describing the childish inhabitants of Flower City—Palatka, as we saw it—which now is interpreted as a metaphor for paradise, the "bright future" the authorities ceaselessly told Soviet citizens they were working toward.

Palatka's buildings of yellow, blue, or red; its flower-shaped street lamps; and its new white miniature church with shiny gilt cupolas all seem to have sprung straight from *Neznaika*'s pages. We turned off the road and parked by a grocery store on the main square. (Radchenko had warned us we should buy provisions there, as there were no restaurants in Ust-Omchug.) At the store's entrance a cornucopia of ice cream, modeled after those kinds beloved during Soviet times—*plombir, eskimo*—caught our eye. Russians take pride in their love of cold treats all year around, but here in this permafrost climate with barely a few summer months, the homage to ice cream seemed more a tribute to the tough Siberian character than to the sweets themselves.

The square featured a collage of slogans heralding the Russian government's program incentivizing eastward migration and inviting newcomers to Siberia to become landowners (we saw this in Blagoveshchensk and Yakutsk as well), a portrait of Putin, and a red hammer-and-sickle monument. A tank that supposedly participated in the annexation of Crimea serves as the main attraction of this serene *Neznaika* village, imported, as far as we could tell, to stir up patriotism and pride in Russia's might—most of all, the might welling up out of Siberia, the country's largest landmass.

Low clouds rolled in. Six hours after departing Magadan, we reached Ust-Omchug, a settlement of some four thousand people centered around an ore-processing plant and a logging company. We could be forgiven for mistaking Ust-Omchug for a vision of the apocalypse.

Ust-Omchug's Lenin statue, next to a yellow wooden hut operating as a church, stood covered in pigeon droppings likely dating back to 1991. Trees surrounding the bronze revolutionary were so overgrown that they threatened to subsume the statue. A block away from Lenin, stray dogs rummaged through piles of garbage at a dumpsite untended for months. Right next to the refuse was a playground where pregnant women watched over their toddlers digging in the gray, dusty earth. In the only real food store, we found a line of already tipsy men and women buying alcohol for the night. The middle-age fire marshal and policeman—we divined their professions from their uniforms—staggered in, bent on buying more booze to pass the brief night ahead.

"It's a ghost town after eight in the evening here," Radchenko explained. "When the alcohol shop closes, so does the town."

Small, formerly industrial towns rarely flourish anywhere, but in centralized Russia, even if a place like Ust-Omchug produces wealth (as it does, subsisting off gold mining), Moscow syphons away most of it. Larger cities are allowed to keep something for themselves, but as we saw in Omsk and Novosibirsk, a lot depends on the governor's will to resist the center's demand for revenue. For example, the former governor of Magadan Oblast, Ukraine-born Pecheny, moved to Siberia to advance his career and so owed no apparent loyalty to the people he was supposed to serve. Moreover, those who complained publicly about the subpar quality of services his government provided and attributed it to the embezzlement of state resources were charged with defamation.[6]

Stocked up on bread, sausage, and bottled water for the night, we drove onto the crunching gravel of an unpaved road—only the Kolyma *Trassa* had asphalt—to the local "hotel," a renovated second floor in a derelict five-story apartment building of soot-streaked cement. The hotel had no name but announced itself with a sign reading HOTEL.

We were, it turned out, the only guests. We flung open the spring-equipped door and climbed the dark crumbling stairway to reception.

"No electricity," said the friendly woman administrator with a sigh.

"Why?" we asked.

"It happens."

"Often?"

"Once in a while," she answered evasively. Best not to go into detail here with outsiders.

We settled into our rooms—which were perfectly serviceable, white-walled and clean, with windows opening onto a vista of cement hovels and gray barren lots strewn with trash, and sweeping away from beyond all this, under a sky of low leaden clouds, the rocky, possibly irradiated slopes of *sopki*. The sense of being lost in the middle of Armageddon was difficult to shake.

Ust-Omchug does have one remarkable feature—a museum substantially dedicated to the Gulag. It owes its existence to Inna Gribanova, a local geologist who lost her job under Yeltsin and found herself reduced to doing janitorial work. Soon after, though, she found a discarded pile of Gulag-related papers in the town's administration office and launched into what would become her life's quest—documenting the labor camps of the Magadan Oblast and particularly of the Tenka region (where Ust-Omchug is located) for the Regional History Museum. It occupies three rooms in a onetime school building and presents the history of the Butugychag camp.

We piled into Radchenko's vehicle for a bumpy ride over potholed dirt roads to the museum. Once inside, we headed for the Gulag section. There we examined rusted buckets and saws, tangled skeins of barbwire, ruined rails from railway lines, and other detritus from the mines, plus yellowed maps, photographs, and books about the most dreaded of all camps, Butugychag. When Russian settlers arrived in the area in the nineteenth century, they discovered *sopki* slopes littered with both the bones and skulls of reindeer and of members of the region's few local people. Uranium- and tin-enriched lands exercised a malignant influence on both man and beast, often leading the living to early deaths. Those locals had branded the area "the valley of death," a name later appropriated by camp inmates. The actual mining of uranium was a deadly occupation, finishing off the laborers assigned to it within a month.

Radchenko explained that in the 1990s, the Butugychag camp itself, like Perm-36, was supposed to become a museum, but authorities scrapped plans for this in the 2000s because of its radioactivity. At least that was the reason the Kremlin advanced. Really, our guide suggested, it just wanted the mine to disappear. With each passing year, the road there becomes less passable as the weather leaves its marks and vegetation encroaches. Likely access to the site will be lost to nature within a decade; the authorities wouldn't need to forbid it. A visit now seemed even more imperative.

The next morning, which broke cloudy and cool, we boarded the UAZ and drove northwest out of Ust-Omchug along the rough gravel Tenka *Trassa*. Hoping to gauge our driver's fitness for what we understood to be a rough journey, we queried Yevgeny Viktorovich and learned his story. He told us that he hailed from the southern town of Krasnoyarsk, just east of Crimea. He often drove this UAZ across Russia, although he owns other—foreign—vehicles.

"Why?" we asked.

"In every village along the way you can get spare parts, even if they are no longer made."

His story hinted at the two Russias we had been seeing on our travels. One, urban, with foreign cars overwhelming the roads of cities. The second, rural, with villages still surviving off the vehicular legacy of the Soviet Union. The Stalin military industrial complex originally manufactured the UAZ, and it and other Soviet-era cars— *Volgas, Zhigulis*—still serve their owners well across the outback of the former Soviet Union.

Thirty-five miles and two hours later, we suddenly veered right and picked up a pair of tire ruts leading to a rocky creek bed through a brushy forest of stunted firs—the track to the mine. Yevgeny Viktorovich, manning the UAZ's two gearshifts, yanked the nobs and switched repeatedly, wrestling with the wheel as we lurched about in the cabin (saved from damaging bruises only by interior handles), water splashing over the windshield, the engine roaring.

"One time we tried to come here with a Jeep," Yevgeny Viktorovich shouted over the crashing and banging. "Afterward it needed major repairs. Its bottom was demolished by the creek's rocks. With this UAZ, I just wash it after the trip and it's ready to go again."

After two hours we had covered only about nine hundred yards—as far as we could go. We lurched up out of the creek bed and onto the bank of the Detrin River, reduced to a trickle by the arid summer months. A black-and-yellow sign warned visitors that they would enter this zone of increased radiation at their own risk. Across from us stood the ruined stone walls of the uranium enrichment plant and just to the south of it, yellow mounds of uranium ore, far too radioactive to approach. Beyond, under a low overcast sky, rose leaden hills bearing only a mangy covering of vegetation. Aside from the trickling of the Detrin's clear waters, we heard nothing but perceived an eerie silence, interrupted only occasionally by the piercing, plaintive screams of airborne eagles.

Arming ourselves with walking sticks fashioned out of branches from alder trees, and now and then whistling loud (to scare bears away; we also carried sound grenades), we set off along the Detrin riverbed, which was, mostly, a rugged channel of rocks. Now and then collapsed wooden shacks appeared above the river.

"Just small administrative offices," Radchenko said. "The mine and prison and living quarters are up ahead of us."

Two hours later, after climbing a steep rocky trail between low alder groves, we came within sight of motley brick walls—the bricks were in fact stones dragged here by the prisoners themselves—invaded by scrawny larches. Elsewhere in Siberia the larch is known as the "queen of trees" for its majesty and height, but here it is stunted, the size of a Christmas tree. The ground of this small plateau presented a soft-hued crazy quilt of grays, reds, and yellows, hinting at the subterranean presence of uranium, tin, and gold. Far above, atop a hill, loomed a black cave—the entrance to the mine itself.

We stepped over tangles of barbed wired and peeked into the

glassless prison windows, between cast-iron bars, to see the wooden shards and latticework of bunks scattered across a common cell. A bit further on, there were the remnants of a library and a scattering of discarded prison shoes, some surprisingly well preserved, some with little remaining save for soles and nails, all weathered into varying shades of sooty gray. Some soles had apertures in the heel—hiding places for matches, coins, or razors.

After the 1993 opening of the Holocaust Museum in Washington, D.C., it became a tradition to display shoes once worn by camp inmates as memorial vestiges of their torment. But here in Butugychag, the same draws few spectators. They do keep alive the memory of the Gulag, but for whom? Almost no one comes to visit, to witness. Even Radchenko guides people here only two or three times a year. What interest there was in the camp is fading.

We looked about us. It is not an exaggeration to say that it did seem that the inmates' souls were trapped here—in these cold stone ruins, within, even, these shoes, in the crannies of their soles, so haplessly strewn over patches of grass and bare rocks. Souls and shoes.

Much else of camp life remained up here: metal ovens, truck tires, a rusted bedpan, a kettle, an aluminum mug. Each rail from the narrow-gauge railway, *uzkokoleika*, that used to carry ore up and down the mountain, was engraved with the words "*Zavod Imeni I.V. Stalina*" (the J. V. Stalin Factory). None here was ever to forget for whom they toiled—to the death.

The next day, riding back to Magadan's airport, we encountered the image of another leader whose presence is constantly felt everywhere in Russia—Vladimir Putin. From a billboard towering over the once deadly Kolyma Route, dressed in khaki fatigues and a naval cap, he wished us, said the caption, "a good trip."

12

PETROPAVLOVSK-KAMCHATSKY

··

THE VERY FAR EAST

TIME ZONE: MSK+9; UTC+12

Before you make fun of children who believe in Santa Claus,
please remember that there are people who believe that the president and the government take care of them.
——A contemporary Russian joke

From the air, the Kamchatka Peninsula, strewn with erupting
geysers and snow-streaked volcanoes, riven by crystalline rivers,
and stalked by bulky brown bears, resembles a lost world, or perhaps
our world at a prehistoric, certainly prehuman, stage. No roads connect the peninsula to continental Russia; there is also no logging, no
pollution. Across its hundred thousand square miles live only 375,000
people, and most of those in a few scattered towns.

Arriving in August in its capital, Petropavlovsk-Kamchatsky, one
steps off the plane onto a runway abutted by a small functional hangar
and feels the sun warm on one's cheeks——an unexpected sensation
given that the city almost shares a latitude with Seattle, across the
Pacific, some 3,300 miles to the east. Alaska is only 1,800 miles
away——Sarah Palin, once the state's governor and the 2008 vice-
presidential nominee, memorably saw Russia from her backyard.

The arc of the Aleutian Islands, divided between Russia and the United States, reaches even closer.

Petropavlovsk-Kamchatsky sits at the edge of Avacha Bay, just beneath the towering Koryaksky Volcano. Koryaksky imposes an atmosphere of precariousness on the town, as if a couple of tectonic jolts from the stony behemoth might, one day, dislodge the city and send it slipping into the sea. The region is in fact seismically active, with the most devastating earthquake in modern times having struck in 1952; it registered nine on the Richter Scale and caused a fifty-foot-high tsunami that killed as many as fifteen thousand people and reached as far away as New Zealand.

The Russians inhabiting this remote territory are in both the literal and figurative senses frontiersmen and women, dwelling in a border region and, also, often wresting their livelihood from its wilderness. Most famous of these are the fishermen, who risk life and limb to haul in the millions of tons of seafood that ends up on dinner plates across Russia and abroad—in Japan, Korea, and the United States.

As many around the world know from the Discovery Channel reality show *Deadliest Catch*, the commercial fishing industry is not for the weakhearted. Each year, it places thousands of workers at the mercy of the most hostile, wave-roiled seas on the planet, and job lists consistently rank commercial fishing as among the most perilous livelihoods. (The U.S. Bureau of Labor Statistics has documented that the industry's fatality rate is three times higher than that of the other most dangerous professions.) *Deadliest Catch* follows American fishermen laboring on the Bering Sea off the Alaskan coast. On the Kamchatka Peninsula their Russian counterparts do the same work but with less advanced technology and equipment, and with inferior insurance. All this they suffer to bring in their catches of king crab and, the most prized of all, the salmon that produces red caviar. Fully a third of the world's Pacific salmon spawn in Kamchatka's pristine streams. This luxury product has made Russia famous throughout the world, but the fishermen themselves say the fish eggs are not worth the dangers they undergo to harvest them.

Before arriving in Petropavlovsk-Kamchatsky, we spoke in Moscow to one of these fishermen, Vladimir, a tall, tough, muscle-bound Kamchatka seafarer in his late thirties with a Popeye-like build and hands as rough as tree bark. (Local fishermen were out at sea during our visit; they pursue salmon mostly during the summer months, as the fish approach the peninsula to spawn.) Vladimir, who seemed to possess a propensity for colorful language, struggled to hide it in a woman's company when he talked, which provided for some funny pauses and stumbles in the most unexpected moments. His face, reddened and chafed, had suffered the ravages inflicted by years of outdoor work in cold maritime winds. He had recently changed his profession and place of residence, having decamped to Crimea to cultivate apples and cherries in the region's famed orchards, which Chekhov celebrated in his play *The Cherry Orchard*.

We asked Vladimir why he left Kamchatka.

"I'm sick of caviar," he replied. "It's hard to get, and to me it tastes like salty red fire in your mouth. Sometimes we would get so much of it that my wife used it as garden fertilizer. Yet for everyone else it was hugely expensive."

Vladimir told us that he had long served as a crew member aboard huge trawlers, often disused craft ready for the junkyard, but bought from Norway or Japan at cut-rate prices, and not always sailing under Russian flags. The captains often, in years past at least, violated the law, heading out into international waters to fish for king crab and salmon; operating in other protected zones or during months when fishing was illegal; or, worst of all, in dangerous weather.

"We surely have an incentive to take risks, earning up to $150,000 a year," Vladimir explained. In doing so, boat owners kept their activities secret from the port authorities and tended to ignore regulations meant to ensure the safety of their crews. The Federal Fishing Agency now administers the business, so illegal fishing, he said, has diminished. Nevertheless, "things in the trade were as chaotic as the Wild West capitalism we had in Russia in the 1990s," when rules were few, profits high.

He was already tiring of practicing his profession in such punishing conditions when the capsizing, in 2015, of a trawler took sixty lives and convinced him that he needed to move on with his life. He and his wife moved to Crimea, a "gift from our great president . . . a dream, really."

The dream had faded since then, though, Vladimir admitted, and so had his admiration for the president, who failed to deliver on promises of the bucolic life described by Chekhov. The Russian government called on Russians to settle the Far East and launched a similar campaign to revive the cultivation of apples, pears, and cherries in Crimea on the Black Sea. Ten-foot-tall apple trees had been left unattended for decades, reflecting the ruinous legacy of Soviet collective agriculture. But with lands now handed over to new Russian owners, the Russian authorities plan to restore to glory the Crimean apples—an uncommonly tasty variety.

"Yet the five-year subsidies," Vladimir complained, "are not enough." The old trees had been neglected for too long—"by the Ukrainians," he added resentfully—to render decent crops, and the new ones they planted on their eight-acre lots would take a few years before they were ready for harvesting. At the moment, he said, the orchard hardly produced anything. Their second crop, gathered in 2017, was meager owing to frosts and summer hail. Whatever they grew, fortunately, a local cooperative bought, and at prices "higher than those for foreign-grown bananas. . . . For now, the sanctions from the West and Russian countersanctions, when we no longer buy Polish apples, have helped local farmers sell on the Russian market, but subsidies they receive will soon be discontinued. And if the weather is poor again, we will not be able to survive." He chuckled. "The tough job of fishing still leaves you more in control of your fortune."

All the uncertainty involved with agriculture has taken its toll on Vladimir, and since our talk he had signed up as a fisherman on a trawler in the Black Sea.

Beside the fishing industry, Petropavlovsk-Kamchatsky hosts the military port where Russia's Pacific fleet is moored. It is also, at least theoretically, a tourist town, a place from which aficionados of rugged outdoor sports embark on adventures into the pristine wilds. We, however, would remain within its urban confines, so we set out to walk, always finding the soft azure waters of the bay within view and the maritime breeze refreshing and welcome given the heat of the summer day.

Petropavlovsk-Kamchatsky is young for a Russian city, having been founded as the settlement of Petropavlovsk by Vitus Bering (a Dane on a mission for the czar, after whom the strait and sea separating the United States and Russia were named) in 1740, and receiving the status of city seventy-two years after that. Backset on three sides by green *sopki*, with a concave seafront, the city sits only a two-hour flight from Tokyo, yet there is little discernible Asian influence, with, rather, a plethora of kebab eateries overseen by owners hailing from Russia's mostly Muslim Northern Caucasus region. True restaurants, we discovered, are few. Grocery stores brim not, as one would expect, with fresh seafood, but rather with fish one might call, charitably, in a phrase from Bulgakov's *Master and Margarita*, "second-hand fresh." The state, as Bulgakov noted, sold truly fresh fish in *Torgsin* stores, where only foreigners and party apparatchiks had the right to shop and had to pay in hard currency. He wrote of the ridiculous incongruity between the communists' promise of a better, more just world, and the government's practice of restricting the sale of certain foodstuffs to a privileged few. *Torgsin* stores exist no more, of course, but the victory of capitalism in Russia now means that fresh fish goes to those who pay top prices for it, which means to big cities in Russia or abroad. Our tour of seafood stores put us in mind of Yeltsin and his moment of discovery in Blagoveshchensk—in a town supposedly chock-full of fresh fish, fresh fish is, in fact, in "deficit."

Except, that is, in one store where we stopped, a grocery coop affiliated with the Lenin Fishery Kolkhoz. There we came across quite a few varieties of salmon and at least a half-dozen types of red caviar ranging in taste from highly salty to hardly salty, with all available for the absurdly low price of 1,000 rubles ($16) a kilogram (2.2 pounds). We remarked on our delight to a stall owner named Natalia, who was busy ordering her wares in a large freezer. In the Soviet era, she told us, centralization and a state-dominated market hardly helped the caviar business, but there were, back then, "many more species of fish, rainbow trout, char, and certainly other seafood products you could buy. You could just head out to a fishing village in the morning and buy everything fresh. These days many suppliers opt out of this coop and try to sell on their own"—something prohibited by law, as fish stocks have diminished with overfishing. At least here they still have red caviar; in the Caspian Sea and Volga, the most prized caviar of all, black, has almost disappeared.

In Lenin Square, in the shadow of the imposing, five-story granite-and-glass Kamchatka Krai Government Headquarters, and not far from a statue of Lenin striking a defiant pose with a cape flaring as if fluttering in the wind, young families push baby carriages and teenagers practice their skateboarding moves. The leader of the world's proletariat shares a space with the recently constructed red-marble column topped by a double-headed eagle—the sight we no longer found surprising. Beneath them, coffee vendors dispense their beverage from stands, and locals sell ice cream from rickety carts. The unmistakable atmosphere of a seaside resort resembling that of Sevastopol in Crimea prevails. One would expect decent beaches here, but a disappointing, gravelly strip of sand runs along the water; people sit and stand tanning, with few venturing into the possibly less than clean sea. Elsewhere, the government has restricted access to the coast for security reasons; this is, after all, a border zone. Although the city hosts all sorts of tourists, the paucity of amenities recalls a salient fact: most visitors use Petropavlovsk-Kamchatsky as a stopover on their way out, by Jeep or by helicopter, into the wilderness yawning just beyond the city's boundaries.

On Leninskaya Street we came upon a statue, erected only in 2008, of Saint Nicholas the Miracle Worker. In accordance with church tradition, the saint faces east, but somewhat untraditionally, he holds aloft a sword in one hand and a miniature cathedral in the other. The message: the formidable holy potentate, backed by the true faith, is warding off invaders. (Legend has it that Saint Nicholas fended off the Mongols for a time.) The monument put us in mind of the aggressive angels who, so said local Solovetsky Islands lore, beat up a fisherman's wife because she accidentally strayed onto God's territory, and of the mighty bronze Saint Nicholas—also armed with a sword and a cathedral—rising above the Preloga River embankment in Kaliningrad. A ways farther down the street, an old, gray Stalinist behemoth of a building, decorated with red hammer-and-sickle flags, hosts both the headquarters of the Communist Party and the Gazprom Bank, the epitome of Russia's capitalist wealth. This seems like a puzzling juxtaposition, but it is not: Gazprom, in supplying hydrocarbons to Europe, was a principle source of hard currency in Soviet days, just as it is now. Political power and money go together.

On our last day, we decided to do what most visitors do: take a boat tour of the coast. We discovered that Russia's confused identity manifested itself once again in the tourist business, which now, privatized, operates solely for profit. Attracted by a sign showing a ship surrounded by cheerful dolphins and playful sea walruses and promising the "true Kamchatka fishing experience," we stopped by a tour company office near our hotel and inquired about schedules for the morrow.

Departure, the young man told us, would be at 8:30 a.m., but "assembly" was obligatory at 8:15, and the cost was a mere $5 per ticket. He showed us pictures of what we would see. We thought we might check out other options—perhaps there was a later trip? We could book by phone at our convenience, he told us. This was fine by us.

So, a few hours later we called to make reservations.

"I can't take reservations until I have copies of your passports."

"What?" we asked. "Why? We're not crossing the border!"

"You heard me, you have to bring me your passports! We will be sailing into the border waters of the Russian Federation!"

"But you said we could reserve by phone!"

"Of course! But you have to bring me your passports! And you can't do that by phone!"

"Can we do that in the morning?"

"Must I repeat myself? I'm not going to spend all afternoon repeating what should be obvious!" he snapped. "I need your passports before I can guarantee you tickets!"

"Why are you being so hostile? We're your customers!"

"Customers have to follow the regulations! We have to comply with the authorities just like everyone else!"

"We will bring you the passports."

Passports are, indeed, a Russian obsession. You need a document to prove your existence—as Bulgakov once memorably stated, in the

Soviet Union "if there's no document, no person exists." This goes
for just about everything—from making a simple bank transaction
to buying a cell phone to voting for president. It comes from the Soviet system of control, of the government's efforts to keep track of its
citizens. In 1991 communism disappeared, but the rules and mentality have remained. This was the case even in the Yeltsin years, and
all the more so now. The state collects information not only for possible use; the constant registration of words and deeds required of
citizens reminds them that the system is watching.

We stopped by the tour office a couple of hours later with, as required, passports in hand. When we tried to pay for our tickets as
well, the man barked, as if we were requesting a special privilege,
"You will pay on the boat, like everyone else! And don't think of showing up for the tour without your passports. You have to show them or
they won't let you on board. Be at the *mekhzavod*"—fur-processing
plant—"gate at 8:15 sharp! Remember, 8:15 at the *mekhzavod*!"

"The *mekhzavod*?" This seemed odd, but then not; furs were probably shipped here from other parts of the peninsula and unloaded,
before being processed, made into clothing, and sent elsewhere.

"Of course! That's where the dock is!"

The next morning a dense fog hung in the warm air, hindering
visibility even on the streets. Down at the *mekhzavod*'s blue gate, passengers, some giddy with excitement, others lethargic from their
early rise, huddled by our tour-company martinet and his female as-
sistant, a young woman with stark red hair and a military bearing.
She examined our passports and led us through the gates where border guards once again inspected our travel documents. Through a
gangplank with a railing, we climbed aboard what looked to be a
tugboat with an observation deck.

We pulled out into the dense mist and began circling around Avacha Bay. From large speakers emanated a prerecorded spiel about

the wonders of the coast, urging us to catch sight of them, to look
right, look left, glance straight ahead. Yet there was only fog and the
cries of birds: of cormorants as they dove into the sea, white with the
fog's reflection, of gulls as they circled above, and of orange-billed
ducks as they paddled by—a lonesome litany of lyrical cries.

Yet soon the sun limned through the fog, clearing the air and leaving us to contemplate green rolling *sopki*, three stark rock outcrop-
pings in the sea dubbed the Three Brothers—a legend has it that they
defended the city from the deadly tsunami and now stand there to
protect it from all misfortunes. Eventually the majestic slopes of three
snow-mottled volcanoes—Vilyuchinsky, Koryaksky, and Avacha—
opened in front of our eyes. We passed out through the bay's narrow
neck and into the Pacific, chugged along for an hour or so, and dropped
anchor.

While we thought of cheerfully waving at Sarah Palin in her
backyard on the other side of the ocean, the rest of the passengers
tossed in their lines, at times retrieving flounders, a local delicacy.

Surprisingly, and uncharacteristically for events such as this (involving strangers, not just friends) in Russia, several of the young
men among us stripped off their shirts and lounged back as they
waited for bites, striking poses resembling those seen in photographs
of Putin in the Siberian wilds, where just a few weeks before he fished
bare-chested, his trip coinciding with our stay in Blagoveshchensk.
They were, one could not help thinking, emulating the Putin power,
the ever-cool James Bond hero of modern Russia.

The sun eventually waned past the meridian, the captain turned
on the motor, and we chugged ahead, heading for the bay's narrow
mouth. We did not get far before halting. Instructions came over the
loudspeaker telling us to fish once again: there would be an unspec-
ified delay.

We waited and waited, floating within view of the volcanoes

and rocks, as gulls flocked and cried out around us. Small private yachts buzzed, passing by us back and forth from the shore. One hour passed, then two. We mounted the stairs to the captain's booth and inquired about the delay.

"For reasons of national security we have to stop here," answered the captain. "We'll be here as long as necessary."

"Any idea how long?"

"As long as necessary!"

And so we floated. And floated. And floated.

Espying the young man from the tour office, we tried to pay for our tickets.

"Can't you see I'm busy?" he barked. "Pay later!"

Two hours after that we pulled into port by the fur plant. The boat's crew, including the tour-company martinet, dispersed, failing to collect ticket fares.

From what we had seen from Kaliningrad to Kamchatka, Bulgakov, were he alive today, would still have much to write about.

THE PAST OF THE RUSSIAN FUTURE

In order to be in control, you have to have a definite plan for at least a reasonable period of time. So how, may I ask, can man be in control if he can't even draw up a plan for a ridiculously short period of time, say, a thousand years?

—Mikhail Bulgakov, *Master and Margarita*

Putin has failed to build us a great future, so he has built us a great past.

—A contemporary Russian joke

Rising from his orderly desk in the Kremlin, Vladimir Putin picked up his navy blue suit jacket from the back of his chair and put it on. Ready for his fourth inauguration, he strode out of his office and down the long white corridors of the Senate Palace, occasionally glancing at paintings of Russia's vast landscapes hung on the walls. He descended a red-carpeted, marble staircase under a magnificent chandelier and soaring ceilings adorned with gold trim. High oaken doors opened before him and he passed out into a courtyard, where he boarded the Russian-made Cortege limousine (instead of a Mercedes-Benz of previous, more Western years) that would take him, surrounded by motorcycles with flashing lights, across the Kremlin grounds to the Grand Kremlin Palace.

Arriving at the Grand Palace as the Kremlin bells struck noon, he exited the Cortege and entered the lavishly decorated halls, where a six-thousand-strong audience of ministers, top businessmen, Orthodox Church leaders, and other members of the country's elite applauded the sixty-six-year-old president as he set off down the red carpet toward Andreyevsky Hall, where the Supreme Soviet once met and where he himself had thrice taken his oath of office. The hall was also the site of festivities for the coronation of three czars. Every channel in Russia was broadcasting these momentous, thoroughly choreographed moments, some set to a song from Mikhail Glinka's patriotic opera, *A Life for the Czar.*

Amid such palatial grandeur the newly reelected president looked small but by no means humble. He certainly looked in charge. Before his previous inaugurations—in 2000 and 2004—Putin, dressed in a leather jacket, had traversed the Red Square, the very image of a young leader destined to modernize Russia. In 2012, following widespread demonstrations against his return to the presidency, his large motorcade ("like Stalin's," some commented at the time) sped through a downtown Moscow blocked off and emptied of pedestrians, presumably to thwart protests.

The inauguration that Russia's state-controlled television stations broadcast aimed to display the lavish traditions and continuity of Putin's presidency. Clever web enthusiasts set the president's walk to the Bee Gees' song "Staying Alive," showing Putin was more of a survivor than a savior, anxiously maneuvering among the pitfalls and perils of Russian politics.

Indeed, Putin's next term, scheduled to last until 2024, could be a dangerous one for him. Segments of the economic elite, hit hard by multiplying Western sanctions, have been grumbling louder than ever, although Putin might find ways to appease or undermine them, as he has before. So far, the 2014 drop in oil prices and the sanctions have not shaken the system, but they may, especially if the economy slides. After all, growth has only twice approached three percent since 2008.

For now, the president's control over politics, the economy, and increasingly society appears secure. However, his growing reliance on authoritarian measures and propaganda may begin to diminish the public mandate he has enjoyed almost since coming to power. State control of television, from where most Russians get their news, has given him an air of omnipotence—he is, truly, as television would have it, the Russian Santa Claus, the miracle worker who has "raised Russia off its knees." Although the Kremlin has failed to prevent tragedies—tragic fires and plane crashes, among other things, show this—the president has certainly restored Russians' sense that they belong to a great world power. The public perception, enhanced by the news reporting, is that the governors, mayors, and other regional authorities, and not the president, should answer for calamities.

Notwithstanding the quasicoronation described at the epilogue's opening, Putin's grip on power might weaken. He has so adeptly manipulated the country's political and economic oligarchs that this hasn't happened—at least openly. Who might replace him, if he gets ousted or quits because he's tired or just plain bored? The names of defense minister Sergei Shoigu or Moscow mayor Sergei Sobyanin have been mooted, although equally as potential candidates for losing their jobs instead—both may have gotten too much power and visibility for Putin's liking. Dmitry Medvedev, the 2008 Putin pick for president and now the prime minister, may be a safe choice that Putin would favor as a replacement once again.

The Russian constitution bars Putin from seeking another, fifth term in office, and no one has talked seriously—so far—about amending it so that he could run again. In any case, should Putin choose to leave the presidency voluntarily, without installing an obedient replacement, he may find himself in jeopardy. He certainly knows the fate of previous KGB leaders. Stalin's dreaded secret police chief Lavrenty Beria found himself, after the dictator suddenly died of a stroke in 1953, sentenced to death for "spying against the state." (Stalin's other two secret police heads met similar ends.) With the exceptions of Khrushchev and Gorbachev, all Soviet leaders died in office; Yeltsin, the first president of Russia, survived by handing power over to Putin.

In his years in power the Russian president has consolidated and strengthened the security forces, intimidated and jailed opponents, and muzzled the media and courts. If he steps down, the system he has created may turn against him, using his own methods.

What we saw during our travels through Russia's eleven time zones gave us little reason to predict doom for Putin, or for the country, at least in the immediate term. People are, as a rule, living better than ever before, freer than ever before, and—where public finances allow—local governments are overhauling infrastructure and bettering life for their citizens. In any case, more than twenty-five years of capitalism and, roughly, a decade of prosperity under Putin have done much to transform Russia from the broken-down, chaotic wreck of a country it was during Yeltsin's time. The people we met criticized Putin or praised him to us, in most places without apparent fear of being monitored by the authorities. (Broadcasting such opinions via the media would probably be another story.) Almost all seemed resigned to Putin's domination of the political scene; in fact, politics, unless we brought it up, was not on people's minds, as it often is in Moscow or Saint Petersburg.

But tentative harbingers of change are appearing—namely, the many anticorruption opposition centers Alexey Navalny has managed to establish around Russia in recent years. Traumatic memories of economic hardship and international humiliation suffered during the

Yeltsin years once mobilized people in support of Putin, but they have, naturally, faded with time; his success abroad, such as in Syria, and his much-lauded annexation of Crimea will eventually lose their capacity to inspire.

Despite Putin's lasting popularity, the Kremlin has certainly recognized the emergence of discontent and its potential for the negative consequences to his power. Hence growing restrictions on the internet and attempts to block social media sites whose traffic the security systems cannot monitor. The police, in curtailing unauthorized demonstrations, have used violence and arrests far more frequently than they did in 2011–2012, when far more protesters turned out. In the last decade, the young in particular have begun to believe that society has not changed in accordance with their expectations, which led to disappointment. In recent years applications for immigration to the United States alone have tripled in number; the American Embassy has received more than 2,500 in 2017, the highest number since the early post-Soviet years.[1] Whether to stay or leave Russia is a frequent topic among members of the middle class, especially in Moscow and other big cities. Even some of those accepting of Putin's policies seem to be yearning for fresh faces. We heard this in Omsk, we heard this in Magadan.

In his brief inauguration speech the president offered the young "a new quality of life, well-being, security, and health."[2] He even ordered the government's youth agency *Rosmolodezh* to report directly to him so as to court this youth away from Navalny. That move has further disclosed the Kremlin's hypocrisy. During his swearing-in ceremony when thousands of those young came out to protest the president's more years in power, they were brutally beaten by the Cossacks. These descendants of the militant conquerors, who once served the czars in defense of the throne and imperial expansion east, today have no formalized role but are used by the Kremlin as

a historic militia of sorts. The Cossacks claim a role of policing patriotism, performing the violent jingoistic pro-Putin duties when
the actual police are still restricted by law.

At the same time, Putin's vision of a Great Russia remains enormously popular. If he were to disappear, his policies would likely
survive. Russians have long believed in the "great man" theory of
history; they remain convinced that individuals at the top more than
circumstances or trends below determine the course of events. Leo
Tolstoy's *War and Peace*, which describes how the Russian empire re-
pelled Napoleon's invasion in 1812, typifies this kind of imperial
thinking.

The well-known Russian tolerance for repression has baffled
Western journalists, economists, and political consultants for decades.
As they suffered through tyranny inflicted on them by some of the
worst despots in world history, Russians, one can say, developed an
almost apocalyptic fear of change—and especially changes of power.
A regime's demise births not hope but dread. Among Russia's ruling
class, this has encouraged, almost more than anywhere else, a reliance on inertia—just the right environment for autocracy. Stalin
could count on this; this was also the secret behind the reelection of
Boris Yeltsin, despite his abysmal popularity ratings. "Better the devil
you know" may be a cliché, but it applies to Russian voters.

If Russian rulers are expected to act in the interests of the country, the Russian people, too, bear a responsibility—to serve their God
and their czar. In this, Russia has followed the Byzantine tradition,
in which there was only the ruler and his serfs. The ruler provides
not guarantees or laws, but gives amnesty, mercy, and the forgiveness of sins. The de facto absence of the rule of law in Russia and the
overwhelming influence of the Supreme Leader over one's freedom
or lack thereof—even, in extreme cases, over whether one lives or
dies—has left Russians ever in search of the Good Czar, whose reign

would usher in, if not paradise, then prosperity and justice for all. Yet, with the state unrestrained by institutions, with civil liberties weak and the czar presiding over all, the result of such an approach to governance is often less than paradisiacal.

Should Russia be classed as European, as Western? Based on our travels from Kaliningrad to Kamchatka we have come to three conclusions. Russia is "coherently incoherent"—in other words, suffering from a split personality disorder. It is driven by its history. It is, for the most part, homogeneous politically, despite its geographic and even ethnic diversity.

The double-headed eagle symbolizes Russia's coherent incoherency. Putin, no fan of revolutions, has kept alive, at least in bronze effigy on squares across the country, Vladimir Lenin, the Father of Revolutions. (Nostalgia felt by the older generation, as well as a justifiable reluctance to destroy historical monuments, have also helped to keep these statues intact.) Devoid of political value today, the Lenin statues stand for continuity, for the century during which Russia, in its Soviet incarnation, was a strong country, a superpower that made the world tremble. Some Stalin images and statues—the bust in Yakutsk, for example—have been thrown in, to firm the memory and aspiration of that superpower status. Then there are the two monuments to Prince Vladimir we saw. The old one in Kiev, commemorating the Ukrainians' own Prince Volodymyr. Another one in Moscow—the new statue, erected in 2016 on Putin's orders and designed to stick it to the Slavic, formerly fraternal country to the south. Even Ivan the Terrible (who famously "gathered"—or retook— Russian lands occupied by the Mongols in the Middle Ages) has been memorialized, with a statue of him raised in Oryol, a town about three hundred miles south of Moscow.

These statues may well be understood as monuments to Putin himself—they represent strong leaders, leaders gathering age-old

Russian territories and standing against enemies foreign and domestic. Stalin enjoyed a cult of personality that saw monuments to him built around the USSR during his lifetime. Putin's cult of personality has taken a more creative approach, expressing itself through the publicly displayed likenesses of other "greats" such as Peter, Catherine, and even Ivan the Terrible.

Russians, we saw, generally accept all these manifestations of power and the contradictory messages they send, picking and choosing from the patriotic kasha in which they dwell. Perhaps this is a survival mechanism. Russians, as we have noted, resemble snowdrop flowers, durable and adaptive. Shaken by crises coming almost as regularly as the seasons, they manage to survive, steering their individual lives across the turbulent sea that is their country, Great Russia.

Russia lives in the past and offers its citizens a less than rosy future; the growing power of the outdated Cossacks is just one example. Russia's frames of reference are old victories or involve settling old scores such as winning World War II or retaking the Crimean Peninsula. The authorities attempt to mold the past to fit the present, with the future also presented as reflecting the past. At the inauguration, the president promised his people a new future, not because it is time for change but because, he said, he felt "responsibility toward Russia, a country of magnificent victories and accomplishments, toward the history of the Russian state that goes back centuries, and toward our ancestors.[3]

"The country's security and defense capabilities are reliably ensured,"[4] Putin stated, his victory parades getting more and more elaborate and symbolically grand with every passing year. In 2017, to public cheers, a new Christmas decoration graced store shelves in GUM, Moscow's Red Square department store—a collection of glass balls titled "Our Heritage," with tanks and fighter jets painted as a theme.

Putin may not believe that war with the West is imminent, but the possibility that it might happen at all only helps him. He certainly gets help from the United States, the former Cold War foe that has now developed its own obsession with Russia. Indeed, Putin possesses a fascinating ability to bring extremely diverse yearnings together— yearnings for monarchy, for the Soviet past, for Russian military glory, for a revived Russian national spirit.

In 2017, by Moscow's main thoroughfare, Sadovoe Koltso—the Garden Ring Road—the Russian Military History Society sponsored the building of a monument to Mikhail Kalashnikov, the inventor of the AK-47. From his pedestal overlooking the road Kalashnikov seems to be ready to shoot at anyone who comes near—yet another striking example of Russia's militant national pride. Part of this composition is an image of the globe, displaying a bas-relief of the Kalashnikov rifle, on top of which stands Archangel Michael slaying a dragon, backset by an imposing Stalinist skyscraper—another sign of Russia's split personality, of Soviet and saintly military greatness aligned.

Russia is largely a homogeneous country, despite its demographic and geographic diversity. Russia does not constitute a separate civilization—it has borrowed too much from the West for that—but in its own way, it seems a world of its own. The multitudinous peoples and cultures composing the country dissolve in a sort of imperial homogeneity. Non-Russians—from the Chechens in the Northern Caucasus to Buryats of Ulan-Ude to the Yakuts of Sakha—make it a diverse land, but they do not influence politics or drive social changes. We saw this from Kaliningrad to Vladivostok.

On the whole, what one experiences does seem imperial, be it in monuments to the many coexisting Vladimirs of the Russian conflicting history. You can sense it in a church, in the Ural Mountains dividing Europe and Asia, where the Bolsheviks brutally murdered the Romanovs, Russia's last royals; or in Magadan, on the Sea of Okhotsk, where a newly built cathedral stands on the site once occupied by the local Supreme Soviet. You can discern it in Russia's coat of arms with its double-headed eagle, whether depicted in amber in Kaliningrad or carved from rare red marble in Petropavlovsk-Kamchatsky. You can even perceive it in a Buddhist temple in Buryatia, when a monk declares with all seriousness that Russia has two thrones, one for the chief lama here and another for Putin in the Kremlin.

This is the Russia of the twenty-first century, so very different from what it was during the communist decades, yet in some way ever the same, unchanging. From the White, the Baltic, and the Black Seas all the way to the Pacific Ocean, the president presides over a neo-Eastern Christian empire—a new Byzantium, if you will—and the majority of Russians continue to applaud his sweeping imperial ambitions.

ACKNOWLEDGMENTS

My utmost gratitude goes to my late mother, Julia Khrushcheva, to whom this book is dedicated. She first made me think about Kremlin politics, its relations to literature, and pretty much everything else. One reason I completed the journeys related herein was to show her that traveling in Russia was not, as so many liberals like her in Moscow believe, such a frightening affair. Initially a staunch opponent of the venture, she soon became a great champion of it. She eagerly awaited my phone calls, during which I would describe every city we visited and tell her the funny stories we accumulated. She was delighted that I would visit some Stalin-era Gulag labor camps. "Grandfather would have been so proud of you," she said, referring to Nikita Khrushchev and his legacy of de-Stalinization.

In June 2017, when we were almost halfway across the country, my mother was killed by a train in Moscow. The rest of the trip was, for me, an exercise in survival, perseverance, professional obligation, and constant inner dialogue with her about life, Russia, power, people, the Gulag, and literature—particularly the work of Mikhail Bulgakov, the author whose satirical writing helped Russians like me understand Stalin's Soviet Union of the 1930s. When we set out to our first cities, Kaliningrad and Kiev, she encouraged me to see people the way Bulgakov would have seen them—as individuals trying to survive state oppression.

I would also like to remember my sister, Ksenia, whose death from cancer in winter 2016 became one of the reasons for my travels. This book is dedicated to her as well. I wish to acknowledge the immense encouragement of her stalwart husband, Igor Makurin, a former journalist who knows Russia well, and to express my gratitude and compassion to Ksenia's children, Maria and Nikita. I now consider them my children.

Special thanks go to Barbara Paca, my wonderful friend, and now a sister really, for her patient listening, thoughtful suggestions, and unwavering support. After the death of my mother, Barbara became a critical and compassionate sounding board. I also would like to thank Nadezhda Azhgikhina, a Muscovite friend of mine and a journalist colleague, who has made invaluable suggestions to me about our Russia story. She has traveled extensively around the country and generously put us in touch with many of the people we met and interviewed along the way.

I am enormously indebted to Steven Lee Myers of *The New York Times*, the author of the best book on Putin, *The New Tsar*, and the newspaper's former Moscow bureau chief, for his kind words of inspiration—in fact, the idea for this book arose from my conversations with him—and for his crucial and careful comments on the manuscript.

I would like to thank my New School mentor Michael Cohen for being one of the early readers of many chapters and for providing some important observations, and Philip Logan for his constant encouragement and support.

My sincere appreciation goes to our agent, Sonia Land, for her backing and assistance, and to Daniela Rapp, our fastidious editor at St. Martin's Press.

I would also like to thank the following people (in alphabetical order) who were kind enough to share their views on Soviet history, Russian politics, and American perceptions of it: Peter Hoffman, Mark Johnson, Kenneth Murphy, Minerva Muzquiz, Alla Shevelkina, and Jeff Wasserstrom.

My profoundest gratitude goes to Vladimir Putin, Russia's longest-serving president, for providing us all with endless material. He has been a constant source of fascination. I do thank and admire the Russian people, my people, for the remarkable patience and endurance they have shown throughout the centuries, though I hope in the future they will learn to surrender less to their "czars."

And lastly but most importantly, I thank Jeffrey Tayler, my tireless companion and coauthor. It was a pleasure to make the journey together.

—Nina Khrushcheva

I would like to thank Nina Khrushcheva, my coauthor, for conceiving the idea for this book, researching the places we visited, and arranging our meetings with people there. Nina's curiosity about Russia was the prime mover for this entire project. Her intellect sparkles on every page. It was an honor to work with her. My gratitude also goes, as usual, to my longtime agent and friend, Sonia Land, for her faith in me and her encouragement. And I would like to thank Daniela Rapp, our editor, for her diligent efforts and useful suggestions about the text. And of course I would like to thank my wife, Tatyana, for putting up with my absences during our journeys. She remains, always, my reason for returning home.

—Jeffrey Tayler

NOTE ON NAMING
AND RENAMING

In Russia, names are often political. Naming your child Maria or Marlen signals a political stance. Maria, of course, is the name of the Christian Mother of God; Marlen, a popular name in the aftermath of the Russian Revolution, is a combination of "Marx" and "Lenin," and naturally brings to mind something less than holy. City streets at times bear the names of political upheavals or memorialize landmark events or, most of all, important leaders. Both 1917 and 1991 were moments of upheaval and great potential for Russia, so one often sees names reflecting those turbulent years—and especially 1917, with its revolution of worldwide import.

Saint Petersburg has undergone renaming more than any other city in Russia we can think of. Built on the orders of Peter the Great, it was first called Sankt-Peterburg—Saint Petersburg—with "burg" harking back to the Dutch origins of the name. In the 1910s, during the upheavals of wars and revolutions, "Saint" was eliminated and the city found itself renamed, in Slavic fashion, Petrograd. After Vladimir Lenin died in 1924, Petrograd became Leningrad. After 1991, the city became Saint Petersburg once again. Some residents now joke that it will soon become Saint Putinburg, since Vladimir Putin hails from the city.

Russia's tradition of naming and renaming may seem exaggerated to outsiders, but it stems from the country's binary spirit, with the currents of history sweeping first in one direction and then in the other. In the twentieth century alone, Russia witnessed two tumultuous political transformations, lurching from monarchy to socialist dictatorship to the chaos of Boris Yeltsin's democracy to the "centralized" democracy that almost inevitably led to the rise of Vladimir Putin, with his initial calls for "a dictatorship of the law." Those were welcome words to Russians wearied by out-of-control oligarchs, organized crime, strikes, and the collapse of infrastructure. Many lessons should have been drawn from such events, but Russian leaders, once victorious, generally seek to annihilate the past from which they could have learned. They have regarded the past not as the foundation for future growth, but as a source of error to be destroyed before it infects their own regime. Total destruction must precede creation, and this obliteration of history manifests itself in statues and names.

Russians have traditionally glorified their leaders, even turned them into demigods, when they were not actually God's anointed vicars on earth, as were the czars. They have also been quick to vilify them when the system of government changes or a new leader arrives. The functionaries of the Soviet system suffered especial peril when their boss in the Kremlin moved on—often, but not always, to the next world. Statues of Joseph Stalin and Lenin used to grace every public square in the USSR, and the bodies of both lay within the mausoleum beneath the Kremlin walls. After Stalin's death and denunciation by Nikita Khrushchev, Stalin's corpse was removed to a more modest location nearby. The authorities then set about expunging his name from street signs and pretty much every public space. Expunge the name and voilà! The crimes the dictator committed against millions vanish.

After World War II and the Soviet annexation, the German name Königsberg became Kaliningrad. It remains Kaliningrad to this day, even though more than half the city's population has no idea that their city was named after Mikhail Kalinin, a Bolshevik revolutionary, Soviet functionary, and Stalin ally. The fall of the Soviet Union prompted many cities to revert to their prerevolutionary names, but this was not an option for Kaliningrad, which had belonged to Germany. Reviving its German name would have hampered its new Russian present. Things were different for Kuibyshev, however, which reassumed its czarist-era name, Samara, even if its main square is still Kuibyshev Square, with its monument to the city's former namesake, Valerian Kuibyshev, another Soviet functionary of the Stalin era, still intact. Similarly, Yekaterinburg, or Sverdlovsk during the Soviet decades, brought back its old name after 1991. Nevertheless, a statue of the Bolshevik Yakov Sverdlov, a Lenin contemporary, remains afoot on Lenin Street, near the Sverdlov State Academic Theater of Musical Comedy. Moreover, Sverdlovsk Oblast has kept its Soviet name even though its capital now is Russian Yekaterinburg.

The incongruity between reality and state-sponsored mythology may trouble foreigners, but it goes almost unnoticed by the Russians, who accept the implicit contradictions as a part of daily life. Like the double-headed eagle next to the Lenin statues, such incongruities characterize Russian culture, which thrives on ambiguity and approximation.

And not only cities and streets get renamed. Russian leaders have at times chosen their own names. The German-born Empress Catherine II or Catherine the Great was once a more modest Princess Sophie Auguste of Anhalt-Zerbst. The current leader of the Russian Orthodox Church, Patriarch Kirill, was Vladimir Gundyaev before donning his robes. Although they claimed to be leading a state founded on scientific Marxism, Soviet leaders followed these same imperial and religious traditions. Hailing from the town of Simbirsk on the Volga, Vladimir Lenin was, first, Vladimir Ulyanov, but after a stint in Siberian exile he adopted the name of Lenin, so impressed was he by the mighty river Lena near which he served his sentence. After Lenin's death Simbirsk was renamed Ulyanovsk, and it is Ulyanovsk to this day. Stalin's original surname was Dzhugashvili. From the small town of Gori in Georgia, then part of the Russian and later the Soviet empire, the young Dzhugashvili decided to harden his image by concocting a name from the word *stal*, Russian for "steel."

Outsiders generally associate Russia with totalitarianism, the epitome of political centralization, and this is not an incorrect assumption. However, much in Russian life also depends on the whim of local authorities, and sometimes even on the people's will. Residents of Ulyanovsk, for example, chose to continue their association with Lenin, rather than renaming their town Simbirsk.

All this naming and renaming can seem baffling to non-Russians. Russians themselves view it as representative of their land's long and complex history, a land of people accustomed to thinking one thing and saying another, a land where roads often lead to dead ends, a land where (for now at least) the Putin-era farrago of symbols from almost all Russia's epochs—Red Victory flags from the Great Patriotic War, red-white-and-blue banners from the imperial period, Soviet-era statues, and emblems from Russian Orthodox Christianity—are tasked with reconciling the irreconcilable extremes of a country where the past is anything but past.

NOTE ON TRANSLATION
AND TRANSLITERATION

Bibliographical references and Russian words cited in this book follow a modified version of the Library of Congress system of transliteration ("ya" instead of "ia," for example). Soft signs are omitted, and names are mostly given in their standard English form (when such exists). Unless otherwise indicated, translations from the Russian are our own.

NOTES

Introduction

1. Igor Zotov, then editor at *Nezavisimaya Gazeta* (Independent Newspaper), in conversation with the authors, August 2016.

2. "Russia Election: Vladimir Putin Wins by Big Margin," BBC, March 19, 2018.

3. "Novogodnee Obrashchenie Prezidenta Rossii" [New Year's Address of the President of Russia], Channel 1, December 31, 2016.

4. "Russia GDP 1989–2018," Trading Economics, https://tradingeconomics .com/russia/gdp.

5. Lauren Carroll, "Obama: US Spends More on Military Than Next 8 Nations Combined," Politifact, January 13, 2016.

6. Yevgeny Kalyukov, "Uroven Bezrabotitsy V Rossii Vpervye Za Tri Goda Upal Nizhe 5%" [For the First Time in Three Years Unemployment Fell to Under Five Percent], RBC, September 19, 2017.

7. Lynn Berry, "Putin's Choice of Words Shed Light on Ukraine," Associated Press, April 17, 2014.

8. Andrew Roth, "Vladimir Putin Secures Landslide Victory in Russian Election," *Guardian*, March 18, 2018.

1. Kaliningrad

1. This and the following quote are from "Transcript: Putin Says Russia Will Protect the Rights of Russians Abroad," *Washington Post*, March 18, 2014.

2. Viktoria Veselova, "Dorogoi Krym: Skolko Stoit Zhit Na Poluostrove?" [Expensive Crimea: How Much Does the Peninsula Life Cost?], Krym. Realii, November 14, 2017.

3. "'I Ne Zatyagivaite': Putin Prikazal Platit Krymchanam Rossiiskie Pensii" [And Make It Quick: Putin Ordered Russian Pensions to Crimeans], NewsRu.com, March 19, 2014.

4. Vasily Marinin et al., "Glavnoe o Krymskom Moste" [The Most Relevant Information About the Crimea Bridge], RBC, May 15, 2018.

5. Alexei Levinson, "86% Za 'KrymNash'" [86% Is for "Crimea Is Ours"], *Vedomosti*, April 3, 2018.

6. I. A. Kurlyandsky, *Stalin, Vlast, Religiya* [Stalin, Power, Religion] (Moscow: Kuchkovo Pole, 2011), 42–43.

7. Damien Sharkov, "Stalin More Popular Than Putin, Russians Say," *Newsweek*, June 26, 2017.

2. Kiev

1. Mikhail Kalnitsky, "Na Pamyatnike Svyatomu Knyazyu Vladimiru Nekotorye Usmatrivayut Prisutstvie Masonskoi Simvoliki" [Some See Masonic Symbolism in St. Vladimir's Statue in Kiev], *Kievskie Vedomosti*, January 22, 2013.

2. Mikhail Bulgakov, *The White Guard*, trans. Michael Glenny (New York: McGraw-Hill, 1971).

3. "Transcript: Putin Says," *Washington Post*, March 8, 2014.

4. Kim Kelly, "Decapitating Lenin Statues Is the Hottest New Trend in Ukraine," *Vice*, May 25, 2017.

5. Ilya Ponomarev, "Segodnya V Dume Rassmatrivaetsya Zakon Ob Internete. Pravda O Zakone" [Today Duma Considers the Law Concerning the Internet. The Truth About the Law] (blog), LiveJournal, July 11, 2012, https://ilya-ponomarev.livejournal.com/512193.html.

6. Miriam Elder, "Russia Passes Law Banning Gay 'Propaganda,'" *Guardian*, June 11, 2013.

7. William Henry Chamberlin, *The Ukraine: A Submerged Nation* (New York: The Macmillan Company, 1944).

3. Arkhangelsk, Solovetsky Islands, Saint Petersburg, and Moscow

1. Yury Brodsky, *Solovki: Labirint Preobrazhenii* [Solovki: The Labyrinth of Transformations] (Moscow: Novaya Gazeta Publishing, 2017).

2. Luke Harding, "Vladimir Putin: Return of the King," *Guardian*, September 26, 2011.

3. "2017 Victory Day Parade in Moscow," Sputnik International, May 9, 2017.

4. Ulyanovsk (Simbirsk) and Samara (Kuibyshev)

1. Ivan Goncharov, *Oblomov*, trans. Stephen Pearl (Charlottetown, CA: Bunim & Bannigan, 2006), p. 128.

2. Ibid., p. 265.

5. Perm, Yekaterinburg, and Tyumen

1. Noah Sneider, "Paradise in Perm," *Economist 1843*, December–January, 2018.

2. "Breakfast with Frost Interview: Vladimir Putin," BBC, March 5, 2000, http://news.bbc.co.uk/hi/english/static/audio_video/programmes/breakfast_with_frost/transcripts/putin5.mar.txt.

3. Cited in Felix Chuev, *Molotov: Poluderzhavny Vlastelin* [Molotov: A Semisovereign Ruler] (Moscow: Olma Press, 2000), p. 422.

4. Gleb Bryanski, "Russian Patriarch Calls Putin Era 'Miracle of God,'" Reuters, February 8, 2012.

5. E. T. A. Hoffmann, *Kroshka Tsakhes Po Prozvaniyu Tsinnober* [Little Zaches, Great Zinnober], trans. from the German by A. Morozova (Moscow: Sovetskaya Rossiya, 1991).

6. Leonid Bershidsky, "Vladimir Putin, the Richest Man on Earth," Bloomberg, September 17, 2013.

7. Eugenia Albats, "Chisto-Konkretnyi Kandidat" [The Concrete Candidate], *New Times*, February 27, 2012; Tatyana Melikyan, "Glavsredstva: Pochemu Yezhemesyachnyi Oklad Tak Malo Volnoval Prezidentov I Gensekov" [Chief Funding: Why Monthly Salary Was Never of Interest to the Presidents and General Secretaries], Lenta.ru, November 15, 2016.

8. Andrei Pertsev, "Borba Za Millionniki: Pochemu Kreml Nachal Nastuplenie Na Ekaterinburg I Novosibirsk" [A Fight for the Million-Population Cities: Why the Kremlin Began Its Offensive on Yekaterinburg and Novosibirsk], Moscow Carnegie Center, June 4, 2018.

9. Ivan Golunov, "270 Millionov Za Gektar: Kak Izmenitsya Moskva V 2017?" [270 Million for a Hectare: How Moscow Will Change in Summer 2017 and Who Will Get Rich?], *Meduza*, May 24, 2017.

6. Omsk: A Mixed Metaphor of Putin's Empire

1. Fyodor Dostoyevsky, *Notes from a Dead House*, trans. Richard Pevear and Larissa Volokhonsky (New York: Alfred A. Knopf, 2015).

7. Novosibirsk

1. Russia has the largest epidemic in Europe and one of the fastest-growing in the world. At least 14,631 Russians died from AIDS-related symptoms in the first half of 2017—an increase of more than 13 percent from the previous year. See Chris Beyrer, Andrea L. Wirtz, George O'Hara, Nolwenn Léon, and Michel Kazatchkine, "The Expanding Epidemic of HIV-1 in the Russian Federation," *PLOS Medicine 14*, no. 11 (2017): e1002462.

2. Vera Fateyeva, "Andrei Travnikov Prokommentiroval Rezultaty Vizita Prezidenta V Novosibirsk" [Andrei Travnikov Commented on the Results of the President's Visit to Novosibirsk], Siberia Online, February 9, 2018.

9. Blagoveshchensk, Heihe, and Yakutsk

1. Simon Karlinsky, ed., *Anton Chekhov's Life and Thought: Selected Letters and Commentary*, trans. Michael Henry Heim (Evanston, IL: Northwestern University Press, 1997), pp. 167–168.

2. "The Far East Has Restored Its Electricity," TASS, August 1, 2017.

3. "Military Power of Russia and China," ArmedForces.eu, http://armedforces.eu/compare/country_Russia_vs_China.

4. Karlinsky, *Anton Chekhov's Life*, pp. 167–168.

5. Micol Flammini, "Quel ponte sullo stretto tra la Crimea e la Russia che fa tremare Kiev: Oggi viene inaugurato il Krymski most, il ponte sullo stretto di Kerch che collegherà la Crimea alla regione di Krasnodar" [The bridge over the Strait between Crimea and Russia that makes Kiev shudder: Today is inaugurated the Crimean Bridge over the Kerch Strait, which connects Crimea to the Krasnodar region, is inaugurated today], *Il Folio*, May 15, 2018.

6. See Kesserwan Arteau, "Interview with Daryana Maximova: Native Yakutian and Researcher," *World Policy Journal* (blog), January 25, 2017; "Yakutskaya Tragediya" [The Yakut Tragedy], Yakutsk History, https://www.yakutskhistory.net.

7. "Alkogolizm V Yakutii V Tri Raza Vyshe Chem Po Strane" [Alcoholism in Yakutia Is Three Times Higher Than in the Rest of the Country], *Sakha News*, August 19, 2013.

8. "Yakutskyi Gubernator Ne Udivilsya Publikatsiyam O Svoei Otstavke" [The Yakutia Governor Was Not Surprised by Reports of His Ousting], RBC, May 24, 2018.

11. Magadan and Butugychag

1. Vladimir Vysotsky, *Vse Stikhotvoreniya* [All Poems], trans. from the Russian by Nina Khrushcheva. (Moscow: Literatura, 2000).

2. Sergei Bondarenko, "Stydnye Voprosy O 1937 Gode" [Embarrassing Questions About 1937], *Meduza*, July 30, 2017.

3. "Spisok I Karta Lagerei Gulag" [A List and a Map of the Gulag Camps], Magadan Jewish Community Site, http://magadanjew.berlev.info/history/gulag/map-legend.htm.

4. "Samyi Nizkii Reiting Vladimira Putina Na Dalnem Vostoke—V Magadane" [Putin's Lowest Rating in the Far East Is in Magadan], *Vesma*, January 10, 2018.

5. Dmitry Olshansky, "Navalny Menyaet Svoi Vzglyady V Ugodu Okruzheniyu" [Navalny Changes His Views Depending on His Surroundings], *Vzglyad*, December 13, 2016.

6. "Zhitel Magadana Obvinen V Rasprostranenii Porochashchikh Svedenii" [Magadan's Man Is Charged with Defamation], Lenta.ru, July 21, 2016.

Epilogue

1. Margarita Devyatkina, Polina Khimshiashvili, "SMI Soobshchili O Rekordnom Chisle Prosb Rossiyan Ob Ubezhishche V SSHA" [Mass Media Has Reported the Record Asylum Applications to the USA], RBC, May 3, 2018.

2. "Vladimir Putin's Inauguration," RT (formerly Russia Today), May 8, 2018.

3. Ibid.

4. Ibid.

INDEX